AN AMERICAN TRAVELER'S
GUIDE TO BLACK HISTORY

# AN AMERICAN TRAVELER'S
# GUIDE TO
# BLACK HISTORY

Also published as
A GUIDE TO NEGRO HISTORY IN AMERICA

⊶⧫⊷

## BY PHILLIP T. DROTNING

DOUBLEDAY & COMPANY, INC.
GARDEN CITY, NEW YORK

*To Meredith, Michelle, Joseph, and Kristina,*
*who suffered in comparative silence*

OTHER BOOKS BY PHILLIP T. DROTNING

Black Heroes In Our Nation's History
Up From the Ghetto (with Wesley South)

# PREFACE

ONE WHO LIVES IN MASSACHUSETTS cannot escape having some appreciation of the role of Negroes in the history of the United States. Monuments recall the death of Crispus Attucks in the Boston Massacre, the signal episode in the chain of events that led to American independence. Another, in Boston Common, pays tribute in the magnificent bronze of Augustus Saint-Gaudens to the valiant service of Robert Gould Shaw and the all-Negro 54th Massachusetts Regiment of Infantry in the Civil War.

Yet, even those who are familiar with these events will find this a startling book. Startling because it portrays a broad sweep of Negro participation in historic events that is beyond anything that educational textbooks or motion picture and television drama have led us to expect.

Its pages reveal that from Lexington and Concord to Dien Bien Phu; from the initial settlement of the Carolina coast to the exploration of the Columbia River by Lewis and Clark; on whaling ships and the Western plains; from Maine to California and Put-in-Bay to New Orleans, Negro and white Americans *together* have helped to make this nation great.

Many of the places, events, and people described in this book have been the subject of writings by others. For the most part, however, what has been written about them has been written by scholars, for scholars. Rarely has an author attempted, for the general reader, to provide a comprehensive overview of the total role of black men and women in American life and history.

Several things should impress you about this book. First, it is a remarkably comprehensive chronicle of the most significant historical contributions—and of the Negroes who made them—told in a highly readable way. In fact, the author deals with history as a good reporter would cover the day's events. He has selected an unusual format; one which ties the past to places that can still be visited today, and thus achieves the effect of bringing history to life. Although some of the events occurred three or four hundred years ago, they seem almost to be happening today.

The author has achieved credibility as well as reality by describing events and people in a thoroughly unemotional and straightforward way. His ability to resist the temptation to overdramatize some of the more surprising information may stem, in part, from the fact that he is not a Negro and hence has less reason to become emotionally involved.

Readers will also be struck by the fact that in a period of great emphasis on the efforts of Negroes in behalf of their own race, this book deals almost entirely with the efforts of Negroes as Americans, in behalf of America. As the author points out, and documents convincingly, Negroes for two centuries have fought for freedom in America, even though—repeatedly—the freedom they have helped to win has not been theirs to enjoy.

Inevitably, because of the broad range of history that it covers, this book can offer no more than delectable samples of the historic role of Negroes in America. Item after item will leave the reader wishing that he had been given more. Hopefully, the experience will whet the appetites of those who read the book for more information on an aspect of our nation's history that has been neglected for far too long.

Mr. Drotning has written a book that can and should be read with pleasure and profit by Negro and white Americans alike. Negroes, particularly those of the rising generation, will find in it a heightened appreciation of what black people of determination and fortitude *can* achieve. White Americans will gain a new understanding of what Negroes *have* achieved for America since the first black colonists touched our shores more than four hundred years ago.

In either event, the book—like the history it describes—will have helped to strengthen our country.

Edward W. Brooke
*United States Senator*

# CONTENTS

# INTRODUCTION

NEGROES HAVE HAD A SIGNIFICANT PLACE in every aspect of American history but one—the history books.

But people leave their mark. The impact of Negroes on our nation's growth and progress is evident across the land in the edifices that have survived our forefathers and the monuments erected by succeeding generations in memory of what they did. This book is a guide to places that bear witness to the role of Negro Americans in making this nation great.

Negroes were with the first Spanish explorers who landed on Florida's coast. One, Estevanico, blazed with wooden crosses the trail that enabled Fray Marcos de Niza to be "the first white man" in Arizona and New Mexico. Negroes were with the founders of Maryland on the Ark and the Dove. They constituted a majority of the original settlers of Los Angeles. And when Captain Robert Gray encountered hostile Indians on his discovery visit to the Pacific Northwest, a Negro in his crew met death at their hands.

The first man killed in the American Revolution was black. When Paul Revere rallied the Minutemen to Lexington and Concord, Negroes were among the first to respond to his call. There were Negroes with George Washington when he crossed the ice-filled Delaware; one, Prince Whipple, was in the general's own boat.

During the War of 1812, when Admiral Oliver Hazard Perry defeated the British in the Battle of Lake Erie, one-fourth of his sailors were Negroes. They died as courageously as they fought. During that conflict Andrew Jackson also praised the courage of the Negroes who helped him achieve victory in the Battle of New Orleans.

Some 166 regiments of Negroes fought to save the Union during the Civil War, but only after they had first fought for the right to fight. Often, during the Indian Wars in the pioneer West, the "white troops" who fought the "red men" were really black.

When Custer fought Sitting Bull in the tragic "Last Stand," a Negro—one who didn't have to be there—was among those who died.

Texas Negroes were with the heroic defenders of the Alamo, and they died with Colonel Fannin at Goliad. They fought and died with Teddy Roosevelt in Cuba in 1898, flanking the famed Rough Riders in the charge up San Juan Hill.

In World War I, Negroes manned the trenches in France. One of them was the first American to win the cherished French Croix de Guerre. A "noncombatant" Negro steward manned a machine gun on the battleship *Arizona* at Pearl Harbor to become one of the first American heroes in World War II. Negroes were among those who won the Medal of Honor in Korea, and today tens of thousands of them are fighting a substantial share of the war in Vietnam. General Westmoreland has twenty Negro officers on his staff; more than 20 percent of those killed in Vietnam have been Negroes.

Negroes sailed on whaling ships in the East and were prominent in the Gold Rush in the West. They were with Lewis and Clark; with Fremont and Ashley and Sublette; with the pioneers on the Oregon and Santa Fe and Mormon Trails. They fought the Apache and the Cheyenne to open the famous cattle trails that led north out of Texas; over five thousand Negro cowboys at one time rode the Western plains.

Negroes have made a place for themselves, despite enormous odds, in literature, the arts, music, sports, medicine, science, business, industry, and education. During the years after the Civil War, they proved their ability in government until their race was systematically disenfranchised, and the Negro office-holders went down in defeat. Today, they are proving it again.

Despite the magnitude of their contributions to the progress of our nation—nearly 180,000 Negro soldiers helped to hold it together during the Civil War—their role has largely gone unsung. Yet, for those who will seek them out, there are memorials and other reminders across the face of America that commemorate the contributions that Negroes have made.

Many of them are described in this book; places that you can visit, monuments that you can see and touch. There are other important events which can no longer be identified with a specific place or structure, and some, no doubt, that have simply eluded the author's search.

Scholars may question some of the details in this book, just as they differ over them with each other. Because Negro history for so long went largely unrecorded, much of it is subject to interpretation and confusion over dates, spelling, and similar details. But a hero is a hero, however his name is spelled, and such discrepancies do not affect the significance or validity of the events themselves.

Historians have been severely criticized in recent years for the absence of Negroes from the pages of American history books. Certainly, to a great extent, they are to blame and so is the social environment in which they studied and wrote. But a word may be entered in their defense. The historian who delves into American history relies on countless manuscripts, newspaper files, and other written materials that survive in libraries and historical collections. Largely, these documents are the product of white men and women for the simple reason that Negroes far more rarely wrote about themselves or to each other.

There is an obvious reason for this. For nearly 250 years the enslaved Negro was frustrated in his efforts to achieve literacy. It was not simply that he was denied access to adequate school facilities; in many states the education of Negroes was actually prohibited by law, and this was true in the North as well as in the South. Prudence Crandall, a Quaker teacher in Canterbury, Connecticut, was only one of many who learned this to her dismay in 1833, when she was jailed for opening a school for Negro girls.

This denial of education was based partly on the fear that educated slaves would revolt. It also stemmed from the psychological need of white persons, in both North and South, to maintain the image of the Negro as a pagan and uneducable subspecies whose lot was improved in servitude. Bruce Catton has stated this need with great clarity:

"White Americans had to believe that the Negro was inferior and in need of restraint, because otherwise the whole idea of slavery was morally wrong from the beginning and the Northerner who tacitly consented to it was as guilty as the Southerners who lived with it."

This desire and need to maintain the Negro in an inferior role by denying him recognition or education manifested itself in other ways, as well. Slave states passed laws prohibiting the migration of free Negroes into their states; other laws drove free Negroes out of slave states; slaveowners were among the leading proponents of efforts to send free Negroes to colonies overseas. The motivation, in each instance, was the fear that educated free Negroes would incite the slaves to revolt.

Inevitably, with all of these restrictions, most Negroes remained illiterate until after the Civil War. As a consequence, there is no great store of letters, manuscripts, or diaries on which the historian can draw. In the preparation of this book the author developed profound admiration and respect for the devoted scholars who have worked in this difficult field. Men such as Charles Wesley, John Hope Franklin, Benjamin Quarles, and others have labored long and hard to establish the facts about Negro participation in the American drama. It is difficult and demanding work.

The historian is also handicapped because for many decades the newspapers maintained the pretense that the Negro, except as a chattel, did not exist. Consequently, there is a dearth of information in old newspaper files about Negro achievements. Often, what is there reflects the prejudice of the editor rather than the facts about the event.

The only really useful sources that remain are official records and documents left by educated whites of the time. Here, too, one who undertakes research in Negro history is in trouble because, unless specific identification is made as to color, it is hard to tell whether the subject is white or black. Historical research is greatly simplified if one begins with the assumption that the entire cast of characters is white. However, this sort of assumption has too long denied the Negro his place in history. Because slaves rarely had anything but one given name, the identification is most often made by some obnoxious preface attached to it, like "Negro" Joe, or "Black" Jim, or "Nigger" Jeff. Sometimes, too, identification of Negro activity is found in surviving geographic place names containing similar epithets, such as "Nigger Bend," in an old gold-mining camp, or "Negro Hill," on the western plains. The fact that Negro births were largely unrecorded causes the careful researcher great anguish over variations in the spelling of names, discrepancies in dates, and similar details.

The reader will observe that far more information is included about eastern states than those of the pioneer West. This is because Negroes were present in the East much earlier and in larger numbers. Moreover, there was less migration to the states that were created after the Emancipation Proclamation was signed and the Thirteenth Amendment adopted; the earlier migrations usually involved fugitives seeking freedom in the North or the Midwest. After the slaves were freed, there was less reason for Negroes to migrate elsewhere.

Nevertheless, the Negro played an important role in the opening of the West, even though he receives little recognition in the fiction and drama that is written about it. Perhaps this oversight is partly justified. The Negroes in the West were rarely two-gun desperadoes or dealers in stud-poker games. Instead, the manuscripts of the time are more apt to recall them for deeds of charity, which is not the dramatic stuff of which horse operas are made.

For example, the pioneer settler in the Puget Sound area of the Pacific Northwest, George Bush, was well known and highly respected among the early settlers. They sought his counsel, and he often staked them with seed, provisions, and supplies. The area in which they settled is still Bush Prairie, but it is doubtful that the origin of the name is known to many of their descendants who are attending Olympia and Seattle schools today.

The hundreds of Negroes who emigrated to the Valley of the Great Salt Lake with the pioneer Mormon parties were also known for the undramatic virtues of providence and generosity. On April 8, 1849, Eliza Lyman noted in her diary that her husband, Amasa, had left on a mission to California, leaving his family "without anything from which to make bread, it not being in his power to get it." She added that, "not long after Amasa had gone, Jane James, the colored woman, let me have two pounds of flour, it being half of what she had."

John Bankhead, who settled in Wellsville, Utah, in 1848, noted that the Negro families always laid in supplies for the winter. It infuriated him that a few improvident white families then "sponged off them" when the cold weather arrived. Bankhead lectured the Negroes for giving up part of their meager stores, "but they were kind and generous-hearted people who shared anything they had with anyone who asked for it."

The records also reveal countless deeds of heroism and examples of devotion on the part of Negroes. When several children fell into a stream along the Mormon trail in 1850, Charlotte, the Negro servant of the Williams Camp family, rescued all of them and then "held them by their heels and rolled them over an old barrel." She said later that if one had drowned she would have jumped into the river again and gone down with him. Similar tales of Negro courage, stamina, and generosity were recorded by pioneers on all of the old western wagon trails.

Up in Cascade, Montana, a noteworthy early resident was Mary Fields, a Negro woman who worked as a teamster and even drove a stagecoach for a while. She was past seventy before she settled down to a less active life as the village laundress, and she is scarcely remembered today. A Negro lady hardly fits the stereotype of the stagecoach driver in Western movies or on television. The same is true of Sarah Campbell, the first woman to enter the Black Hills of South Dakota. That state's history records Annie Tallent as the first *white* woman to enter the Black Hills. "Aunt Sally" Campbell, who preceded her by several months, is remembered only on a marker in an isolated cemetery at Galena, which today is a near-ghost town. It took a search by this author, seeking information about this hardy Negro pioneer, to win belated recognition of "Aunt Sally's" achievement in the Deadwood newspaper in 1967.

It is impossible to escape becoming partisan in the course of research on a work of this kind, for the conclusion is inescapable, according to recent historical scholarship, that Negroes deliberately have been written out of our nation's history. Inevitably, because this is an effort to write them back into it, this may appear to be a one-sided book. It may be hoped that in the future, the history of America will be presented as it happened; as the combined effort of Americans—black and white—who lived, worked, fought, and died together in the nation's cause.

Meanwhile, the nation must write new history based upon a society that lives by a philosophy of unity, patience, tolerance, and understanding. This may be the time for white America to recall the philosophy Abraham Lincoln expressed at a meeting in Chicago in 1863. Commenting on the service of Negro troops in the Civil War, he said: ". . . Negroes, like other people, act upon motives. Why should they do anything for us if we will do nothing for them? If they stake their lives for us they must be prompted by the strongest motive, even the promise of freedom, and the promise being made must be kept."

PHILLIP T. DROTNING
*Glenview, Illinois*
*October 1, 1967*

AN AMERICAN TRAVELER'S
GUIDE TO BLACK HISTORY

# ALABAMA

*Coleman Hill*, southwest of Courthouse Square, was the site of one of four hundred and forty-nine military encounters of the Civil War in which Negro units were engaged. Nearly one hundred and eighty thousand Negroes displayed their skill and courage in the Federal Army; more than sixty-eight thousand died. Nearly thirty thousand sailors, about one-fourth of the men who served in the Federal Navy, were Negroes. It is estimated that some two hundred thousand others served the Federal forces in supporting roles.

In this engagement, a clever deception achieved by the South's greatest military strategist, General Nathan B. Forrest, deprived the members of the 111th Colored Infantry Regiment of the opportunity to fight. The Confederate general arrived at Athens with a cavalry and artillery force of forty-five hundred men. He convinced Union Colonel Wallace Campbell that he had twice that number by exposing his unmounted men as infantry, and then putting them on horses to ride another section of the line as cavalry.

Believing that nine thousand Confederates were pitted against his smaller force of Negro and white soldiers, Campbell surrendered. His troops spent the remainder of the war amid the hardships of a military prison camp.

## FLORENCE

*Handy Heights Housing Development and Museum* marks the birthplace of composer W. C. Handy, "Father of the Blues." The museum, in his restored cabin, houses his piano, trumpet, and other mementoes.

Handy's first published song, "Memphis Blues," was originally written as a campaign song for the notorious Memphis political boss,

E. H. Crump. His most famous song, published in 1914, was "St. Louis Woman"; other favorites include "Beale Street Blues" and "Careless Love."

Handy went to New York to become a music publisher in the 1920s. Although he lost most of his sight, he was still active when he died in 1958 at the age of eighty-five.

## MOBILE

*Fort Gaines,* on Dauphin Island, was one of the outer defenses of Mobile during the Civil War. It was captured by Admiral Farragut's fleet in August 1864, during the Battle of Mobile Bay. Farragut's flagship, the *Hartford,* had been under fire from the fort's batteries when it entered its historic duel with the Confederate ironclad *Tennessee.*

John Lawson, one of the first Pennsylvania Negroes to volunteer for Navy duty, had already been in action during the capture of New Orleans, and at Port Hudson and Vicksburg. Early in the encounter a Confederate shell landed in the midst of his six-man powder crew. Four men were killed outright, and Lawson was wounded in the leg. He refused medical attention, and with incredible effort kept his guns going for several hours, despite his injury. He was awarded the Medal of Honor for his courage, which may have saved the *Hartford.*

Work on Fort Gaines was begun in 1821, but its completion was delayed until the late 1850s. A huge anchor and chain from the *Hartford* are on display a few yards from the entrance.

*Fort Morgan,* in Baldwin County on Alabama 180 at Mobile Point, was another outer defense captured by Farragut. There are a number of historical markers in the restored fort recalling the battles that led to the fall of Mobile. Its architecture is as interesting as its history, for it was patterned after an ancient structure in Florence, Italy, designed by Michelangelo.

The Mobile Bay engagement was the first in which torpedoes and smoke screens were used in naval warfare. The torpedoes were not self-propelled, but their use accounts for the often-quoted exclamation of Admiral Farragut, "Damn the torpedoes; full speed ahead."

Negro infantry and artillery units were also with Farragut during the capture of Forts Morgan and Gaines. Less than a year later, on April 9, 1865, they were also on hand to storm the ramparts of Fort Blakely and capture Mobile. A marker in the fort notes the landing of thirty-two thousand men with Union General Canby, who moved up the east shore of the bay and joined another thirteen thousand Union soldiers from Pensacola for the assault on Mobile.

Only a few hours after General Robert E. Lee surrendered at Appomattox, the major defense of the city, Fort Blakely, crumbled under the onslaught of a Federal force that included nine Negro regiments in General John Hawkins' 1st Division. They marched for eleven days to get in the fight.

Of seven divisions in the assault this one was the smallest, yet its casualties were the heaviest of all the divisions engaged. The commanding officer of the 50th U. S. Colored Regiment praised the Negro soldiers in his official report, which concluded: "The conduct of none could be criticized to their discredit, and the behavior of the men . . . was convincing proof that the former slaves of the South cannot be excelled as soldiers."

This defense of the Negro's capacity as a soldier grew from the long controversy over whether Negroes should be allowed to enlist. For two hundred years they had so vigorously resisted their enslavement that many whites feared retaliation if Negroes were given weapons. They based their objections, however, on the argument that Negroes were cowards who would not fight. Even after Negroes had displayed their skill and courage in many battles, their commanders still felt compelled to defend them from allegations of cowardice.

Fort Blakely was once a prosperous town, rivaling Mobile in population. Today, nothing remains except a few markers in the old cemetery, but Civil War buffs, equipped with copies of the official map of the engagement, still prowl the site looking for buried shells and other relics of the battle.

*Magnolia Cemetery.* The National Cemetery in the southwest corner contains the remains of Union soldiers who fell during the attack on Fort Blakely in the final assault on Mobile. Among them are soldiers who died storming the ramparts with Hawkins' 1st Division. This is one of many National Cemeteries established by the Congress in July 1862, with the approval of President Lincoln.

SELMA

*Arsenal Place,* a monument at Water Avenue and Church Street, marks the site of a Civil War arsenal on which the Confederacy depended heavily during the Civil War. Of four hundred workers in 1865, three hundred and ten were Negro. The Confederate ironclad *Tennessee,* which engaged Farragut's flagship in Mobile Bay, was one of several vessels built here at the Naval Foundry, Water Avenue and Sylvan Street.

## TALLADEGA

*Talladega College.* The American Missionary Association founded a primary school here in 1867. It grew into the first college for Negroes in Alabama. Today the college is an outstanding liberal arts institution, housed in sixteen major buildings.

The Savery Library has three panels of frescoes by Negro artist Hale Woodruff depicting the incident in which Joseph Cinque led a revolt on the *Amistad* that liberated a shipload of slaves. (See Farmington, Connecticut.)

Woodruff, who now teaches art at Atlanta University, studied at the John Herron Art Institute in Indianapolis, and in France. One of his teachers was renowned Negro artist Henry Ossawa Tanner.

## TUSKEGEE

*Tuskegee Institute.* Tuskegee Institute opened July 4, 1881, with a two-thousand-dollar appropriation from the Alabama legislature, a single shanty, thirty students, and a faculty of one: Booker T. Washington. Washington, a former slave who headed Alabama's first normal school for the training of Negro teachers, had previously established a night school at Hampton Institute, Virginia. In 1882, Washington moved Tuskegee to a one-hundred-acre plantation and instituted a program of self-help that enabled the students to earn part or all of their expenses. Most of the early buildings were constructed with student labor.

Tuskegee now covers nearly five thousand acres and has more than 150 buildings. In its early years the Institute offered secondary education as well as teacher training. It also developed the agricultural and manual training courses for which it and Washington became famous. Today Tuskegee is an internationally known center for agricultural research and extension work.

Next to Washington himself, the most famous person associated with Tuskegee was George Washington Carver. He joined the faculty as director of agricultural research in 1896. Working with students and local farmers, Carver finally persuaded many farmers to substitute peanuts, sweet potatoes, and other crops for cotton, which was rapidly depleting the soil. Carver then proceeded with research programs that developed three hundred products from peanuts, and

118 from sweet potatoes. Long before the development of modern plastics, he succeeded in making a synthetic marble from wood pulp. His research was invaluable when the arrival of the boll weevil forced farmers to turn to crops other than cotton.

Notable places to visit at Tuskegee are the Founder's Marker at the site of Washington's original shanty; the Booker T. Washington Monument, and the George Washington Carver Museum. Washington's den at The Oaks is still maintained as he left it; on display are several valuable Oriental antiques which he treasured.

The Carver Museum houses the scientist's extensive collection of plants, minerals, and birds; exhibits of products he developed, including paints and clays, and some of his paintings. It also houses a valuable collection of African art and many of Carver's papers.

The Institute is also the home of the George Washington Carver Foundation, a research center started by Carver in 1940. In 1966 the Interior Department designated the Institute as a National Historic Landmark.

# ALASKA

**FAIRBANKS**

*Pioneers Home.* One of the few surviving Negro pioneers in Alaska is Mattie Crosby, a cheerful, warmhearted woman of eighty-three who now lives in the home.

Mattie came to Alaska in 1900 with a Maine family that had adopted her. They also adopted twenty-six other children. In a family that size one learns to share, and Mattie is known throughout Alaska as a woman with a generous heart.

Except for two years when she went "outside," she has lived in Alaska for sixty-seven years. For many years she operated what was considered "the finest bathhouse in Alaska," and won a reputation as one of Alaska's finest cooks. Mattie was a good businesswoman, but her generosity kept her from getting rich. For years she grubstaked every prospector who needed help.

The population of Alaska in the early days was never great, and Negroes were few in number. The gold rush brought some Negroes to the territory, and others worked on the boats that brought its supplies, but as a Negro pioneer who came early and stayed late, Mattie is almost unique.

"Once I went seventeen years without seeing anyone of my race," Mattie says. "Most of the time if I wanted to see another dark face I just looked in the mirror."

Although Mattie (her friends are more apt to call her "Tootsie") is now confined to a wheelchair, she is quick-witted despite her years. Some years ago she wrote a book about her life and gave it to some friends to be typed. She didn't get it back. Today, despite her age, she's writing it all over again!

---

# ARIZONA

---

APACHE

*Geronimo Monument.* Nearby is Skeleton Canyon, the site of Apache Chief Geronimo's surrender on September 5, 1886.

Between 1881 and 1886, Geronimo led several Apache war parties. The last outbreak lasted about a year and cost some one hundred lives before Negro cavalrymen under General Crook finally brought Geronimo's career to an end. Geronimo and his tribe were escorted by the Negro cavalry to imprisonment at Fort Pickens, Florida; but after about two years he was returned to Fort Sill, Oklahoma, where he died.

After the Civil War four Negro regiments were formed to protect wagon trains, railroad construction workers, and settlers from attack by Indians on the western plains. The 9th and 10th Cavalry and the 24th and 25th Infantry Regiments fought Indians for some twenty-five years before the Apache, the Cheyenne, the Comanche, the Ute, and many other tribes were finally subdued. To the Indians they were known as the Buffalo Soldiers; their officers, usually white, called them the Brunettes. Both considered them to rank with the best troops in the West.

Lieutenant Henry O. Flipper, the first Negro to graduate from West Point, was assigned to the 10th Cavalry in 1877 as the regiment's first Negro officer.

## BISBEE

*Chiricahua National Monument.* It is believed that Negroes were with Coronado when his expedition entered the territory in 1540. Guiding the Coronado party from Mexico City was Fray Marcos de Niza, who had learned the route a year earlier from the Negro guide, Estevanico (See Phoenix).

De Niza, in the report on his expedition, had sought to confirm the existence of the "Seven Golden Cities of Cibola." Coronado, on his return, informed the viceroy with some disgust that his predecessor had "said the truth in nothing that he reported . . ." Instead of gold and jewels he had found only "great houses of stone."

## BONITA

*Old Fort Grant,* three miles from town, is now a state industrial school, but from 1858 it was an outpost for Negro cavalrymen who protected settlers and immigrant wagon trains from the Indians. It became inactive in 1898 when the Negro troops were withdrawn for service in Cuba during the Spanish-American War.

In May 1889, the all-Negro 24th U. S. Infantry left here with the payroll for Fort Thomas. The soldiers encountered bandits who, firing from a ridge alongside the road, took a deadly toll of the wagon drivers and their escorts. Sergeant Benjamin Brown was caught in the open during the fight, and shot through the abdomen. He fell, but grabbed a rifle dropped by another wounded soldier and continued to shoot until a second bullet hit him in the arm.

Corporal Isaiah Mays finally left the shelter of the wagons and braved the bandits' fire to go to a nearby ranch in search of help. By the time he returned, the bandits had made off with the payroll.

Major J. W. Wham, the paymaster in charge of the expedition, later reported that he had "never witnessed better courage or better fighting than shown by those colored soldiers."

Mays and Brown were each awarded the Medal of Honor for their roles in this action. More than half a century later, halfway around the world in Korea, another Negro of the same regiment became the first of his race to win the Congressional Medal since the Spanish-American War.

This twentieth-century hero was Private First Class William Thompson, of Brooklyn, New York. Unlike Mays and Brown, however, he was not alive to receive his medal. When the enemy launched a surprise attack on his unit, Thompson set up his machine gun and held them off long enough for some of his comrades to organize a defense. He was soon wounded, but he kept up the devastating fire even after other soldiers tried to drag him away from his weapon. He was finally killed by an enemy grenade.

Later in the Korean conflict, Sergeant Cornelius H. Charlton was awarded the Medal of Honor for gallantry. When the officer of his unit was wounded, the twenty-one-year-old Bronx Negro led a group in several attacks on Hill 542, an enemy stronghold. He wiped out several emplacements with grenades, but was finally wounded in the chest.

Charlton refused medical attention and led still another charge, but even then the stubborn enemy on Hill 542 refused to yield. Finally, bleeding to death, the courageous soldier made a last, desperate, one-man assault on the enemy position. This time he succeeded. The price was his life, but his unit took the hill.

BOWIE

*Ruins of Fort Bowie*, twelve miles from town on Apache Pass Road, are all that remain of a fort established in 1862 at the eastern entrance to Apache Pass, which may have been the most dangerous spot on the wagon trail to California.

Many soldiers and migrants were slaughtered in the canyon by such fabled Apache leaders as Cochise and Mangas Coloradas. Even the Negro cavalry and infantry troops, long experienced in Indian warfare, dreaded a trip through the narrow mountain defile.

The old cemetery here once contained the graves of many victims of the Apache. The old markers, long since removed by souvenir hunters, bore such legends as, "Killed by the Apaches," or "Tortured to Death by Apaches."

FORT APACHE

*Old Fort Apache*, one mile from town, is another fort at which Negroes served during the Indian wars. The 10th Cavalry returned here in 1913, after service in Cuba and the Philippines.

The Negro troopers were sent on a punitive expedition against the Mexican terrorist, Pancho Villa.

The fort is now a trading post, government school, and Indian sanitarium.

From this point the highway to San Carlos follows what was probably the route taken by Estevanico on his expedition of discovery to New Mexico.

FORT THOMAS

*Site of Camp Thomas.* Moved here in 1878 from nearby Geronimo, Camp Thomas was a base from which the 9th and 10th Cavalry Regiments moved into many actions against the Apache.

Sergeant William McBryar, of Elizabethtown, North Carolina, was stationed here when he became the only Negro of the 10th Cavalry to win the Medal of Honor for service in the Indian wars. Only ten days before the end of the Apache campaign he left here with a scouting party in search of a band of renegade Apache. Just as the soldiers were entering a narrow canyon, they found the Apache. The Indians were well concealed in the surrounding cliffs, and a bloody battle ensued.

McBryar's commanding officer noted that he had demonstrated "coolness, bravery, and good marksmanship" under trying and hazardous conditions.

HOLBROOK

*Mormon Settlements,* south on State 77. The area between Holbrook and McNary Junction was settled largely by Mormon families. Many arrived with Negro slaves or servants in their party. One of these was Jeff, who worked as a cowboy for Thomas and Ellen Greer, who had a ranch near here.

The Greer family historian recalled Jeff as an extremely proficient ranch hand who could not only handle horses and cattle, but cooked at roundup camps, and braided rawhide ropes for the other cowboys. Her gentle account of Jeff overlooked some of his more hazardous exploits during the periodic warfare with Mexican sheepmen. Jeff was wounded in one gunfight with Mexicans in St. Johns. The Mexicans invited Greer to St. Johns to buy cattle cheaply, but when he and his cowboys arrived, they ran into an ambush. In the ensuing gunfight Jeff was shot, but managed to escape.

In a later episode, perhaps stemming from the same event, Jeff was seized by sixteen Mexican deputies in Holbrook, and held captive in a hotel. They said they were going to return him to St. Johns for trial, but Jeff expected to be shot along the way. He was spared that fate when a group of cowboys surrounded the hotel and freed him.

After twenty years on the ranch Jeff made a trip to Los Angeles with one of the Greers and saw his first taxicab. He decided he would rather drive a cab than ride a horse, so he stayed in California. No one knows what happened to him after that.

PHOENIX

*State Capitol,* West Washington and 17th Avenue. Eight murals by Jay Datus depict the *Pageant of Arizona Progress.* One portrays Estevanico, the Negro guide of Fray Marcos de Niza, who led a Spanish expedition into Arizona in 1539.

Estevanico preceded the group into what is now Arizona and New Mexico to become the first man, other than the Indians, to behold the territory. Searching for the fabled "Seven Golden Cities of Cibola," the Negro found, instead, death at the hands of Zuni Indians at one of seven pueblos near the present town of Gallup, New Mexico.

SAN CARLOS

*San Carlos Indian Reservation.* The Tribal Council of the San Carlos Apache meets here now, on the reservation to which Geronimo and the Warm Springs Apache were brought by units of the 10th Cavalry in 1876.

It was from San Carlos that Geronimo broke out again in 1881, headed for Mexico, and began the raids that made his name a synonym for terror throughout the Southwest. Units of the 10th engaged and trailed him throughout the campaign that followed. They were among the troops under General Crook when he surrendered, only to escape again.

The 10th escorted most of the Apache warriors and their families to exile in Florida.

SIERRA VISTA

*Site of Fort Huachuca,* established in 1877 to protect settlers from the Apache. It frequently quartered troops of the 9th and 10th Cavalry Regiments. Elements of the 10th Cavalry also served here in the years immediately preceding World War I.

More than twenty-five years later, during World War II, the men of the all-Negro 92nd Division trained here and then went on to Africa and Europe to win more than twelve thousand decorations and citations—among them two Distinguished Service Awards, sixteen Legion of Merit Awards, ninety-five Silver Stars, and nearly eleven hundred Purple Hearts.

After the war the fort became the U. S. Electronic Proving Ground.

## SPRINGERVILLE

*Apache National Forest,* twelve miles southwest of town. The drive from Springerville is almost all uphill to the summit of the White Mountains at eight thousand feet.

The Indians on the adjacent Fort Apache Indian Reservation are peaceful now, in sharp contrast to their behavior in the days when the Negro "buffalo soldiers" were charged with keeping them in hand. It was here in the White Mountains, on September 18, 1886, that the men of the 10th Cavalry captured one of the most ferocious of the Apache chieftains, Mangas Coloradas.

Even during the Indian wars, Americans had apparently developed a policy of being most generous to their most vigorous adversaries. The Apache were the most dangerous opponents of western settlement. They were also one of the few tribes to salvage a decent piece of land to call their own. This reservation contains three and one-half million acres of choice cattle land.

## TOMBSTONE

*John Swain Grave in Boot Hill.* John Swain was born a slave in 1845. He came to Tombstone in 1879 as a cowhand for John Slaughter, who later became sheriff.

Tombstone, headquarters of such notorious frontier characters as the Earp brothers and Doc Holliday, was a turbulent town until Slaughter took over as sheriff. Slaughter chased many offenders out of Tombstone, but rarely brought one back alive. Old-timers recalled that he usually reported having chased the outlaw "clean out of the territory," but curiously, they never reappeared in Tombstone—or anywhere else.

John Swain worked for Slaughter in a day when ranchhands had to defend their cattle from rustlers and from such notorious Indians as Apache chief Victorio. A near-giant of a man, Swain was an expert rider and cattleman, and he had nerve to match his strength.

One of Tombstone's notorious killers, Frank Leslie, once tried to jump his mining claim. The Negro cowboy challenged him, but Leslie withdrew to look for an easier victim. In 1884, Swain fought John L. Sullivan for one round. He lost.

Swain died in 1945, three months short of his one-hundredth birthday. He was buried with honors by the City of Tombstone, which provided a special marker for the grave of this "worthy pioneer."

## TORTILLA FLAT

*Site of the Battle of the Caves,* about sixteen miles from town, off State 88, near Horse Mesa Dam. Only a hardy soul will try to find this site. The trip is not recommended because it is hard on cars and people. After a drive on a dirt road, the cave can be reached only on foot. Visitors must climb a mountain, cross a lava bed, and then descend a torturous trail over the rim of the gorge and down the face of the cliff.

That should discourage tourists, just as the Apache thought it would discourage the Negro cavalrymen. The Indians considered it one of their safest hiding places.

From 1872–73 General Crook launched a campaign against the mountain retreats from which the Apache had been conducting surprise raids. On a December night in 1872, the Negro soldiers, covered by darkness, climbed to within fifty feet of the cave without being detected.

In the morning, when the Apache emerged, the soldiers opened fire. Some Indians were killed, but others retreated into the cave. They were finally dislodged by a murderous barrage fired into the mouth of the cave against the ceiling and walls. The ricocheting bullets ended the encounter. Seventy-six Indians died and eighteen were captured.

# ARKANSAS

*Poison Spring State Park.* Here, on April 18, 1864, Confederate forces routed a large Federal supply wagon train under the command of Colonel James M. Williams. Losses by the 1st Kansas Colored Regiment were its heaviest of the war, with 117 dead and sixty-five wounded. After the fighting there were reports that the Confederates had shot captured and wounded Negroes, which allegedly led to a vow by the Kansas Negro troops that they would retaliate by taking no more Confederate prisoners.

HELENA

*The Battle of Helena* is noted by seven markers at significant points. This was the home of seven Confederate generals, and a highly prized target of both armies during the Civil War. Sometimes called "the only seaport in Arkansas," its location on the Mississippi River made it of great strategic importance to both North and South.

The city was occupied by Union General Samuel Curtis in 1862. In July 1863, when three Confederate generals joined in an unsuccessful effort to retake it, Negro soldiers fought shoulder-to-shoulder with white troops.

Although President Lincoln had given approval for the use of Negroes as soldiers only six months earlier, thirty regiments had been recruited by mid-1863. The defenders here included the untrained and untried members of the 2nd Infantry Regiment—African Descent. This unit had been recruited in Arkansas, and at the time of the engagement had not even been formally mustered in. A contemporary observer commented that they followed their officers, "even in charges or assaults of great peril, far more readily than white soldiers."

The South also employed Negroes in the Civil War, usually in the construction of fortifications or other menial roles. Many plantation owners relinquished their slaves for duty with great reluctance, for they were valuable property. The story is told, perhaps apocryphal, of the Southerner whose son had taken one of his slaves off to war with him. The father wrote a letter cautioning his son not to allow the slave to "get too near the battle" because he was worth one thousand dollars.

The record of one unit stationed here, the 56th U. S. Colored Troops, provides a vivid example of the dreadful toll of disease among those who fought in the Civil War. Most of the 56th's service was as garrison; it fought in only three minor engagements during the war, losing four officers and twenty-one men. Meanwhile, six officers and nearly six hundred and fifty men died from disease.

LITTLE ROCK

*Philander Smith College.* Although one of the younger Negro colleges, this institution is symbolic of the eager struggle of young Negroes for educational opportunity. The school was opened in 1877 as the first educational institution of the Southwest Annual Conference of the Methodist Episcopal Church. Named Walden College, in honor of the first corresponding secretary of the Freedmen's Aid Society, it began operations in a converted livery stable and later moved to larger quarters over a store.

In 1882 a gift from the widow of Philander Smith led to the renaming of the institution and construction of Budlong Hall, its first brick building. This building and Webb Hall, both since razed, were built largely with student labor. Today the campus has modern classroom and dormitory buildings and an accredited four-year liberal arts program.

NEW EDINBURGH

*Mark's Mill Battlefield.* On April 25, 1864, Confederate forces under General John S. Marmaduke attacked a 240-wagon supply train carrying supplies to General Frederick Steele at Camden. As in other Arkansas engagements, Southern soldiers displayed great bitterness toward their ex-slave adversaries.

In a report of the action, John Edwards, a member of Confederate General Jo Shelby's division, wrote: "The battlefield was sickening to behold. No orders, threats, or commands could restrain the men from vengeance on the Negroes, and they were piled in great heaps about the wagons, in the tangled brushwood, and upon the muddy and trampled road."

## PINE BLUFF

*Portis House,* 216 East Second Avenue; *Thompson House,* 519 West Barraque Street; and *Bocage House* are varied examples of homes built between 1844 and the end of the Civil War. Much of the construction of homes such as these was done with slave labor, and the Negroes who built them often were exceptionally fine craftsmen. In some instances, their heritage of African wood carving may have contributed to their artistry in working with wood.

## SHERIDAN

*Jenkins Ferry State Park,* 11.5 miles southwest on State 46. Two weeks after the engagement at Poison Spring, on April 30, 1864, the 50th Indiana was relieved at this spot by the 1st and 2nd Kansas Colored Regiments. The Negroes—shouting "Remember Poison Spring"—charged a battery of three Confederate guns located along the Sabine River. They overran it and killed one hundred and fifty Confederates, losing only fifteen killed and fifty-five wounded themselves.

The engagement occurred when General Steele's force was attacked during its withdrawal after the Battle of Mark's Mill. After half a day of fighting, Steele's troops finally crossed the river on pontoons and returned to Little Rock.

# CALIFORNIA

## ARCADIA

*Santa Anita Race Track*, Huntington Drive, is one of the nation's most famous tracks, with a grandstand that seats thirty thousand and a season that includes four one-hundred-thousand-dollar purses. The track and the town occupy what was once part of the E. J. "Lucky" Baldwin ranch.

One of those credited with a major role in the development of the thoroughbreds at Rancho Santa Anita was John Fisher, a Negro who began life as a slave, became an expert horseshoer, and finally a breeder and trainer of great knowledge and skill.

Lucky Baldwin lured Fisher away from a job in St. Louis, after overcoming Fisher's fear of "wild Indians," and ultimately made him foreman of a ranch that employed more than four hundred men. The ranch has long since been broken up, and the land where Baldwin and Fisher's horses grazed is now some of the state's highest priced real estate. But Santa Anita Race Track lives on as a sort of memorial to the Negro who was instrumental in establishing a place for California in racing history.

## BECKWOURTH

*Beckwourth Pass*, State Highway 70, east of junction with U. S. 395. This is the lowest pass through the Sierra Nevada Mountains. It was discovered by—and named for—James F. Beckwourth, one of several Negroes among the pioneer traders and trappers known to American history as the Mountain Men.

Beckwourth was born in Charlottesville, Virginia, in 1789, of a slave mother and a Revolutionary War officer. He first visited the Rockies in 1824 with General W. H. Ashley's fur-trading expedition. Later he guided many other expeditions through the mountains.

There are many legends about Beckwourth, some of which he started himself. One of the more romantic tales did not originate with Beckwourth; it sprang up after his death.

In his sixties he killed a man in an argument in Denver and was held in jail until he was acquitted on a plea of self-defense. He went to the Crow Indians, the story says—Beckwourth always claimed to be a Crow chief—and was warmly welcomed because the tribe believed he brought them good luck.

According to the legend, that belief sealed his doom. When he talked of leaving, the Crows were determined not to let him go, taking their good luck with him. They held an elaborate feast in his honor but poisoned his stew and thus by his death kept their good luck with them forever.

The facts are a good deal less glamorous. Apparently Beckwourth, having left Denver, died on the trail two days before he was to rendezvous with the Crow. Still, his exploits—more of them real than mythical—live on in the history of the West.

## BEVERLY HILLS

*Beverly-Wilshire Hotel* was designed by Paul R. Williams, perhaps the most accomplished of Negro architects. Williams specializes in business structures—others here are those of Twentieth Century-Fox and Saks Fifth Avenue—but he has also designed homes for many well-known Hollywood personalities. Among them were the palatial residences of Grace Moore, Zasu Pitts, and Columbia Broadcasting System chairman William S. Paley.

Williams won the Spingarn Medal in 1953, awarded by the NAACP to Negroes of outstanding accomplishment.

## DOWNIEVILLE

*The Pioneer Museum.* You'll have to use your imagination here, because no physical evidence remains, but there were ten Negroes with William Downie when he and his party found gold here in 1849.

Major Downie (or Downey) is referred to by a Downieville old-timer as a "wanderer on the earth." He was born in Glasgow, Scotland, in 1819, and arrived in Monterey in 1843. He went on to Downieville after being told that Indians were panning gold in baskets made of willow and lined with pitch.

Little is known of the members of his party, but local histories recount one incident in which a party of nine of Downie's men went to the Sacramento Valley for provisions, and only one came back. His name was Jim Crow.

When Downie and his party arrived here they found the river-bed so rich in gold that they immediately began panning it, although the sandbars were snow-covered and the river filmed with ice. A woman who ran a tent restaurant found flecks of gold while sweeping the dirt floor, promptly folded the tent, and became a miner instead of a restaurateur.

One of the early miners here was Waller Jackson, a Negro who came "around the Horn" from Boston in 1849.

### FOLSOM LAKE

*"Negro Bar" Marker* recalls the old mining camps now flooded by Folsom Lake. This place name is typical of those that often provide the historian with his only clue to a Negro accomplishment. The Mormon Island Pioneer Cemetery contains the remains of mining camp pioneers who were reburied here before the lake was formed by Folsom Dam.

Negroes were with Hernando de Alarcon when this Spanish navigator explored the Gulf of California and the lower reaches of the Colorado River in 1540. On several occasions during the fall of that year he crossed the river at a point near here.

### FREMONT PEAK

*Fremont Peak State Park.* The park and nearby Fremont's Ford are named for John C. Fremont, a soldier, explorer, mapmaker, writer, and politician; and a key figure in the development of California and the war that brought it into the Union.

Fremont was several times a hero and several times in disgrace. His career was marked by controversy and contradiction.

He led four exploratory and mapping expeditions. Kit Carson was his guide on all but the last, which ended in tragedy. Negroes were members of the second and fourth expeditions.

Jacob Dodson, a free Negro and a servant of Fremont's father-in-law, Senator Thomas Hart Benton of Missouri, was a member of the second expedition, which made Fremont a national figure.

Saunders Jackson, also a Benton servant, volunteered for the fourth. He went because he needed seventeen hundred dollars to purchase his family out of slavery.

Accounts of this expedition are contradictory. It appears to have been marked by several unexplained blunders, made more serious by bad weather and deep snows. The party became lost in the Sierra Nevada Mountains and was forced to turn back. Eleven men died in the ill-fated assault on the mountain range. Some of the survivors accused others of cowardice and cannibalism.

Fremont and some of those who survived, including Jackson, went on to California by a southern route. When they arrived in 1849, gold had been discovered on land Fremont had purchased during an earlier visit. He discovered he was a millionaire.

Jackson was given permission to mine a section of the land and reportedly dug his seventeen hundred dollars out of the ground in a few days. He returned to Missouri, bought his family out of slavery, and disappeared from history.

Fremont was named one of California's first senators in 1850. Although he was a Georgian by birth, he was anti-slavery by politics, and his views cost him re-election. During the Civil War he was military commander of the Union forces in Missouri. In 1861 he issued a proclamation freeing all the slaves held by Missourians fighting for the South.

HOLLYWOOD

*Grauman's Chinese Theatre,* 6925 Hollywood Boulevard. Patrons of this historic theater have watched the Negro role in motion pictures evolve from one of stereotyped idiocy to a realistic view of the contribution of Negroes to American life, and the casting of Negroes in roles worthy of their talent.

In 1939, Hattie McDaniel won an Academy Award for a supporting role in *Gone with the Wind* that still portrayed the Negro in the degrading "Uncle Tom" role. More than twenty-five years later, in 1965, Sidney Poitier won the best actor award for a highly respectable role in *Lilies of the Field.*

Hollywood actors have long felt that they have "arrived" when Grauman's Chinese Theatre invites them to place their footprints in a square of wet concrete in the forecourt. On June 23, 1967, Sidney Poitier finally became the first Negro actor to do this; it was as much a triumph for Negroes in the film industry as it was for him.

HORNITOS

*Gold Mining Camp,* fourteen miles off State 49 from Mount Bullion, was the home of Moses Rodgers, a Negro who owned a group of mines in nearby Quartzburg, and who was a partner in the Sweet Vengeance mine in Brown's Valley. Rodgers was known as one of the best engineers and metallurgists on the Pacific Coast, and his services were much in demand by other miners.

Many slaves worked in the mines to buy their freedom. The 1850 California census recorded 962 Negroes, most of them men. This was about 1 percent of the total population. While they were not numerous, many of the Negroes were very successful. One, Robert Anthony, owned what may have been the first quartz mill in the state, located on Horn Cut Creek in Yuba County. Allen B. Light, another Negro, was appointed by the government agent to prevent illegal otter hunting.

Among the camps where Negroes are known to have mined gold were Placerville, Grass Valley, Negro Bar, Mormon Hill, Murphy's Diggings, Diamond, and Mud Springs. Near Tuttletown in Tuolumne County a Negro named Dick found a vein so rich he soon had one hundred thousand dollars. Like many white miners, he succumbed to temptation, lost his fortune at the gambling tables in Sacramento, and killed himself in remorse.

LOS ANGELES

*Los Angeles County Museum of Natural History* has a diorama depicting the founding of Los Angeles. The American Revolution was nearing its end in the eastern colonies when the first settlers arrived on September 4, 1781. Contrary to popular opinion, they were not Spanish grandees.

Eleven families, totaling forty-four people, were recruited in Mexico by Fernando de Rivera y Moncada for the original colony. Twenty-eight of the settlers were Negroes.

The site of the original Pueblo de Los Angeles is the Plaza on North Main Street. The original title, proclaimed by Governor Don Felipe de Neve, was El Pueblo de Nuestra Senora la Reina de Los Angeles de Porciuncula (The Town of Our Lady the Queen of the Angels of Porciuncula).

MOKELUMNE HILL

*Gold Discovery Marker.* Negroes were on hand in most of the gold rush communities of California, including this one. Here, legend has it, white miners tried to play a joke on a Negro who asked them where to dig. They pointed to the most barren and unpromising hillside in town, but the humor backfired. He returned a day or two later to thank them, carrying a sack of gold.

"Mok Hill" was one of the principal California gold camps, but many of the others are little more than ghost towns today. Things were livelier here in the days of gold fever, when ten to sixteen square feet constituted a mining claim, and many were willing to kill or die for one. During one period, a man was killed here every weekend for seventeen consecutive weeks, and in another week five men died with their boots on.

OAKLAND

*Oakland Art Museum,* 1000 Fallon Street, specializes in California art "from the earliest times to the present." A number of Negro artists are represented in the collection. One of the finest pieces is a painted wood sculpture by Sargent Johnson, "Forever Free."

The museum has many examples of the work of Grafton T. Brown, believed to be the first Negro artist in California. Some of his first work was done in the 1850s, and in about 1872 he opened his own business as a lithographer. One of his apprentices established a lithography firm that is still prominent in California today, but nothing is known of Brown's fate.

The work of Brown displayed here consists mostly of lithographs. The artist specialized in drawings of western towns, and several views of San Francisco and Virginia City are included.

RED BLUFF

*Oak Hill Cemetery* is the final resting place of Alvin Aaron Coffey, a true pioneer of California, the only Negro to join the Society of California Pioneers, who became one of its most devoted members.

Coffey came to California in 1849 as a slave. His grandfather, a Kentuckian, was an officer under Andrew Jackson in the Battle of New Orleans. Coffey's master told him that he could purchase his freedom for one thousand dollars, so Coffey worked by day mining his master's claims, and by night cobbling shoes for other miners. At one point he had accumulated half the amount, but his owner appropriated it.

Eventually, Coffey was forced to return to Missouri with his owner, who then sold him. He persuaded his new master to allow him to return to California to earn the money to buy his own freedom, and that of his wife and children. He agreed, and Coffey's family remained in Missouri until he had earned enough money to set all of them free.

Coffey farmed near Red Bluff for many years, and many of his children remained in the area. One son became an engineer in San Francisco. The Pioneer's Society Library in San Francisco has many Coffey papers which reveal him as a highly respected pioneer. When he died in 1902 his obituary was a glowing one.

He is buried here with his wife, Mahalia, and several of their children.

*John Brown House,* 135 Main Street. After the abolitionist was hanged for his raid on Harpers Ferry (see West Virginia), his widow and three daughters lived here from 1864 to 1870. Local citizens, many of them Negroes, raised money to assist them. This is now a private home, but a state historical marker has been placed here.

### SACRAMENTO

*St. Andrew's African Methodist Church,* 2131 Eighth Street, was the first African Methodist Episcopal church on the Pacific Coast. It was organized in 1850 and operated in a private home until it acquired its original site on Seventh Street.

The first church and parsonage were built for three thousand dollars. On May 29, 1854, Mrs. Elizabeth Thorn Scott opened the first public school for Negroes, Indians, and Mongolians in the church basement.

*Sutter's Fort,* 2800 L Street, is the reconstructed fort established in 1839 by John Augustus Sutter to protect his Mexican land grant of seventy-six square miles. At least one Negro, Fisar, is known to have lived here in 1847.

### SAN BERNARDINO

*Pioneer Cemetery.* A granite monument in this cemetery reveals nothing of the incredible story of Elizabeth Rowan, whose name it bears. From birth, on the plantation of William Love in North Carolina, she was simply called "Liz." When Agnes Love married James Madison Flake, she received Liz as her father's wedding gift. The child was only five years old.

In 1844 the Flakes joined the Church of Jesus Christ of Latter-Day Saints and traveled to Nauvoo, Illinois. They spent the winter of 1846–47 in a dugout, awaiting the spring journey across the plains to the Valley of the Great Salt Lake. Throughout the summer Liz and the three small Flake children herded the loose cattle across hundreds of miles of plains, arriving in the valley in October 1848.

Two years later James Flake died, and Mrs. Flake decided to join a company that was leaving to begin a settlement in Southern California. Once again they started out, this time across mountain and desert, with Liz driving two yoke of oxen. Arriving in 1851, Liz helped the boys make the adobe brick for the first house built by Mormons in the San Bernardino Valley. Soon after it was finished, Mrs. Flake became ill and died. Liz kept house and took care of the children until 1855 when she and the boys went to live with another family.

When William Flake, one of the boys, returned to Utah, he gave Liz her freedom, and Liz married a free Negro named Charles H. Rowan. He owned and operated a barber shop in the Grand Union Hotel for more than forty years, and the couple acquired some property in the main business section. Meanwhile, they had three children.

Their daughter, Alice, became a teacher in a white school in Riverside—perhaps the first instance in the country of a Negro girl teaching white children. William Flake's descendants still treasure the set of fine silver that Elizabeth Flake Rowan, his mother's slave, sent him for a wedding gift.

## SAN FRANCISCO

*Leidesdorff Street.* This downtown street was named for William Alexander Leidesdorff, a native of the Danish West Indies who was of Negro and Danish ancestry. He came to California in 1841 as master of a trading vessel, and settled here as a merchant. Subsequently, he bought a steamer which was the first to pass through the Golden Gate.

In 1845 he was appointed United States vice-consul, and after the American conquest of California became a member of the San Francisco city council, city treasurer, and a member of the school committee. He died more than one hundred years ago, in 1848, and was buried at Mission Dolores, located on Dolores Street between 16th and 17th Streets.

*The Presidio* was settled in the name of the King of Spain in 1776. Originally a walled square containing about one hundred buildings, it is now an Army post. Only one of the original buildings remains.

Negroes were here very early in California history. The records disclose that there were at least two Negroes at the post in 1790—Justa Altamarino, from Sonora, and an eighteen-year-old girl, Maria Garcia.

*Site of Terry-Broderick Duel,* south of the city off U. S. 1, at the southern tip of Lake Merced. Two granite shafts here mark the site where Senator David C. Broderick and State Supreme Court Justice Terry faced each other on September 13, 1859, at dawn, thirty paces apart.

Broderick was a devoted supporter of civil rights for Negroes. One of his most trusted associates was his confidential aide, a Negro named John Jones.

The duel grew out of a public attack on Broderick by Terry, who ridiculed him for sharing the views of Negro abolitionist Frederick Douglass. Broderick replied in kind, and the duel ensued. Broderick, the abolitionist, got off the first shot, which entered the ground nine feet in front of Terry. Terry's bullet hit Broderick in the chest, and he died three days later.

A crowd of thirty thousand people gathered in Portsmouth Plaza in San Francisco for Broderick's funeral. Although California's 1849 Constitution prohibited slavery, there was considerable animosity between the abolitionists and the pro-slavery forces. Those who favored slavery opposed the admission of another free state, and delayed Congressional approval of California's admission to the Union.

# COLORADO

### BRECKENRIDGE

*Barney Ford Hill,* just southeast of the city limits, was named for a runaway slave who came to Colorado in 1860 in search of gold. He had already made and lost a fortune in the hotel business in Nicaragua and had operated a station on the "underground railroad" in Chicago, twice becoming involved in the exploits of John Brown.

Ford found gold, but it did not make him rich. He was cheated out of his claim and driven off by outlaws. He spent what little gold he had getting back to Denver, but a legend grew that he had buried a fortune on the hill that now bears his name.

When Ford later became wealthy in the hotel and restaurant business, many people insisted his wealth came from his buried treasure on the hill. Over a period of nearly thirty years, the hill became pockmarked by the frustrated attempts of miners and others to locate Barney Ford's "buried treasure."

CENTRAL CITY

*"Aunt Clara" Brown Chair*, Central City Opera House, is dedicated to a Colorado pioneer who was about eighty-five when she died here in 1877. It is believed that she was the first free Negro resident of the territory.

Born a slave in Virginia, she saw her husband and children sold before her master took her to Missouri. When he died he left a will that set her free. "Aunt Clara" moved first to Leavenworth, Kansas, and then, in 1859, to the Colorado gold fields. She opened the first laundry in Colorado Territory and began saving money to purchase freedom for her husband and children.

Before she had saved enough they were freed by the Emancipation Proclamation. Mrs. Brown went to Missouri and returned to Central City with a group of thirty-eight relatives. She lived here for the rest of her life, becoming revered for her deeds of charity. When she died, the other members of the Colorado Pioneers Association buried her with honors.

The chair in her name was dedicated in 1932. The memory of Aunt Clara is also honored with a bronze plaque in St. James Methodist Church, noting that before it was built, "services were held in the home of 'Aunt Clara' Brown."

COLORADO SPRINGS

*U. S. Air Force Academy*. Many Negroes have attended this youngest of the service academies since the first three were enrolled in 1959.

The first cadet to win the Major Richard I. Bong Award as the outstanding student of Military History was a Negro, Roger B. Sims, of the Class of 1963. Another Negro cadet, Fletcher H. Wiley, of the Class of 1965, was awarded a Fulbright Scholarship at the University of Paris.

CRAIG

*Site of Thornburgh Battlefield.* Seventeen miles south of Craig on State 13, turn left eleven miles to a side road, then right 0.6 mile to a low granite shaft erected in memory of Major T. T. Thornburgh and the men of his command who were slain by the Ute Indians in 1879.

Thornburgh, with an infantry and cavalry force of 160 men, was surrounded and pinned down here by a large war party of Ute. Most of the Army horses were killed, and soon fifty-six men, including Thornburgh, were also dead or wounded.

Messengers were sent to secure help, and forty-four men of the 9th Cavalry Regiment, led by Captain Francis S. Dodge, were the first to respond. They slipped into the trenches during the night without losing a man. In the morning the Ute renewed their attack, killing most of the Negroes' horses, but the added strength was enough to hold off the Indians for three days until four more troops of cavalry and a company of infantry arrived. They had been summoned by a scout who rode 165 miles in twenty-eight hours.

Sergeant Henry Johnson, a 9th Cavalryman who risked his life repeatedly to care for white and Negro wounded, won the Medal of Honor in this engagement.

DEARFIELD

*A Negro Community* was established here in 1910 by C. T. Jackson, a Negro who came to Colorado in 1887 and was employed in the governor's office.

Jackson read *Up from Slavery,* by Booker T. Washington, and, with encouragement from the territorial governor, selected a site near Boulder for a Negro farming colony. Seven families built homes there in 1911, and after some difficulty, developed successful farming operations.

DENVER

*Colorado State Museum,* 14th Avenue and Sherman. Operated by the State Historical Society of Colorado, the museum has many relics of the pioneer days of Colorado. Included in the collection are paintings by Robert Lindneux depicting the Thornburgh battle, and Forsyth's encounter with Chief Roman Nose at Beecher Island. These were two of the major Indian battles in Colorado in which Negroes figured prominently.

*Inter-Ocean Hotel*, 16th and Market Streets. This hotel, now only a shabby shadow of its former self, was built by Barney Ford in 1873. It was for many years the most elegant and famous hotel between St. Louis and San Francisco, host to miners, millionaires, statesmen, and Presidents.

Ford, a runaway slave, had previously operated a hotel in Nicaragua, prospered, and then went broke during a rebellion. He returned to Chicago and later went to Colorado seeking gold. When that failed to make him rich, he opened a barbershop, then a restaurant, then a series of hotels. The Inter-Ocean became so popular that he was asked to build another hotel in Cheyenne, Wyoming. Many believed the second Inter-Ocean surpassed the first, but it has since burned.

Ford's last years were spent in modest retirement. He died in December 1902, while shoveling snow. He is buried beside his wife, Julia, in Denver's Riverside Cemetery.

*Julia Greeley Grave*, Mount Olivet Cemetery. Buried here is Julia Greeley, who came to Colorado as a servant in the home of the first territorial governor, but became known and remembered as the "Colored Angel of Charity."

A Catholic convert, Julia Greeley's charitable works were so admired that on her death she was accorded the highest honor ever paid to a Colorado Catholic layman. Her body lay in state in the Sacred Heart Church from three until eight o'clock, and a contemporary account said that "while she lay there, limousines and touring cars carried the rich to her side, and the poor flocked to the church to pay their last tribute to the Colored Angel of Charity."

FORT GARLAND

*Old Fort Garland*, Costilla County, U. S. 160. The state has restored this old fort, which was once commanded by Kit Carson. The 9th Cavalry Regiment was stationed here during the Negro troopers' campaign against the Ute Indians in the late 1870s. Dioramas have been constructed and frontier relics are on display.

GEORGETOWN

*Old Mining Camp.* This entire town, and others in the area, are monuments of sorts to the pioneer prospectors who discovered gold in the area beginning about 1859. Some, like nearby Central City, have been rejuvenated for tourists, who are busily returning the gold that was removed long ago.

Among the first to prospect Leavenworth Mountain, near here, was a Negro, Jerry Lee. He discovered many lodes that are well-known locally—the O.K., Argentine, Jenny Lynd, George Law, and others; several produced fortunes after they passed from his possession.

With a partner, Professor Bowman, Lee built the Red, White, and Blue smelter in Leavenworth Gulch, and the first road over Burrell Hill. The road was used for many years to haul out millions of dollars' worth of ore.

Lee was born in Virginia in 1829, moved to Illinois and Missouri, and at seventeen went off to fight in the Mexican War. In 1850, he was mining gold in California. He returned to the East, but the gold fever got him again in 1859 and he came to Colorado. The Negro miner crossed the western plains nine times before a railroad was built, but finally settled down to a comfortable life in Central City, where he owned considerable mining property.

PUEBLO

*El Pueblo Museum,* 905 S. Prairie Avenue. The museum houses a re-creation of the Gantt-Blackwell Fort, which Jim Beckwourth, the Negro scout and trader, claimed he founded in 1842. Beckwourth made a number of such claims, not all of which have been upheld, but this one probably was the truth.

Like most of the mountain men, Beckwourth had a reputation as a teller of tall tales, but as explorer, scout, and guide, he made a contribution to the opening of the West that needed no embellishment.

WRAY

*Beecher Island Battle Marker,* on Route 53, is at the site of another episode in which Negro cavalrymen rescued greatly outnumbered white units during the Indian wars. Colonel Forsyth and fifty scouts were trapped along the Arickaree River here by several hundred Indians led by Chief Roman Nose. The siege lasted eight days, with the soldiers subsisting on meat from their dead horses and water scooped from holes in the sand.

Roman Nose was killed early in the fight, and an officer and four scouts had been killed and eighteen men wounded when the 10th Cavalry arrived from Fort Wallace and drove the Indians off. The site is marked by a twenty-foot cement obelisk and five flanking gravestones.

# CONNECTICUT

## FARMINGTON

*First Church of Christ, Congregational.* This historic structure was dedicated in 1772. It was the only church in Farmington in 1839 when a group of Africans arrived in the village to await trial for mutiny aboard the slave ship *Amistad.* Led by a fiery Negro named Joseph Cinque, they had rebelled against their captors, seized the ship, and brought it into the harbor at Montauk, Long Island.

The Negroes spent two years in Farmington. They worshiped in this church and attended a church school in rooms above a store that still stands on Mill Road. They were quartered in another nearby structure. One of the party died here and is buried in the Farmington Cemetery. The inscription on the marble marker reads:

Foone
A native African who was drowned while bathing in the Center Basin, Aug. 1841. He was one of the Company of Slaves under Cinque who asserted their rights and took possession of the vessel after having put the Captain, Mate and others to death, sparing their Masters Ruez and Montez.

Cinque and the others were convicted in their initial trial. The conviction was overturned by the United States Supreme Court after a brilliant argument by former President John Quincy Adams.

After the acquittal, local citizens raised funds to return the group to Africa and supply them with equipment and money. The Negroes established, near Sierra Leone, a mission called Mendi, named for the place in Africa from which they had been abducted and sold into slavery. Joseph Cinque, who risked death to avoid servitude, lived at the mission and served as an interpreter until his death in 1880.

*Underground Railroad Stations.* Connecticut once ranked third among the New England colonies in the slave trade. In 1660 it barred Negroes from military service, and in 1690 passed laws prohibiting Negroes from being on the streets at night or leaving their town without a pass. On the eve of the Revolutionary War its Negro population was larger than that of any other New England colony.

After the Revolution, in which Connecticut Negroes served valiantly along with those of other states, a law was passed for the gradual abolition of slavery. By 1830 the census showed only twenty-three slaves in the entire state. Subsequently, strong abolitionist sentiment developed, and many white citizens began assisting Negro slaves in their flight to freedom. At least eight of Farmington's leading residents were active in aiding slaves. Homes here that are known to have been used as "underground railroad" stations include that of Horace Cowles, on Main Street; Lyman Hurlburt's, on High Street, and Elijah Lewis's, on Hartford Road. The town became the junction point of Connecticut escape routes; Horatio T. Strother, in his exhaustive work on the subject, called it the Grand Central Station of Connecticut's underground railroad lines.

GROTON HEIGHTS

*Fort Griswold State Park.* When a British force under Benedict Arnold moved on New London in September 1781, the Americans withdrew to Fort Griswold, across the Thames River, where they conducted a murderous defense. The British were so enraged by their heavy casualties that when the Colonial troops surrendered they were shown no mercy.

The American commander, Colonel William Ledyard, offered his sword to a British officer, who promptly stabbed him with it. A Negro named Lambert Latham, who had volunteered shortly before the battle, avenged Ledyard's death by killing the British officer. Then he himself died of thirty-three bayonet wounds.

Jordan Freeman, Ledyard's Negro orderly, speared British officer William Montgomery with a pike as he scaled the walls. He was one of those slain after the surrender.

A tablet in the park depicts Freeman in the act of slaying the British officer.

MYSTIC

*Mystic Seaport.* This reconstruction of a nineteenth-century coastal village has on display the old whaling vessel *Charles W. Morgan.* The crew lists of this and other whalers reveal that many Negroes served on board the sailing ships that spent months and even years at sea in pursuit of whales. Negroes also helped build the ships and make whaling equipment.

NEW HAVEN

*Temple Street Church* was founded by two of the most active agents of the "underground railroad," the Reverend Simeon S. Jocelyn, and the first Negro pastor of the church, Amos G. Beman. New Haven was literally a haven for countless slaves who stopped here on their flight to freedom before and during the Civil War, and who were helped on their way to Canada by some of the town's leading citizens.

*Yale University.* This old Ivy League institution has educated a number of America's leading Negroes.

The Library houses a collection of the books and papers of James Weldon Johnson, Negro novelist, poet, and civil rights advocate.

The first Negro to win a Ph.D. in America, Edward A. Bouchet, received it here in 1876. He was also the first Negro member of Phi Beta Kappa, the national honor society. After graduating, he taught at Negro schools in Philadelphia and in Texas.

The Reverend Adam Clayton Powell, Sr., the former congressman's father, attended the Yale Divinity School.

NEW LONDON

*The United States Coast Guard Academy* was founded in 1876 to train and educate career officers for the service that guards the nation's ocean frontiers in war and peace. The Academy numbers Negroes among its six hundred cadets, and among its faculty, as well.

# DELAWARE

*Delaware State House,* situated on the east side of the Village Green, is the second oldest state house still in use.

It was the captain of a ship owned by Peter Minuit, who came to Delaware with a Swedish expedition in 1638, who brought the first Negro slave into the colony a year later. The slave, Anthony, became a favorite servant of Governor Printz.

Many of the slaves owned in Delaware in the seventeenth century were freed before 1700, and by the time the state constitution was adopted here in 1776, anti-slavery sentiment prompted inclusion of a declaration against slavery. In 1787 a law was passed declaring that any Negro slave brought into the state would be freed.

In 1790 there were four thousand free Negroes in the state, and nearly nine thousand slaves. By 1860 fewer than two thousand Delaware Negroes remained in slavery, and nearly twenty thousand were free.

*Governor's House,* King's Highway and Pennsylvania Avenue, is also known as Woodburn. This old mansion bears a marker asserting that it was used as an underground railroad station to assist escaping slaves prior to the Civil War.

A more romantic legend about the mansion holds that it once figured in the career of the notorious murderer and slave kidnaper, Patty Cannon. Allegedly, a group of her raiders entered the house by a staircase window in order to carry off some Negroes who were, with the owner's permission, having a dance. The would-be kidnapers were driven off.

ODESSA

*Friends Meeting House,* on Main Street, was built in 1783 but has been closed since 1880. During the days when most of the plantation owners of the surrounding countryside owned slaves, the members of this church used it as an underground railroad station. The slaves were hidden in the loft and fed until they could safely move on to the north.

## WILMINGTON

*Asbury Methodist Episcopal Church,* Third and Walnut Streets, was dedicated by Bishop Francis Asbury in 1789, but the congregation was founded several years earlier.

There is a tradition that Methodism was not socially acceptable to some of Wilmington's leading citizens who, nonetheless, wanted to hear Asbury, a distinguished orator. They compromised by listening from a distance rather than entering the church. On one occasion, Asbury had his Negro servant, Harry, give testimony at the beginning of the meeting. The distant listeners, impressed by the Negro's eloquence, thought it was the bishop.

Originally the church included Negro members, but when a decision was made in 1805 to compel them to worship in the gallery, the Negroes withdrew and formed their own church.

# DISTRICT OF COLUMBIA

## WASHINGTON

*American Red Cross,* Seventeenth Street between D and E Streets, N.W. This is the headquarters of the organization that has served soldiers, sailors, and disaster victims of all races since 1881. One of its most significant contributions was made possible by a Negro physician and scientist, Dr. Charles Richard Drew.

An Amherst graduate, Dr. Drew went to McGill Medical School, and then taught pathology at Howard University. In 1940, while working on a D.Sc. degree at Columbia University, he wrote a dissertation on "banked blood." He developed techniques for separating and preserving blood, and contributed much of significance in the field of blood plasma research.

He achieved such stature that he was invited to London to set up the British Blood Bank. Later he directed the Red Cross blood donor project in World War II. The lives saved as the result of his work undoubtedly number in the millions.

After the war Drew became Chief Surgeon of Freedmen's Hospital in Washington, but his life ended tragically in an auto crash in April 1950, at the age of forty-six.

*Association for the Study of Negro Life and History,* 1538 Ninth Street, N.W., was organized in 1915 by Dr. Carter G. Woodson, a pioneer Negro historian. In 1916 he began publishing the *Journal of Negro History*. Later the association launched its own publishing firm, Associated Publishers, Inc.

In 1926 Woodson conceived and the association launched "Negro History Week," which is still observed annually, primarily in schools. Woodson, who died in 1950, was the author of many books on Negro history. Some of them were written in collaboration with his successor as director of the association, Dr. Charles H. Wesley. Dr. Wesley was formerly president of Central State University in Wilberforce, Ohio.

*Constitution Hall,* 18th and D Streets, N.W., the largest auditorium in the District of Columbia, is owned and operated by the National Society, Daughters of the American Revolution. Most of the important concerts and lectures in the city are staged here.

In 1939 national attention was given to the refusal of the hall's management to permit an appearance by the great Negro contralto, Marian Anderson. Without defending the merit of its policy, the DAR asserted that it was simply conforming to local custom in excluding Negro artists—a point that was reinforced when the District of Columbia public school system also refused to allow Miss Anderson to appear.

The DAR had, in fact, permitted Negroes to appear on its stage during an earlier period: Roland Hayes in 1931, the Hampton Institute Choir, and other Negro groups. The public furor over the incident compelled the District's places of amusement—and the local government—to re-examine their segregation policies. Washington amusement places were soon integrated, including this one.

Marian Anderson appeared here in 1953, 1954, 1955, 1956, 1958, 1960, and at the start of her farewell tour in 1964. The tour climaxed a brilliant career during which she served as an alternate delegate to the United Nations and was awarded the nation's highest civilian honor, the Presidential Medal of Freedom.

*Emancipation Statue*, Lincoln Park, is the oldest memorial to Abraham Lincoln in the Washington area. It was erected and paid for by former slaves.

When Mrs. Charlotte Scott, a former slave from Marietta, Ohio, heard of Lincoln's assassination, she donated the first five dollars she had earned in freedom toward a Lincoln memorial. Others recently freed from bondage joined in making contributions.

Congress set aside the grounds and provided a pedestal for Thomas Ball's statue of Lincoln breaking the chains of slavery.

*Ford Theatre and Lincoln Museum*, 511 Tenth Street, N.W. Restored for visitors are the theater in which Lincoln was shot and, across the street, the bedroom in which he died.

*Frederick Douglass Home*, 1411 W Street, S.E. The twenty-room home in which Frederick Douglass lived for the last thirteen years of his life has been preserved as a monument to the great abolitionist.

Born a slave in Maryland, Douglass ran away to New York in 1838. After an impromptu speech at an anti-slavery meeting in Nantucket, Massachusetts, in 1841, he was hired as an agent of an abolitionist society and soon became famous.

From 1845 to 1847 Douglass lectured in England, Ireland, and Scotland, raising money for the abolitionist cause. During this period, friends in the United States raised money to pay for his freedom. He was able to return home without fear of being taken under the Fugitive Slave Act.

After his return, Douglass started publication of *The North Star*, later known as *Frederick Douglass' Paper*. He continued writing and lecturing in the anti-slavery cause until the outbreak of the Civil War, when his efforts focused on securing for Negroes the right to serve as soldiers. He helped win that right for two of his own sons and about 180,000 others.

After the war Douglass was active in aiding the newly freed slaves. He was secretary of the commission to Santo Domingo in 1871, and a presidential elector in 1872.

From 1877 to 1881 he was a District of Columbia marshal, then

Commissioner of Deeds until 1886. In 1889 he was named minister to Haiti. He died February 20, 1895.

His home has been preserved much as it was on the day he died, and includes some priceless antiques, among them a desk presented to Douglass by Harriet Beecher Stowe. It also has a museum.

*Georgetown University,* Thirty-seventh and O Streets, N.W., is the oldest Catholic university in the United States, and in a sense traces its origin to March 25, 1634, when the Reverend Andrew White, S.J., and the Reverend John Altham Gravenor, S.J., arrived in Maryland with the pioneer colonists. Although Lord Baltimore founded the colony on the principle of religious freedom, anti-Catholic laws were soon passed that thwarted successive attempts to establish a Catholic school.

After the Revolution, the Most Reverend John Carroll, the first Catholic bishop in the United States, began collecting funds for an academy at "George Town, on the Patowmack, Maryland." The first building was built, and in 1789, the year the U. S. Constitution became effective, a larger parcel of land was purchased.

Georgetown's period of greatest progress began in 1868 when Father Patrick Francis Healy, a Negro, became prefect of studies there. Father Healy was an imperious, hard-driving Jesuit who would settle for nothing less than perfection in himself and those around him. He was born in Georgia, the son of a slave and a poor Irish immigrant who built a fortune from land, slaves, and cotton. His mother was a household servant, born on a nearby plantation. Healy, captivated by her intelligence and beauty, bought her freedom, married her, and they settled in Georgia and raised seven sons and three daughters.

As prefect of studies, Father Healy began expanding the curriculum at Georgetown, and undertook the construction of a new building which now houses the college administrative offices, and is named in his honor. He became rector (president) of the university in 1874, and died in 1910. He is buried in the Jesuit campus cemetery.

Father Healy was unique in being the first Negro president of an American Catholic university, but his greater distinction lies in the service he rendered. The Reverend Joseph T. Durkin says in his history of the university: "Georgetown as a University may be said to have really begun in the late 1870s. The advance was effected mainly by a man and a building. The man was Patrick Healy, and the building was the structure that bears his name."

*Howard University*, 2400 Sixth Avenue, N.E., was founded in 1867 and became the largest of the centers of higher education for Negroes established after the Civil War. Now integrated, its enrollment is approaching the ten-thousand mark.

The Howard campus covers more than fifty acres on one of the highest elevations in the District of Columbia, and the physical plant is valued at more than forty million dollars. The university has a College of Liberal Arts, School of Music, School of Social Work, School of Engineering and Architecture, School of Religion, School of Law, College of Medicine, College of Dentistry, and College of Pharmacy. It is supported by congressional appropriations, endowments, gifts, and fees.

The Founders Library at Howard contains more than three hundred thousand volumes, including the Moorland Collection, one of the largest and finest collections of Negro Americana.

Howard has graduated some of the nation's most distinguished Negro citizens, among them George H. White, of North Carolina, the last Negro to serve in Congress of the twenty-two who were elected during the years following the Civil War. Following White's election in 1901, Congress was without a Negro member until the election of Oscar DePriest of Illinois, also a Howard graduate, in 1928.

Federal judge William Henry Hastie, the first Negro appointed to this office, was formerly dean of the Howard Law School. He was also the first Negro governor of the Virgin Islands.

*Lincoln Memorial.* A visit to this magnificent shrine is an emotional experience for every American, Negro or white. Perhaps the most moving occasion here was a concert by Marian Anderson, on Easter Sunday 1939, after she had been denied access to Constitution Hall and the District of Columbia public school facilities. Washington dignitaries turned out in force, and when Miss Anderson sang "Nobody Knows the Trouble I've Seen," Walter White, the NAACP leader, commented that "A new affirmation of democracy was felt by all those present."

Apparently it was felt by private and public officials in Washington, as well, for public facilities in the District were soon opened to all entertainers, regardless of race.

In 1968, the mall before the Memorial became the site of "Resurrection City," the encampment of participants in the "Poor People's March" that Dr. Martin Luther King had scheduled before his death. Dr. King's widow and other officials of the Southern Christian Leadership Conference spoke here on several occasions.

*National Gallery of Art,* Sixth Street and Constitution Avenue, N.W. Here, the art lover will find some of the world's greatest paintings, housed in a huge gallery donated by Andrew Mellon. Among the paintings is one by the first American Negro portrait artist, Joshua Johnston, called "The Westwood Children."

Johnston was most active between 1796 and 1824. Tradition had it, in many families that owned his work, that he was a slave, but the Baltimore directory for 1817 lists him as a "Free householder of color." This was a designation employed in the slavery era to identify a Negro who was his own master.

*Phillips Gallery,* 1612 Twenty-first Street, N.W., has thirty of the sixty panels on the "Migration of the Negro," done in oil by Negro artist Jacob Lawrence. The others are in the New York Museum of Modern Art.

Perhaps the foremost of contemporary American Negro painters, Lawrence was born in Atlantic City in 1917, and studied at the American Artist School and Harlem Art School. He has done several series of panels on Negro historical themes. His work is also displayed in New York's Metropolitan Museum of Art, Museum of Modern Art, and the Whitney Museum.

*Phillis Wheatley YWCA,* 901 Rhode Island Avenue, N.W., was named to honor the Negro girl who came off a slave ship in 1761 at the age of eight, but grew up to become a poet. Her first book of poetry was also the first book by a Negro woman and the second by an American woman. During her earlier years, Miss Wheatley was accepted in the most proper Boston circles, and the environment is reflected in her literary style. It strongly resembles that of the British author, Alexander Pope, whose work she greatly admired.

A poem written by Miss Wheatley in honor of George Washington's appointment as commander of the Continental Army won an invitation to visit him at his headquarters. He also wrote a message of appreciation that is a classic example of nonstop Colonial-era hyperbole. It read: "Thank you most sincerely for your polite notice of me, in the elegant lines you enclosed; and however undeserving I may be of such encomium and panegyric, the style and manner exhibited is striking proof of your poetical talents; in honor of which, and as a tribute justly due to you, I would have published the poem, had I not been apprehensive that, while I only meant to give the world this new instance of your genius, I might have incurred the imputation of vanity."

Miss Wheatley enjoyed an international reputation, but her work today has greater historical than literary importance.

*Post Office Department,* Twelfth Street and Pennsylvania Avenue, N.W. Philatelists will find a complete collection of U.S. postage stamps on display here, including those issued in honor of George Washington Carver, Frederick Douglass, and Booker T. Washington.

*The Smithsonian Institution* is one of the most comprehensive museums in the world, and its collections contain many items that illustrate Negro contributions to America.

In the Hall of Physical Sciences is a display showing Benjamin Banneker surveying the boundary of the District of Columbia in 1791, when he helped Pierre L'Enfant lay out the city. Dr. Daniel H. Williams is honored in the Hall of Medicine for performing the first open heart operation in 1893. The Division of Cultural History has exhibits dealing with the African background of Negro Americans, and displays of early Negro craftsmanship in the United States.

The National Collection of Fine Arts has a painting by Negro artist Jacob Lawrence, "The Library," and the Museum of Natural History has an exhibit of African cultural materials from a collection of about twelve thousand specimens.

*Tidal Basin Bridge,* which commands a magnificent view of the cherry blossoms each spring, was engineered and built by a Negro, Archie A. Alexander, who later became governor of the Virgin Islands, and engineered and built many other municipal structures, highways, and airports.

Alexander worked his way through the State University of Iowa, and later was voted the outstanding graduate of the Class of 1912. He employed workers of both races, and on one job, where separate rest rooms were provided for "White" and "Colored," he took down the signs and put up new ones reading "Skilled" and "Unskilled."

*U. S. Capitol Building.* The two houses of Congress meet here, each in its own wing. Negroes serve in both houses. During the Reconstruction period following the Civil War many southern Negroes were elected to Congress—including one who succeeded Jefferson Davis, President of the Confederacy—but this era ended as laws were passed depriving the Negro of the right to vote.

Present Negro members are from primarily urban areas. The only Negro in the U. S. Senate, Edward W. Brooke of Massachusetts, represents a state with less than 2 percent of Negroes in its population.

The sessions of the two houses are opened with a prayer. The first Negro to deliver one was the Reverend Dr. Henry Highland Garnet, Pastor of the Fifteenth Street Presbyterian Church, on February 12, 1865. He was also the first Negro to enter the House of Representatives, and one of the founders of the Liberty Party, the first political organization opposed to slavery.

*U. S. Supreme Court Building.* From this building have come many of the landmark decisions establishing civil rights for Negroes. John S. Rock, of Boston, Massachusetts, was the first Negro admitted to practice before the Court.

Thurgood Marshall, who tried more cases before the Court than any other lawyer, is now sitting as its first Negro member. A former U.S. solicitor general, he graduated at the head of his Howard Law School class in 1933. He won the NAACP's Spingarn Medal in 1946.

*The White House,* 1600 Pennsylvania Avenue, N.W., is a must for every visitor. Adjacent is the Executive Office Building, which houses the presidential staff. In recent years, many Negroes have served in staff positions of importance. The Cabinet, of which Robert C. Weaver, former Secretary of Housing and Urban Development, was the first black member, meets here.

---

# FLORIDA

---

APALACHICOLA

*When the River Was King.* A marker here notes the growth and importance of cotton in the Florida economy during the first half of the nineteenth century. Between 1836 and 1840 cotton receipts at this port jumped from 55,000 to 130,000 bales per year, and Apalachicola became the third largest cotton port in the United States.

The importance of cotton in the southern economy was largely responsible for its dependence on slave labor, and its resistance to the anti-slavery demands of the more highly industrialized northern states.

The last action by Negro troops in Florida during the Civil War was an expedition from Barrancas to Apalachicola by the 82nd Colored Infantry Regiment on May 31, 1865.

## CHARLOTTE HARBOR

*Ponce de Leon Marker* notes that Juan Ponce de Leon visited here on his first voyage to Florida in 1513. He and his party, both white and Negro, spent several weeks near the mouth of Charlotte Harbor, but returned to Puerto Rico when they were attacked by Indians.

The Spanish explorer returned in 1521 with two shiploads of colonists. The colonists, beset by illness and Indian attacks, abandoned Florida after five months. Ponce de Leon was wounded and died in Cuba shortly thereafter.

## DAYTONA BEACH

*Bethune-Cookman College.* This school is itself a monument to a dedicated and tireless advocate of improved education for Negroes. The college was founded by Mary McLeod Bethune in 1904, in a rented shack. She had a dollar and a half, a few soap boxes for furniture, five little Negro girls for pupils, and a brave dream.

Born on a plantation near Mayesville, South Carolina, of parents only recently out of slavery, Mrs. Bethune was eleven before her community had a school for Negroes. After securing her own education, she determined that she would establish a college for the training of more Negro teachers. Bethune-Cookman College is the result of her dream and her tireless effort. Today, the college has a student body of more than one thousand, and is one of the leading Negro teacher-training institutions. Three-fourths of its graduates enter the teaching profession.

Mrs. Bethune died in 1955, a few weeks before her eightieth birthday. During her full life, she had also found time to establish the National Council of Negro Women, and to serve as an adviser to Presidents Roosevelt and Truman.

JACKSONVILLE

     *Little Talbot Island State Park.* The fishing pier here is dedicated to a local Negro, David H. Dwight, described as "perhaps the outstanding colored leader of this community during his lifetime . . . universally respected by all the people of this community."

Dwight is but one of the local Negro citizens honored in similar ways. The Joseph H. Blodgett Housing Project was named for a civic leader who was probably Florida's first Negro millionaire. There are thirty-five Negro millionaires in the United States today.

In 1967, a nursing home was named for Dr. Eartha M. White, on her ninetieth birthday. Dr. White established and maintains the Clara White Mission, named for her mother, which serves needy Negroes in many ways. Her work has often been compared with that of Jane Addams, founder of Chicago's Hull House, the first social settlement in the United States.

Also here is the James Weldon Johnson High School, named for the gifted Negro poet and critic who died in 1938. Johnson was born in Jacksonville in 1871, and was educated at Atlanta and Columbia Universities. Among his best-known works are *God's Trombones,* a book of folk sermons in verse, and his autobiography, *Along This Way.* Johnson also served as U.S. consul in Venezuela and Nicaragua.

During the Civil War, one of the first Negro units to serve, the 1st South Carolina Volunteers, captured Jacksonville on March 10, 1863, without firing a shot. They held the city only briefly, however, for the need for troops in the North was so urgent that they were recalled. A year later, when the Union Army returned to Jacksonville, it was with a force of twenty thousand men, who encountered great difficulty before they retook the city.

OLUSTEE

     *Olustee Battlefield Historic Memorial.* You can visit the positions held by the opposing forces in this Civil War battle in a short walking tour. The Negroes who fought here had a rougher time of it. They marched 110 miles in 108 hours to get in the fight.

Three Negro and six white regiments were in the Federal forces that fought at Olustee in February 1864. Some of the Negroes were seasoned veterans, others raw recruits. Among the untried soldiers were the men of the 8th U. S. Colored Troops, some of whom had never had a day of practice loading or firing their weapons. What they lacked in experience they made up in courage as they "stood to be killed or wounded—losing more than three hundred out of five hundred and fifty."

An officer of the veteran 54th Massachusetts Regiment later described its role in the action in a letter to a friend, written three days after the battle:

"Before going into battle we were double-quicked for a mile, and as [we] went in General Seymour said to Colonel Hallowell, 'the day is lost; you must go in and save the corps.' We did go in and did save it, checked the enemy, held the field, and were the last to leave —and covered the retreat."

Colonel Hallowell, in his report, disagreed on only one particular. He said the men marched double-time for *two* miles. Negro Sergeant Stephen A. Swails was cited for courage in this action, and later was the first Negro to be commissioned in the 54th Regiment. After the battle the Federal troops retreated to Jacksonville, which they held until the end of the war.

The battlesite also features an interpretative museum.

## ST. AUGUSTINE

*Mission Nombre de Dios.* A marker has been placed at the site where, on September 8, 1565, Pedro Menendez de Aviles landed with a band of white and Negro settlers. They founded St. Augustine, the first permanent Christian settlement in the United States, and the first Catholic mission. Father Francisco Lopez de Mendoza Grajales, Spanish diocesan priest, offered here the first Mass in the nation's first Catholic parish.

## ST. MARKS

*San Marcos de Apalache.* A museum and the ruins of a fort here commemorate the arrival, late in 1528, of Pamphilo de Narvaez and a party of three hundred men. Narvaez left Spain in 1527 on a mission to explore the northern shore of the Gulf of Mexico. He landed on April 14, 1528, probably in Sarasota Bay.

The party made their way overland to this point near the mouth of the St. Marks River, where they beat swords into tools to build and launch the first ships made in the New World. They endured extreme privation, eventually eating their horses and even each other.

Four men survived: Cabeza de Vaca, Castillo, Andres Dorantes, and Estevanico, his Negro servant or slave. For six years they were prisoners of the Indians, but finally escaped to travel west and cross into Mexican territory in 1536. (Estevanico's further adventures are described in the New Mexico section.)

## TALLAHASSEE

*Old City Cemetery* was established by the Florida Territorial Council in 1829. Many pioneers and their slaves are buried here. The cemetery also contains the graves of Confederate and Federal troops—both white and Negro. They were among those killed in the Battle of Natural Bridge in 1865, which was the last Northern attempt to seize the Florida capital during the Civil War.

## TAMPA

*Port of Embarkation,* Spanish-American War. A marker notes that from April to June 1898, Tampa served as embarkation point for U.S. troops on their way to Cuba. Although most of the glory has gone to Teddy Roosevelt's Rough Riders, much of the fighting was done by four all-Negro units—the 9th and 10th Cavalry Regiments and the 24th and 25th Infantry. Five men from these units won the Medal of Honor for heroism, but at El Caney, Las Guasimas, and San Juan Hill, most of the Negroes were heroes.

In one episode, en route to Santiago, the 10th Cavalry saved the Rough Riders from almost certain disaster. At El Caney, the 25th Infantry led the charge alone, and Negro Private T. C. Butler was the first man in the enemy blockhouse. He got the Spanish flag for his regiment. At Las Guasimas, Roosevelt's Rough Riders were trapped until the 9th and 10th Cavalry came up, destroyed the blockhouse, and drove the Spaniards off.

In the famous charge up San Juan Hill the Negro troops fought on to victory under the leadership of Negro noncommissioned officers after most of the white officers had been wounded or killed. Said Teddy Roosevelt, shortly before the Americans entered Santiago: "I don't think that any Rough Rider will ever forget the tie that binds us to the Ninth and Tenth Cavalry."

## WOODVILLE

*Battle of Natural Bridge,* six miles east, off U. S. 319. A monument, markers, and the battlefield earthworks here commemorate a battle on March 6, 1865, in which the Florida 2nd Cavalry and the 2nd and 99th U. S. Colored Infantry Regiments, with naval support, sought to capture St. Marks and Tallahassee. Home guards and even West Florida Seminary cadets joined Confederate regulars to halt the advance. Because they succeeded, Tallahassee was the only Confederate capital not in Federal hands when the war ended a month later. Federal losses were twenty-two killed, forty-six wounded, and thirteen missing.

# GEORGIA

## ANDERSONVILLE

*Andersonville National Cemetery, and Andersonville Prison Park*. Much has been written about the hardships endured by the Federal soldiers who were imprisoned here during the Civil War. Many of them died, including Corporal James Henry Gooding, of the all-Negro 54th Massachusetts Regiment. He was seriously wounded and taken prisoner in the Battle of Olustee, Florida.

Some time earlier Gooding had written President Lincoln protesting the fact that enlisted Negroes of all ranks were being paid at the rate of seven dollars a month while white troops drew from thirteen to thirty dollars. The men of the 54th refused to accept their pay at this discriminatory rate. Gooding's complaint and that of other Americans—Negro and white—was finally heeded by Congress in July 1864, and pay was equalized.

It was too late for Corporal Gooding; he died on July 19, 1864, without ever drawing a day's pay for giving the "last full measure of devotion" to his nation's cause.

## ATLANTA

*The Atlanta University System* is a leading center of higher education and one of the most beautiful campuses in the South. It includes Atlanta University, Morris Brown, Clark, Morehouse, and Spelman Colleges.

Atlanta University is the third oldest predominately Negro institution of higher learning in the country, and the oldest in the South. The first classes were held in 1865 in a boxcar, brought in from Chattanooga by the American Missionary Association. It is now exclusively a graduate school, with four professional schools. The School of Business Administration is headed by Dean Harding B. Young, the first Negro to receive a doctorate in the field from Harvard University.

The other Atlanta schools offer four-year under-graduate courses.

The Trevor Arnett Library at Atlanta University contains important collections of Negro Americana and books on Africa. It has the world's largest collection of works by Negro American artists.

An exhibition of paintings, sculpture, and prints by the nation's leading Negro artists is held each spring.

*Booker T. Washington High School,* 45 Whitehouse Street, has a monument erected by teachers and students of the school and Negro and white citizens of Atlanta. A group of bronze figures, executed by George Keck of New York, depicts Washington lifting the veil of ignorance from his race. On the marble base are inscribed his words: "We shall prosper in proportion as we learn dignity and glorify labor and put brains and skill into the common occupations of life."

*Ebenezer Baptist Church,* 413 Auburn Avenue, N.E. The late Reverend Dr. Martin Luther King, Jr., long the most ardent spokesman for the nonviolent Negro protest movement, was associate pastor here. It was in this church that he gained stature as a civil rights leader before becoming president of the Southern Christian Leadership Conference.

Dr. King's efforts in behalf of his race and his country earned him the Nobel Prize for Peace in 1964. He was the second Negro to win the award. The first went to Dr. Ralph J. Bunche in 1950 for his work, as a representative of the United Nations, in settling the Arab-Israeli dispute in 1948.

Dr. King was returned to this church after his life was extinguished by an assassin's bullet in Memphis, Tennessee, on April 4, 1968. Five days later a mule-drawn wagon, symbolic of his efforts in behalf of the poor, carried him from his church for the last time. With hundreds of admirers and many of the great and near-great of the world in the procession, the wagon rattled through Atlanta's streets to the noted black leader's alma mater, Morehouse College.

There, on a sunwashed lawn, an estimated one hundred and fifty thousand persons paid their last respects to Dr. King.

A memorial will be erected on the Morehouse campus in his honor.

*Henry Rutherford Butler School,* 89 Yonge Street, N.E. Formerly the Yonge Street School, the name was changed to honor the husband of the founder of the National Congress of Colored Parents and Teachers. The meeting from which this organization grew was called here at the request of Selena Sloan Butler, who became the first national president of the Congress.

*South View Cemetery.* This is the last resting place of Dr. Martin Luther King. He is entombed in a marble crypt on which are inscribed the words from an old slave song which he had himself borrowed to conclude his speech on the steps of the Lincoln Memorial during the 1963 Civil Rights March on Washington. They read:

Free at last, free at last, thank God Almighty I'm free at last.

It is an appropriate burial place, for the cemetery was organized in 1886 by Negroes who refused to be buried in the rear of the city burial ground. Dr. King first won national attention by leading Montgomery, Alabama, Negroes in a protest against being compelled to sit in the rear of the bus.

AUGUSTA

*Paine College.* Originally known as Paine Institute, this was the first educational institution for Negroes to be sponsored in the South by southern churchmen of both races. John Wesley Gilbert was the first graduate. He also became the first Negro faculty member, following further study at Brown University and on a scholarship at the American School of Classical Studies in Athens, Greece. Dr. Gilbert also accompanied Methodist bishop Walter Russell Lambuth on the journey that brought Christianity to the central Congo.

*Springfield Baptist Church* is one of the nation's oldest Negro Baptist churches. It was organized on August 12, 1793, by the Reverend Jessie Peters and George Liele, of the Silver Bluff Baptist Church in South Carolina, the nation's oldest Negro church of this faith.

*William Makepeace Thackeray* marker is on the site of the first Masonic temple in Augusta, where the British author lectured in February 1856. The marker, erected by the Georgia Historical Commission in 1954, quotes from a letter that Thackeray wrote home during his visit:

"Nice quaint old town Augusta, rambling great street 2 miles long, doctors and shopkeepers the society of the place, the latter far more independent and gentlemanlike than our folks, much pleasanter to be with than the daring go ahead northern people. Slavery no where repulsive, the black faces invariably happy and plump, the white ones eager and hard. I brought away 60 Guineas for 2 hours talking, a snug little purse from snug little Augusta."

Thackeray, in his observation of the "happy" black faces, did not find slavery repulsive, but this could not be said of those forced to endure it. The resistance of Georgia Negroes to their enslavement had been going on since before the Revolutionary War. A slave conspiracy in Augusta was betrayed in 1819, but not until Negroes, desperate for freedom, had fired the town. Several persons were executed and a Negro slave, Paul, was sentenced to 250 lashes, the branding of his cheek with the letter R, and the removal of both ears.

Augusta was put to the torch again in 1829, and several slaves were adjudged guilty and executed. In 1841, a group of slaves led by a white school teacher planned a revolt, which was also discovered, and at least one man was executed.

Still, the myth of the happy, submissive slave persists.

### CATOOSA COUNTY

*Chickamauga Battlefield,* on U. S. 27, nine miles south of Chattanooga, was the scene of one of the major actions of the Civil War. Near the end of the century Negro troops were trained at Camp Thomas here before going on to Tampa to embark for Cuba and valiant action in the Spanish-American War. (See Florida.) The site of their camp was Dyer's Field, where General George Thomas won the title "Rock of Chickamauga," during the Battle above the Clouds. He later led Negro troops in many major actions of the Civil War.

The visitors' center has a Civil War museum.

### COLUMBUS

*"Blind Tom" Marker,* U. S. 27A, six miles north. Nearby is the grave of Thomas Wiggins, better known as "Blind Tom" Bethune, who thrilled audiences here and abroad with his remarkable piano concerts. The son of slave parents, Tom was blind

from birth. His owners discovered his musical gift when they heard exquisite music in their home near Columbus and found the little blind boy at the piano. His ability to reproduce perfectly on the piano any sound or composition that he heard won him the opportunity to play before royalty.

"Blind Tom" also thrilled audiences in his own country. He was one of the first professional musicians to appear in Colorado, and the first whom Coloradans judged to be better than second-rate. An account of his appearance in Denver in 1872 reported on his "exciting the wonder of the people as he always does."

*Bragg Smith Marker*, Columbus Colored Cemetery. The text of this marble memorial reads: "Erected by the City of Columbus to mark the resting place of Bragg Smith, who died on September 30, 1903, at the age of thirty-two, in the heroic but fruitless effort to rescue the city engineer from a caving excavation . . ."

"Honor and fame from no condition rise. Act well your part, there all the honor lies."

## DALTON

*Battle of Dalton Markers*, on U. S. 41, near the site of the first Civil War action for the 14th U. S. Colored Troops. This new unit was led into action here from August 14–15, 1864, by Colonel Thomas Morgan. They were more than a match for the attacking Confederate cavalry. A contemporary report recalls that when Morgan's Negro troops returned from the engagement, the men of the white regiment "swung their hats and gave three rousing cheers."

## DARIEN

*Saint Andrew's Episcopal Church*. A marker here recalls that the original building "was burned in 1863 when Darien was put to the torch by Federal troops stationed on St. Simon's Island." The church was rebuilt in 1872. Only two buildings in Darien were standing when the Federal troops left the town—the Methodist Church at Vernon Square, and one residence.

The troops involved in this raid were Negroes of Colonel Robert Gould Shaw's 54th Massachusetts Regiment, one of the first Negro units organized in the Civil War. In command of the expedition, however, was Colonel James Montgomery. He had already acquired a reputation for his destructive raids on the rivers of southern

Georgia. Local legend has it that the sacking and burning of Darien was done by the Negro troops "without orders," when they "got lickered up and just decided to burn off some energy."

History records a different version. Colonel Shaw, the heroic Massachusetts officer who is immortalized along with his Negro troops in a St. Gaudens statue in Boston Common, was on the scene. He was horrified by what took place. He reported that Montgomery ordered foraging parties to loot the town, and when this had been accomplished, he turned to Shaw with a "sweet smile" and said: "I shall burn this town. Southerners must be made to feel that this is a real war, and that they are to be swept away by the hand of God like the Jews of old." Montgomery ordered Darien destroyed.

Shaw protested Montgomery's action to his superiors, arguing that his Negro troops had been promised honorable duty, and hadn't come south to destroy the homes of defenseless civilians. Stronger voices in the North joined in his objections, which may have been why no similar expeditions were demanded of the men of the 54th after the Darien raid.

The behavior of these early Negro regiments was, in fact, exceptional. Colonel Thomas W. Higginson, who wrote a book about his experience as commander of the all-Negro 1st South Carolina Volunteers, led many similar raids. He was astonished by the restraint of his men, who left untouched bulging warehouses filled with household valuables.

Subsequently, when the Federal troops withdrew from Jacksonville, one large section was burned. The New York and Boston newspaper correspondents reported that the section was burned by the white troops that occupied it, and that "the Negro troops took no part whatever in the perpetration of this vandalism."

MARIETTA

*Marietta National Cemetery.* Heroes of all the nation's wars, including the Revolution, are buried here, but by far the greatest number were Federal soldiers who fell during Sherman's march in late 1864 and early 1865. Many Negroes are among them, including the men of the 14th U. S. Colored Troops who died in the action at Dalton. Of nearly ten thousand Civil War soldiers interred here, about three thousand are unknowns whose bodies were gathered from battlefield cemeteries throughout the area.

OXFORD

*Kitty's Cottage Location.* Kitty was a Negro slave willed to Bishop James O. Andrew, President of the Board of Trustees of Emory College, which is located here. The will provided that at the age of nineteen she was either to go to Liberia or remain as free as the laws of Georgia would permit, which wasn't very free. She elected to remain in Oxford, technically the slave of a Methodist bishop.

This became a matter of controversy at the General Conference of the Methodist Episcopal Church in New York City in 1844. It was one of the issues that caused the organization of the Methodist Episcopal Church, South, in 1845. In 1938, Kitty's cottage was moved to the Salem Campground, near Covington, where annual camp meetings are held by the Atlanta-Decatur-Oxford Methodist District.

SAVANNAH

*Fort Pulaski National Monument,* on Cockspur and Mc-Queens Islands, at the mouth of the Savannah River, seventeen miles east of Savannah on U. S. 80, was named in honor of the Polish nobleman Casimir Pulaski. Count Pulaski was induced by Benjamin Franklin to aid the colonies in the Revolutionary War. He commanded French and American cavalrymen during the siege of Savannah, and died of wounds received here on October 9, 1779.

During the Revolution most American Negroes fought in integrated units, shoulder-to-shoulder with white troops. The practice of segregating units by race did not become general until the Civil War. The siege of Savannah and the Battle of Rhode Island were the only major actions of the American Revolution in which all-Negro units participated. At Savannah, the French allies under Count d'Estaing included a group of 545 Negroes recruited not long before in Santo Domingo. Commanded by Viscount de Fontages, they were called "Fontages' Legion."

The assault on the British was ill-advised. They had warning of the impending attack and used three thousand captured slaves to strengthen the fortifications. The attacking forces were slaughtered when they tried to take them. The most brilliant action was that of Fontages' Negro soldiers when the attacking forces withdrew.

Knowing that the American forces were badly battered, British Lieutenant Colonel Maitland launched an attack on the retreating troops, intending to annihilate them. The charge was met by the Negro soldiers, whose determined resistance saved the army.

In later years some of them were leaders in the revolt that gave independence to Haiti. Henri Christophe, who was a bootblack on the streets when he was recruited by Fontages, was wounded at Savannah. Later he became the King of Haiti.

The fort itself was not built until after the War of 1812, and at the start of the Civil War was believed by the Confederate leadership to be impregnable. Their confidence was shattered in April 1862 when Federal forces, armed with the new rifled cannon, began a bombardment which breached the thick brick walls and forced the fort to surrender.

The engagement was a significant development in military history, proving that the old type of brick and masonry fortifications could not stand up to modern artillery.

*Rev. George Liele Monument,* at First Bryan Baptist Church, dedicated to the first Negro Baptist missionary. The church is named for Liele's understudy, Andrew Bryan, who assisted him in organizing the first Baptist church in Georgia in 1779. When Liele went to Jamaica, Bryan continued his work, preaching to Christians of all races. The Baptist church in Georgia stemmed from this first congregation.

# HAWAII

## HONOLULU

*National Memorial Cemetery of the Pacific.* This cemetery, dedicated on the fourth anniversary of V-J Day in 1949, contains the remains of more World War II dead than any other national cemetery. It is situated in Punchbowl Crater, one of three large extinct volcano craters on the island of Oahu. The Hawaiian name of the crater is *Puowaina,* meaning "reverence in the highest degree."

About one million Negroes served in the armed forces in World War II. At its peak strength, there were more than seven hundred thousand Negroes in the Army alone. Many are buried here. Many, also, were among those whose names are listed in the eight "Courts of the Missing" in the Memorial erected here. Honored are more than eighteen thousand men from World War II and over eight thousand from the Korean conflict, whose bodies were never recovered.

At one point, in Korea, Negroes constituted 30 percent of the American troops in the field. Two of them, Sergeant Cornelius H. Charlton and Private First Class William Thompson, won the Congressional Medal of Honor.

*Arizona Memorial.* Built on the superstructure of this battleship, which was sent to the bottom in the Japanese sneak attack on Pearl Harbor on December 7, 1941, is a memorial to the men who gave their lives in that engagement.

One of those aboard the *Arizona* that day was a Negro Messman First Class, Dorie Miller, of Waco, Texas. He was on deck when a Japanese plane dove toward the ship and released a bomb on its deck. Miller was knocked down by the explosion. When he got to his feet he saw a wounded man nearby. It was his commander, who was bleeding badly from a stomach wound. Miller picked him up and carried him through a hail of machine gun bullets to receive medical attention in a protected location.

Miller then found an unmanned machine gun. As a messman he was not supposed to use it and never had, but before the attack ended he had shot down three enemy planes. For his courage he was awarded the Navy Cross.

Little more than a year later Miller went to his death with the torpedoed aircraft carrier *Liscome Bay.*

Prior to World War II Negroes were recruited only for noncombatant roles in the Navy. Other "noncombatant" Negroes decorated in the Second World War were Leonard R. Harmon of the U.S.S. *San Francisco* and William Pinckney of the U.S.S. *Enterprise,* both of whom won the Navy Cross, and Elbert H. Oliver of the U.S.S. *Intrepid,* awarded the Silver Star.

# IDAHO

*Idaho Historical Society,* 610 North Julia Davis Drive, has an early photograph of the blacksmith shop operated here by George Washington Stitts, a colorful Negro who figures prominently in local lore about the period immediately following the Civil War. Stitts was one of a handful of Negroes who left their mark on the city during that period.

Joe Allen arrived from Newburyport, Massachusetts, during the 1860s with a one-horse dray that he had bought in San Francisco, and operated the city's dray service until 1869. He left because his children were not permitted to attend the local school. Another Negro, John West, was tried for shooting a man in a card-game altercation, but the jury freed him because of the unsavory reputation of his victim. A familiar and popular figure on Boise streets was a Negro known simply as "Old Bill." In an era when communications media were virtually nonexistent, he served as "Town Crier," keeping the populace informed by moving through the streets ringing a loud bell and announcing important events.

West, "Old Bill," and another Negro named John Seavy were the principal characters in an election drama which demonstrated the importance of the individual vote. In 1870, Congress extended universal suffrage to Idaho Territory, and in the next election Lute Lindsay, a Democrat, ran for sheriff against William Bryon, a Republican, in a lively contest that ended with Lindsay the victor by one vote. The Republicans discovered, however, that the election judges had thrown out the votes cast by the three Negroes. They challenged Lindsay's election in court, and the Negroes were asked to testify how they had voted. All three said they had voted Republican, and Bryon was declared sheriff by the court, with a margin of two Negro votes.

## LEWISTON

*The First Capital* marker notes that this was the capital of Idaho territory in 1863 and 1864. Two sessions of the legislature met here before the capital was moved to Boise.

Negroes were never numerous in Idaho. In 1869, of twenty thousand people in the state, only sixty-eight were Negroes, but there were fifty-six hundred Indians and nearly forty-three hundred Chinese. Even as late as 1910 there were only about 650 Negroes in the state, and in 1960 the Negro population barely exceeded fifteen hundred.

## LOLO PASS

*Lewis and Clark Trail*, U. S. 12. Numerous points on the trail have been marked by the Idaho Department of Highways. The expedition crossed the Bitterroot Mountains here on September 13, 1805, and traveled west to the *Canoe Camp Site*.

Lewis, in his journals, makes numerous references to his Negro aide, York. On one occasion, he wrote: "Some of the party had also told the Indians that we had a man with us who was black and had short curling hair, this had excited their curiosity very much. And they seemed quite as anxious to see this monster as they were the merchandize which we had to barter for their horses."

It might be supposed that the Indians would find Lewis's white skin more of a curiosity than the black skin of York. However, Lewis also describes finding it necessary to "strip up his shirt" to show the Indians that he was white, "for my face and hands which have been constantly exposed to the sun were quite as dark as their own."

## OAKLEY

*Gobo Fango's Story.* There is no memorial to this Negro, but his story needs to be told. Gobo Fango came from South Africa, and was the slave of the Lewis Whitesides family at Kaysville, Utah. He slept in a shed in cold weather and his feet were frozen, so he limped all of his life.

Eventually, Gobo went with some of the Mormon pioneers to herd sheep near here, during a period when a cattle- and sheepmen's war was in progress. One day two cattlemen rode up to Gobo and, after pretending friendship, shot him and left.

Gobo did not die at once. He managed to crawl back to camp. There he found a piece of paper, dipped a stick in his own blood, and wrote his will.

He had saved his money—five hundred dollars—and his blood-smeared last testament gave it to the Grantsville Relief Society.

OROFINO

*Canoe Camp Site,* near U. S. 12. This is one of several Lewis and Clark expedition campsites located within the huge Nez Perce National Historical Park. The explorers camped here from September 26 to October 7, 1805.

They had used pack horses to cross the mountains after leaving the Upper Missouri River. Here they made canoes and returned to water travel, leaving their horses to be cared for by the friendly Nez Perce Indians.

As usual, the lone Negro in the party, who acted as hunter and guide, attracted a great deal of attention. He and the white men danced for the Indians, as they had at other points along the trail.

York apparently tired at this point of the Indian curiosity about his color, which had been so useful to the party in previous encounters with Indians. When one of them moistened his finger to see if the black would rub off, York drew his knife. As Indian legend records it, he "make big eyes much white in eyes and look fierce at Chief."

The Indians called York Tse-mook-tse-mook To-to-kean, which is Nez Perce for "black white man." York, like many others in the party, took an Indian wife while here. On his return York learned that his temporary bride had given birth to a child. Among contemporary Nez Perce Indians are some who claim they are descendants of York.

SILVER CITY

*Old Ghost Town,* twenty-two miles off State 45, in Owyhee County, rivaled Boise in size and prominence during the years following the discovery of gold on Jordan Creek in 1863. Today only a handful of people remain to recall the days when ore from the Poorman mine was yielding as much as four or five thousand dollars in silver per ton.

In its heyday, Silver City, perched in the mountains at six thousand feet, was the seat of a county larger than the two smallest eastern states combined. One of its leading citizens was "Silver" Walker, a Negro barber who was one of the state's leading horsemen in the early 1870s. In those days, many Idaho towns had racetracks, and Walker owned a string of horses that raced, and often won, at most of them.

Walker was known and respected throughout the state, and active in Republican politics as well as horse racing. Silver City could have used his political skill in 1934, to keep nearby Murphy from taking over as county seat.

# ILLINOIS

## CHICAGO

*The Art Institute of Chicago*, South Michigan Avenue, is one of the nation's great art galleries. In its collection, although not always on display, is the painting "The Two Disciples at the Tomb," by Henry Ossawa Tanner, a famous Negro artist who was fond of biblical subjects. The museum also has two sculptures by Negroes: "Hero Construction," by Richard Hunt, and "Man of Sorrows," by Marion Perkins.

Tanner, who was born in Pittsburgh, studied at the Pennsylvania Academy of Fine Arts and the Julian Academy in Paris. Winner of many awards, he achieved fame with his paintings titled "Daniel in the Lion's Den" and "The Resurrection of Lazarus," which were purchased by the French government.

*Chicago Historical Society*, in Lincoln Park, has extensive Lincoln and Civil War Collections, including material on Illinois Negro units that participated in the Civil War.

Portraits of two distinguished Chicago Negroes, both by Aaron E. Darling, are on exhibit. One is of John Jones (1811–79), who settled in Chicago in 1845 and became a successful businessman and the first Negro to hold elective office in Cook County, as a county commissioner from 1871 to 1875. Also pictured is his wife, Mary Richardson Jones, who, like her husband, was a tireless worker for repeal of the Illinois Black Laws, and for improved conditions for Negroes in Illinois.

Among the museum exhibits are a diorama that traces Lincoln's career and his interest in the slavery question; a replica of the cabin built prior to 1790 by Jean DuSable, Chicago's pioneer settler; numerous exhibits related to the days of slavery; memorabilia of the abolitionist, John Brown, and the table on which Robert E. Lee signed the surrender document at Appomattox Courthouse.

*Civic Center Plaza* features a huge steel statue designed by Pablo Picasso which was dedicated in 1967. There was great local controversy over the impressionistic work, and many agreed with the suggestion that a more popular choice would have been a statue of Ernie Banks.

This view was not shared by Gwendolyn Brooks, Chicago's Pulitzer Prize-winning Negro poet. She was asked by the city to compose a poem and read it at the unveiling. She chose, in the verse, to chide critics of Picasso's work.

Miss Brooks is the only Negro who has won the Pulitzer Prize, which she received in 1950 for a volume of poetry titled *Annie Allen*. Her first book of poems, *A Street in Bronzeville*, was published in 1945 and brought her selection by *Mademoiselle* as one of that year's ten outstanding American women.

A fellow of the American Academy of Arts and Letters since 1946, Miss Brooks has been awarded two Guggenheim fellowships. In January 1968, she was named official poet laureate of Illinois.

*DuSable Marker*, Pioneer Court, Michigan Avenue. Chicago's first non-Indian settler was a Negro, Jean Baptiste Point DuSable. It is believed that he was born in Santo Domingo, and that he migrated to Chicago sometime between 1772 and 1779. He built a log cabin on the north bank of the Chicago River and helped a village grow around it. In the late eighteenth century he moved to Peoria. He died in St. Charles, Missouri, about 1814.

*Milton L. Olive Park*, on the lakefront at Ontario Street, was named in honor of a Vietnam Medal of Honor winner, Private First Class Milton L. Olive, III.

On October 22, 1965, Private Olive's platoon was pursuing Vietcong in the vicinity of Phu Cuong. He and four comrades were moving through the jungle when a grenade landed in their midst. According to his citation:

"Private Olive saw the grenade and then saved the lives of his fellow soldiers at the sacrifice of his own by grabbing the grenade in his hand and falling on it to absorb the blast with his body. Through his bravery, unhesitating actions, and complete disregard for his own safety, he prevented additional loss of life or injury to the members of his platoon."

Private Olive was awarded the Medal of Honor posthumously for "conspicuous gallantry, extraordinary heroism, and intrepidity at the risk of his own life above and beyond the call of duty."

When the twenty-year-old soldier's father learned of the award he wrote these words to President Johnson:

"Our only child and only grandchild gave his last full measure of devotion on an international battlefield 10,000 miles from home. It is our dream and prayer that some day the Asiatics, the Europeans, the Israelites, the Africans, the Australians, the Latins, and the Americans can all live in One-World. It is our hope that in our own country the Klansmen, the Negroes, the Hebrews, and the Catholics will sit down together in the common purpose of good will and dedication; that the moral and creative intelligence of our united people will pick up the chalice of wisdom and place it upon the mountain top of human integrity; that all the earth, shall resolve, to study war no more!"

*Museum of African-American History and Art,* 3806 South Michigan Avenue, was founded by a Chicago public school art teacher "to inspire African-American people by acquainting them with contributions other members of their race have made to society in the past." The teacher, Mrs. Margaret Burroughs, directs the museum.

In addition to books and periodicals, the collection includes numerous exhibits related to Negro history in Africa and America. Among the treasures are the powderhorns carried during the Revolutionary War by the Negro fifer, Barzillai Lew.

*Provident Hospital,* founded by Dr. Daniel Hale Williams, established the nation's first training school for Negro nurses.

In 1893, in a spectacular operation here, Dr. Williams devised a method for suturing the human heart. The Negro surgeon also discovered a method by which the delicate tissues of the spleen could be ligated to prevent hemorrhage.

Dr. Williams was a cobbler's apprentice at eleven, later a barber and roustabout on a lake steamer. He graduated from Chicago Medical College in 1883 and began practicing medicine in Chicago. When he was unable to get his patients admitted to the

Chicago hospitals, he founded this one and opened it to all races. Later he became a charter member and fellow of the American College of Surgeons.

Dr. Williams died in 1931.

*Underground Railway Marker,* 9955 South Beverly Avenue, is at the site of one of many underground railroad stations in the state. Another was at Jacksonville, where the Reverend D. Pat Henderson published *The Statesman,* believed to be the first anti-slavery paper west of the Allegheny Mountains.

Underground railroad routes to Chicago led from both Quincy and Rock Island. It is said that at Plainfield, Illinois a "station keeper" on the underground hid fugitives in a room he built in the center of a woodpile.

Most of the escaping slaves made their way on to Canada, where they were assured of freedom, but some remained in Illinois. The state also acquired other Negro residents who had purchased their freedom.

One of these was Frank McWorter, a Kentucky slave who arranged to pay his master an annual fee so that he could keep his own labor. He manufactured and sold saltpeter, and at forty had saved enough money to buy his own freedom, but his wife, Lucy, and their thirteen children were still slaves.

After saving more money Frank bought freedom for his wife. They had three free-born children and in 1829 took them to Illinois where they became the first settlers in Hadley township. They left thirteen slave children behind.

Frank acquired the surname McWorter, by special act of the Illinois legislature. He became a successful farmer and used his income to purchase freedom for the thirteen oldest children and two grandchildren he had left in Kentucky. On his death in 1854 he left a will providing for the purchase of freedom for four more grandchildren.

In all, he spent more than ten thousand dollars purchasing freedom for himself and his family.

*Victory Monument,* 35th Street and South Park Way, was created by Leonard Crenelle as a memorial to the Negro soldiers of Illinois who served in World War I. Two blocks south is Ida B. Wells Home, named for the famed civil rights advocate, and a quarter-mile east on Thirty-fifth Street are the monument and tomb of Stephen A. Douglas, Lincoln's presidential opponent, who once owned much of the land in the area.

EL PASO

Campbell House Marker, E. Front Street: "On this site
. . . David A. Strother voted in the city election Monday, April 4,
1870, the first legal Negro vote cast in the United States."

(On March 31, 1870, Thomas Mundy Peterson, a Negro, voted
in a special election in Perth Amboy, New Jersey.)

FARMER CITY

Maple Grove Cemetery. A simple headstone here marks
the grave of a man whose life symbolized the truism that you don't
have to be a leading citizen to be a good one. The marker says,
simply:

"Corp. T. W. Johnson
Co. F, 8 Ill. Inf.
1870–1936"

That's probably what Tom Johnson would want it to say, for certainly he regarded his military service as his greatest contribution to
mankind.

Johnson was a Negro, brought to Farmer City by the Garvey family when they came here to open a drugstore. He drove a horse and
wagon, delivering kerosene, and in his spare moments did the jan-
itor work. When the Garveys died and the store was sold, he went to
work at the Woodward Livery Barn, driving the carriage to meet the
train and working in the stables.

When the Spanish-American War came Johnson signed up with
a number of other Farmer City men. They came home heroes,
pitched their tent in City Park, and spent a few days shaking hands
and accepting the congratulations of their neighbors. After all, there
hadn't been any fresh heroes since the Civil War ended about thirty-
five years before.

For the rest of his life Johnson marched in the Memorial Day Parade, sometimes next to old Tom Williams, a Civil War veteran with
a long white beard. It was an inspiring sight, for Tom Johnson was
a Negro and Tom Williams had fought on the Confederate side.

When Tom Johnson died in 1936 he had never, by customary
standards, accomplished very much except to make a lot of friends.
He made a few more when they read his will: Somehow, during a
lifetime of menial jobs, he had saved twelve hundred dollars.

He left it all to the Farmer City Library, the only private bequest
that storehouse of knowledge has ever had.

OTTERVILLE

        *Dr. Silas Hamilton Monument,* in the local schoolyard, bears this legend:

"Erected by George Washington. Born in Virginia a slave. Died Otterville, Ill., April 15, 1864. A Christian Freeman.

"To the memory of Dr. Silas Hamilton. His former Master, Born in Tinmouth, Vt., May 19, 1775. Died at Otterville, Ill., Nov. 19, 1834. Having in his lifetime given freedom to Twenty-eight Slaves. At his death bequeathed four thousand dollars for the erection and endowment of the Hamilton Primary School."

QUINCY

        *Augustus Tolton Memorial,* in St. Peter's Cemetery, marks the resting place of the first Negro American ordained a priest.

Father Tolton was born in April 1864, in Missouri, of slave parents. He later fled with his mother, brother, and sister to Quincy. Ordained in Rome in 1886, he was installed as pastor of St. Joseph's Church in Quincy, established a Negro school in the basement, and soon began attracting white residents to his services. He later served in Chicago.

On his death in 1897 Father Tolton was buried here at his own request.

SPRINGFIELD

        *Lincoln Home State Memorial* is the only home ever owned by Abraham Lincoln, who lived here from 1844 to 1861.

One of Lincoln's friends during his years in Springfield was William de Fleurville, a Haitian Negro who had arrived in New Salem, virtually penniless, in 1831. Lincoln befriended him and introduced him to others, from whom he earned some fees as a barber. Later, de Fleurville moved on to Springfield, where he worked until he had saved enough money to open his own barber shop in 1832.

"Billy the Barber's" shop became a favorite haunt of local businessmen, including Lincoln. The future President also became de Fleurville's lawyer, and visited his shop to bid him goodbye before he left for Washington.

The Negro barber was a leading citizen of the town. He supported his own church and those of several other faiths, represented his race in community matters, played the clarinet in the military band of the Springfield Artillery Company, and entertained at social gatherings with his flute and violin.

---

# INDIANA

---

## BLOOMINGDALE

*Underground Railroad Marker,* one mile northeast on U. S. 41, is one of several markers on routes used by fugitive slaves in Indiana. Most of the slaves continued on to safety in Canada, but some remained in the state.

One of these was William Trail, who escaped from his master in Maryland in 1814. Although he was pursued and captured on two occasions, he was finally freed by the courts. He established a prosperous farm in Union County.

## FOUNTAIN CITY

*Levi Coffin Home,* North Main Street. This building, still being used as a residence, was once the home of Levi Coffin, a Quaker abolitionist sometimes called "The president of the underground railroad."

Coffin used the house as a station on the underground. Between 1827 and 1847 he hid more than three hundred slaves here as they passed through Indiana on their journey to freedom in Illinois, Michigan, and Canada.

Coffin was born in North Carolina in 1798 and moved to Fountain City, then called "Newport," in 1826. He moved to Ohio in 1847 or 1848, and continued his abolitionist work there. In all, he helped more than three thousand slaves escape to freedom, and continued to help the freedmen long after the Civil War. Coffin was a founder of the Freedmen's Bureau in 1863. He died in Avondale, Ohio, in 1877.

GREENCASTLE

*DePauw University.* Many victims of arthritis live in greater comfort because of the discoveries of a brilliant Negro scientist who studied here before going on to Harvard University and the University of Vienna.

The son of a Montgomery, Alabama, railway clerk, Dr. Percy L. Julian worked as a waiter in a fraternity house, sleeping in the attic, while he attended school here. He graduated Phi Beta Kappa in 1920, as valedictorian of his class.

Dr. Julian developed processes that reduced the cost of cortisone to bring it within the reach of millions who suffer from arthritis. In 1935 he found a way to synthesize the drug commonly used in the treatment of glaucoma. He operates his own research company, Julian Laboratories, in Chicago, where he was once named "Man of the Year."

Among them, Dr. Julian and his five brothers and sisters earned fourteen college and university degrees. It is ironical that their grandfather was a slave whose right hand was mutilated as punishment for learning to read.

INDIANAPOLIS

*Crispus Attucks High School* was named to honor the first American to die in the Revolutionary War. In 1940 it graduated the first Negro to be commissioned in the regular United States Navy, John Wesley Lee.

After attending Indiana and DePauw Universities, Lee entered the Navy as a steward's mate in April 1944, and a year later was commissioned as a reserve midshipman. On graduation from Reserve Midshipmen's School at Northwestern University he was commissioned an ensign in the Naval Reserve and assigned to a fleet oiler in the Pacific. Two years later, in July 1947, he was commissioned in the regular Navy.

Lee had a brilliant Navy career, rising to lieutenant commander, and holding several commands, including that of Chairman, Joint Planning Team, Allied Forces Central Europe. He retired from the Navy in June 1966, at the age of forty-two.

PENNVILLE

*Eliza Harris Marker,* one mile north. A stone cairn and bronze plate commemorate the escape route of Eliza Harris. She was the prototype of the character Eliza, in *Uncle Tom's Cabin.*

# IOWA

## AMES

*Iowa State University.* George Washington Carver was graduated here in 1894 and joined the faculty while continuing his studies. He later became director of the Department of Agricultural Research at Tuskegee Institute.

Carver was primarily responsible for persuading southern farmers to turn to crops other than cotton, which was depleting their land. Among his discoveries were nearly three hundred uses for the peanut.

## BURLINGTON

*Old Zion Methodist Church Marker* on North Third Street. A parking lot now occupies the site of the Old Zion Methodist Church, in which the Iowa Territorial Supreme Court met.

The court's first case involved a Missouri slave named Ralph, whose master had authorized him to go to Dubuque to work in the mines and earn the money to purchase his freedom. When his owner sought his return the case was tried here with David Rorer, of Burlington, handling the Negro's defense.

The court ruled unanimously that since Ralph did not come to Iowa as a fugitive, and since the law prohibited enslaving anyone in Iowa, he could remain free. The decision handed down by Chief Justice Charles Mason in July 1839 was almost directly opposite that handed down in the Dred Scott case less than twenty years later.

## CLINTON

*Site of Underground Railroad Station,* Sixth Avenue South and South Second Street. A small house that stood here before the Lafayette Hotel was built often was a refuge for slaves who escaped into Iowa from Missouri.

Slavery had been barred from this territory under the Ordinance of 1787 and the Missouri Compromise. Anti-slavery sentiment in the state was strong among the many Quakers who had come from the East, and their influence encouraged development of an efficient underground railroad network.

## DES MOINES

*State Capitol Building,* East 12th Street, displays the battle flags of the Iowa military units that fought in the Civil War. Among them is that of the 60th United States Infantry, which was originally recruited as the 1st Regiment, Iowa Colored Infantry.

The regimental history records the eagerness with which Negroes here and throughout America responded to the opportunity to fight, once they were permitted to do so:

"At that time there were probably less than fifteen hundred persons of African descent living within the boundaries of the State of Iowa. There was an ardent desire, however, on the part of the Iowa men of Negro blood, to assist in accomplishing the defeat of those who were engaged in an attempt which, if successful, meant the perpetuation of human slavery in the Southern states. . . ."

A total of 1153 Negroes—"almost every man of African descent in the state who was capable of military service"—enrolled in the regiment. Before the war ended, 344 of them were dead.

## INDIANOLA

*Simpson College.* Were it not for the friendship and understanding of the administration, faculty, and students at this institution in 1890, the world might have lost one of its greatest agricultural scientists.

George Washington Carver came here that year, seeking admission as a student, but with little hope that he would be accepted. In 1885 he had been accepted at Highland College, in northeastern Kansas, only to be told when he arrived on the campus that a mistake had been made—the school did not accept Negroes.

During the next several years Carver worked on farms, homesteaded a land claim, cooked in a hotel, and finally was persuaded by a white friend to try again at Simpson. He walked twenty-five miles from Winterset to Indianola with his worldly goods tied in a small bundle. To his delight, he found he was welcome at this all-white school. When he had paid his fees, he had ten cents left.

Carver bought corn meal and beef suet with his last dime, and found lodging in a woodshed. Someone loaned him a washtub, and he began doing laundry for other students, refusing all offers of charity. Initially, his greatest interest was in art, but when it became apparent to him that he could render a greater service in scientific agriculture, he transferred to Iowa State College at Ames.

Throughout his life, however, he held great affection for this school, which took him in when others had refused. "It was in high school that I first learned what it meant to be a human being, and at Simpson that I could truly believe I was one," Carver said later.

The Science Building here is named in honor of the genius who was probably Simpson's most distinguished alumnus. A marble memorial inscription and bronze plaque pay tribute to him in the foyer.

## SIOUX CITY

*Pearl Street*, this city's first major thoroughfare, was named for a pioneer Negro woman who arrived, as did many other migrants to western river towns, on one of the boats that were the major form of transportation a century ago. The honor paid her suggests that if Pearl was not a good cook, she must certainly have been a popular one.

Pearl had competition, however, from another Negro cook who arrived here in the 1860s. She was called Aunty Wooden. Soon after her arrival she established such a reputation for her opossum dinners that leading citizens competed for invitations to them.

The most remarkable early-day Negro in Sioux City was Henry Riding, a veteran of the Civil War who established a successful hotel and acquired other real estate in the town. He gained fame and respect by holding the track layers at bay with a shotgun when the railroad tried to cross his land without permission. The railroad finally paid him twenty-one thousand dollars for the privilege.

Sioux City was also a refuge for slaves seeking to escape from forced servitude in Missouri. One of the underground railroad stations stood on the site on which the Lafayette Hotel was built in later years.

## SPRINGDALE

*John Brown Headquarters Marker*, three miles northeast. A huge granite boulder with a bronze tablet marks the site of an old farmhouse where John Brown quartered some of his band during the winter of 1857–58. The inscription reads:

"Here was the home of William Maxon,
a station on the Underground Railroad where John Brown of Ossawatomie
recruited and trained 11 men for the
raid on Harper's Ferry.

Let some poor slave mother whom I
have Striven to Free
With her children, from the gallows-
stair put up a prayer for me.

WHITTIER"

Many Quakers had settled in Springdale, and Brown made a deep impression on them despite the conflict between their belief in non-violence and his determination to abolish slavery by any means necessary. When Brown left here to go to Chicago, the Quakers joined at the Friends Meeting House in a prayer for his success.

TABOR

*Todd House* was used by John Brown as a headquarters between 1854 and 1856. The home has been purchased by the Tabor Historical Society.

*John Brown's Camp Ground.* A marker in the village park notes that this was the abolitionist leader's camp ground in 1858–59. Tabor was an active station on the underground railroad.

# KANSAS

BAXTER SPRINGS

*Baxter Springs National Cemetery.* Parts of the 3rd Wisconsin Cavalry Regiment and fifty men of the 2nd Kansas Colored Infantry Regiment were surprised here in October 1863 by forces of the notorious guerrilla leader from Missouri, Quantrill.

The men were eating when the attack began and had to fight their way through the attackers to get to their weapons. Nine of the defenders were killed. After they had driven the raiders away, Lieutenant James B. Pond, the commander of the Wisconsin cavalry unit, reported that the Negro troops "fought like devils. Thirteen of them were wounded in the first round, and not one but fought the thing through."

This was the second action for Kansas Negro soldiers at Baxter Springs. Earlier, on May 18, the 1st Kansas Colored Regiment was attacked by forces of another Missouri guerrilla leader, Major T. R. Livingston. Twenty of the Negroes were killed in action and several were captured. Livingston's men killed one of the Negro captives; Colonel James Williams, the Federal commander, promptly had one of his Confederate prisoners shot in retaliation.

Most of the Federal troops who were killed battling Quantrill's guerrillas are buried in the Baxter Springs National Cemetery. A monument has been erected in their honor.

BEELER

"*Homestead of a Genius*," State K-96 near Beeler. This inscription marks the site homesteaded by George Washington Carver when he was twenty-two. Carver came here disappointed by the refusal of white colleges to admit him as a student. Ultimately, however, his determination to obtain an education prompted him to borrow $300 on his property and go to Iowa.

For a time after his arrival there he worked as a cook in a hotel. His brilliant career began when the authorities at Simpson College in Indianola, an all-white school, accepted him as a student and encouraged his work.

DODGE CITY

*Fort Dodge,* five miles east on U. S. 154, was established in 1865 to protect settlers, westward pioneers, and cattlemen from the Indians. Units of the 10th U. S. Cavalry saw a great deal of action in the area, not all of it against the Indians.

Dodge City, in those days, was almost as tough as contemporary fiction and drama recall it. Crooked gamblers, thieves, confidence men, cattle rustlers, and killers found the wide-open town to their liking.

Not all of the men killed here were the intended victims. One who died in the early days, a Negro named Tex, simply happened to be in the way of a stray bullet during a shooting spree. A great many men were killed on purpose, however, and even the formation of a vigilance committee did no good. The criminal element soon took it over and turned it to their own ends.

Law and order finally came to Dodge City after another Negro, named Taylor, was murdered. Taylor was employed by the commanding officer at Fort Dodge, who promptly occupied the town with troops. Soon thereafter a county government was formed and in subsequent years Dodge City became relatively peaceful as it was policed by a succession of fearless and competent, if somewhat unorthodox, peace officers like Bat Masterson and Wyatt Earp, whose names have gone down in history.

Many Negro cowboys visited Dodge City as they came north on cattle drives, and many Negroes were among the pioneers on the wagon trains. As might be expected, not all the Negroes were of sterling character.

Dodge City was the home of one remarkable Negro confidence man, Ben Hodges, who swindled a great many ranchers out of cattle and horses. His most elaborate swindle was one in which he posed so convincingly as the heir to a huge Spanish land grant in the area that he got financial backing from many prominent citizens, including the local bankers. His scheme was found out only when he tried to obtain capital from some less gullible bankers in New York.

Hodges is remarkable because, unlike most of the bandits of the Old West, he did not die of "lead poisoning," or at the end of a rope. Instead, he lived to regale the youngsters of the new generation with tales of his exploits, finally died a natural death, and was buried in Maple Grove Cemetery among Dodge City's distinguished pioneer citizens.

FORT SCOTT

*Fort Scott.* Several buildings survive at this Civil War home of the 1st Kansas Colored Volunteers, who were organized in August 1862. This was the first Negro unit under fire in the war. It repulsed a superior Confederate force in a battle at Island Mound, Missouri, October 28, 1862.

Prior to the Civil War the fort was a meeting place for abolitionists, including John Brown. The museum in the old headquarters building was badly damaged by fire in 1967, but the National

Park Service plans to develop the fort as a historic site, and it presumably will be restored.

There is also a National Cemetery here, which was established in 1862. Many of the headstones bear the letters USCT, for United States Colored Troops.

## KANOPOLIS

*Fort Harker Museum* is in the old stone guardhouse of this frontier military post. Three other buildings remain in use as residences.

The fort was abandoned in 1873 after only nine years of use. During that period it was the occasional headquarters for Negro cavalrymen who protected settlers and Union Pacific construction workers from the Indians.

The museum contains many relics of the Indian wars, including a horse-drawn ambulance used to bring wounded troopers in from the plains. It also displays a picture of Mose Buckley, a Negro who was orderly for General Nelson A. Miles, one of the outstanding cavalry commanders in the early history of the West.

## LARNED

*Fort Larned National Historic Site.* Troopers of the 10th U. S. Cavalry Regiment were stationed here in 1868, soon after they had been assigned to duty on the plains. Their encounters with Indians were few, but one party of ten Negro cavalrymen engaged a band of hostile Indians in November and killed two of them in a twenty-mile running battle.

As was often the case among military units in the last century, disease was their most dangerous adversary. Epidemic cholera claimed many lives. Rabid wolves were another hazard, as Negro Private Willis Mason of the 10th Cavalry learned when he was bitten in the foot by one while he was stationed here.

## LAWRENCE

*Oak Hill Cemetery,* 13th Street. Buried here is Senator James Lane, one of the first to advocate, and then do something about, the use of Negro soldiers in the Civil War. Lane began recruiting Negro troops in August 1862, at a time when the War Department and President Lincoln had specifically forbidden it. He argued that if the Southern troops objected to being killed by Negroes, "let them lay down their arms."

Lane's was the first Negro unit to see action in the war, meeting a force of guerrilla troops near Butler, Bates County, Missouri. The Leavenworth *Conservative* commented: "It is useless to talk any more about Negro courage. The men fought like tigers, each and every one of them, and the main difficulty was to hold them well in hand."

LEAVENWORTH

*Fort Leavenworth,* three miles north on U. S. 73. One of the nation's oldest military posts, established in 1827, this was the first home of the 10th U. S. Cavalry Regiment. Between the Civil War and the late 1890s, this Negro unit participated in many of the important engagements of the Indian wars. Later its men served with great valor in the Spanish-American War in Cuba.

It was also here that the unique Independent Kansas Colored Battery was mustered in 1864. It was the only unit in the Civil War with Negro officers. One of them, Captain H. Ford Douglass, son of Negro abolitionist Frederick Douglass, was also one of the first Negroes to enlist during the war. He joined the Illinois Volunteers in 1862.

*Fort Leavenworth National Cemetery.* Many of the men of the 9th and 10th U. S. Cavalry Regiments are buried here. A monument to General Edward Hatch, erected by the men of the 9th U. S. Cavalry, lists more than fifty battles and skirmishes—mostly with Indians—in which he and his soldiers took part during his twenty-three-year Army career.

Some men of the Negro cavalry regiments were truly western pioneers. One, Edward L. Baker, was born in a wagon train near the North Platte River in Wyoming in December 1865. He grew up to serve with the 9th and later with the 10th U. S. Cavalry here at Fort Leavenworth. During his career he fought Geronimo, the renowned Apache chief, and earned a medal for bravery in the Santiago campaign.

MANHATTAN

*Fort Riley,* ten miles southwest on State 18, was once the headquarters of General Custer and the 7th U. S. Cavalry. It was also the first real home of the 10th U. S. Cavalry Regiment, and in 1880 became the headquarters post for the 9th. One assignment of these regiments was the protection of settlers and wagon trains from marauding Indians on the Oregon and Santa Fe Trails.

## NICODEMUS

*Nicodemus Colony*, U. S. 24, two miles west of the Rooks-Graham County line, is the sole survivor of three colonies founded by the Exodusters, groups of Negroes who homesteaded in Kansas in the 1870s. It was not named for the biblical character, but for a slave who, legend says, prophesied the Civil War.

The first settlers arrived in 1877 and spent their first winter in dugouts and burrows. They built their first homes above ground the following spring.

From the beginning, the Negroes were plagued by bad luck. A long series of crop failures included the destruction of one crop by searing winds which left most of western Kansas unharmed.

At its peak the village had fewer than five hundred residents, but it produced several teachers, ministers, politicians, and civil servants. Today it is virtually deserted. The state has placed a roadside marker in a park in the town.

## OSAWATOMIE

*John Brown Memorial State Park* contains the cabin in which John Brown lived and hid fugitive slaves during his Kansas days. His statue is also in the park.

## WALLACE

*Site of Fort Wallace.* Only a roadside marker and the old post cemetery remain to identify this pioneer military post at which members of the 10th U. S. Cavalry Regiment once served. Among the actions against hostile Indians that began at this post was one in September 1868 when the Negro troopers galloped off to rescue a force of volunteers from Chief Roman Nose at Beecher Island (see Wray, Colorado).

One ironic episode that began here involved Major Eugene A. Carr, a white officer who arrived at Fort Wallace to take command of the 5th Cavalry. Two years earlier, Carr had refused a command with the Negro cavalry units. He now found that his new all-white unit was in the field searching for a Cheyenne war party, and he was given an escort of Negro troopers to take him to his regiment.

When the party reached Beaver Creek they were attacked by hundreds of Indians. The Negro soldiers of the 10th Cavalry, long experienced in Indian warfare, formed their wagons in a horseshoe on top of a small hill and poured a fusillade of bullets on the Indians from their seven-shot Spencer rifles.

The Indians were driven off and the unit returned to Fort Wallace the next morning. The Negro cavalrymen had marched 230 miles in nine days, killed ten hostile Cheyenne, and convinced Major Carr, whose scalp was still intact, of their skill and courage.

# KENTUCKY

## CAVE CITY

*Mammoth Cave National Park,* 9.6 miles west on State 70, was first discovered about 1800, and its development as a tourist attraction began in 1837, when it was purchased by Frank Gorin.

Much of the exploration of the huge caverns has been done by Negro guides. The first of these was Stephen Bishop, a slave who devoted his life to exploring the cave until his death in 1859. He was succeeded by Matt Bransford, another Negro slave who also spent his life working in the cave, and then passed on his knowledge to other successors.

The cave, which has several entrances, is noted for its size and beauty. Rivers flow at several levels, allowing the adventurous Negro guides, for well over a century, to explore some cave areas by boat.

## LANCASTER

*Site of the Kennedy House,* 8.4 miles east on State 52. Only the foundation remains of what was once one of the largest plantations in the South. General Thomas Kennedy owned fifteen thousand acres and two hundred slaves, several of whom were proto-types of characters in *Uncle Tom's Cabin*.

Harriet Beecher Stowe visited here while gathering material for the book. General Kennedy's daughter, Nancy, is said to have in-spired the character Little Eva. The George Harris of the story was a Negro slave named Lewis Clark, who later escaped and went to Cambridge, Massachusetts, where he lived for many years in the household of the author's sister.

## LEXINGTON

*Man o' War Park* is the last resting place of two of the greatest names in thoroughbred racing—one a horse and the other a man.

The man was Isaac Murphy, one of the greatest jockeys of all time. He was reburied here two days before the running of the Kentucky Derby in 1967. His remains had been in a neglected grave in a nearby abandoned Lexington Cemetery that will become a parking lot.

Isaac Burns Murphy was born on the Tanner farm near here in 1861, probably of free Negro parents, although historians disagree on this. The son—his friends called him "Ike"—learned to ride in 1873 and entered his first race in 1875. He won his first one in Lexington in 1876.

Ike apparently liked the taste of victory because, during the rest of his career, he won 44 percent of his races—628 of 1412. He won the Kentucky Derby three times, a record that was not equaled until Earle Sande won his third on Gallant Fox in 1930. It was not broken until Eddie Arcaro won his fourth Derby on Citation in 1948.

Murphy rode all of the great horses of his time, but he also rode many that were not so great, and often won with them. Thus, he won a reputation as "the poor owner's friend." He always advised other jockeys to "be honest and you'll have no trouble and plenty of money."

Ike lived by this rule, and when he died at the age of thirty-six he had plenty of friends. Five hundred of them—including many of the greatest names in racing—were at his funeral.

The great Negro jockey sleeps now only a little way from the great horse, Man o' War. Eddie Arcaro, who attended the ceremony in 1967, spoke for a lot of jockeys when he said: "If I had lived in Isaac Murphy's time I am sure we would have been good friends.

When they take me away . . . they can put me right here . . . next to Isaac Murphy."

*Patchen Wilkes Stock Farm,* on Winchester Pike, was once the home of the stallion, Peter the Great, one of the fabled horses of harness racing. This great horse sired so many blooded horses of championship stature that at the age of twenty-one he still sold for fifty thousand dollars.

Much of the credit for the success of this horse and his offspring belonged to Ed Willis, "a born colt handler," who was the trainer at Patchen Wilkes Farm. In 1914, when the farm was in its glory, *Trotter and Pacer* magazine credited Willis with being "responsible for the many extremely fast records and so many championship honors" credited to the offspring of Peter the Great.

The magazine noted that Willis, a Negro, "had charge of Peter the Great from the day of his advent there, and . . . broke, gaited, educated and started on the road to fame almost every great performer which has gone out from the farm . . ."

## LOUISVILLE

*Churchill Downs,* South 7th Street and 7th Avenue, is the site of the most famous thoroughbred race of them all, the Kentucky Derby.

Negro jockeys had a prominent role in the Derby during its first thirty years. Isaac Murphy won it three times, and three other Negroes won it twice: Willie Simms on Ben Brush in 1896 and on Plaudit in 1898; and Jimmy Winkfield on His Eminence in 1901 and on Alan-a-Dale in 1902.

Simms also gained fame by becoming the first American jockey riding an American horse to win an English Sweepstakes.

There were eleven Negro winners beginning with the very first Kentucky Derby, held in 1875. It was won by Oliver Lewis, riding on Aristides. In this race thirteen of the fourteen riders were Negroes.

The other Negro Derby winners were: Billy Walker, 1877 on Baden Baden; Garrett Lewis, 1880 on Fonso; Babe Hurd, 1882 on Apollo; Ike Murphy, 1884 on Buchanan; Erskine Henderson, 1885 on Joe Cotton; Isaac Lewis, 1887 on Montrose; Ike Murphy, 1890 on Riley; Murphy again, 1891 on Kingman; Alonzo Clayton, 1892 on Azra (in this Derby all three starting horses were ridden by Negro jockeys); James "Soup" Perkins, 1895 on Halma. The last Negro jockey to ride in the Derby was Jess Conley, in 1911. He came in third on Colston.

Another famous Negro rider, the only man to win six out of six races in one day, was Monk Overton. He accomplished this feat at Washington Park, in 1891.

The first Negro jockey on record was known as Abe. He won the initial Jerome Handicap at Belmont in 1866 on Watson, and the first Travers Stakes that same year on Merrill at Saratoga.

The Belmont Stakes was won by Pike Barnes in 1890 on Burlington and by Willie Simms in 1893 on Comanche and in 1894 on Henry of Navarre.

*Site of Crowe's Livery Stable*, 224 South 3rd Street, marks the spot where the phrase "Jim Crow" came into the American language. In the early nineteenth century Thomas Crowe operated a livery stable here at which a number of Negro slaves served as stable hands. Among them was an elderly Negro named Jim Crow, who had a stiff left leg. He was fond of singing and dancing as he worked, but because of his deformity, he finished each verse with a sort of jump. The refrain of his favorite folk tune was:

> Wheel about, turn about,
>  Do jes so;
> An' every time I wheel about
>  I jump Jim Crow.

The livery stable was located near the city theater, and in 1828 Thomas D. Rice, a member of a stock company playing there, visited the livery stable and heard Jim Crow sing and dance. He made himself up as a Negro and worked the song into his act. For more than a decade he sang the song and did other Negro impersonations around the country, and the name eventually came to be applied as a symbol of segregation.

## MOUNT STERLING

*Yellow Rose Farm* was operated until his death in 1926 by Peter Lee Hensley, a Negro who owned and bred trotting horses. At fourteen he found employment as a wagon driver, and at nineteen he owned a grocery store and a restaurant.

Hensley became interested in trotting, bought a horse, and eventually the Yellow Rose Farm. One of his horses, Temple Bar, won twenty-four out of twenty-five races; another, Aloyo, won seventeen events in a row.

NICHOLASVILLE

*Camp Nelson Military Cemetery*, seven miles south on U. S. 27, is the burial place of more than five hundred soldiers who died in the Battles of Perryville and Richmond during the Civil War.

Nearby is the site of Camp Nelson, which was a major center for the enlistment of Negro troops during the war. Nearly twenty-four thousand Kentucky Negroes served with the Federal forces.

# LOUISIANA

ALEXANDRIA

*Colonel Bailey's Dams.* Portions of the Confederate earthworks on the outskirts of the city remain as reminders of the Civil War, although the fort they protected never saw action. It was in an earlier engagement here that the ingenuity of a Wisconsin engineer and incredible effort by Negro soldiers saved Union General N. P. Banks' gunboats.

During the Red River campaign of 1864 Confederate General Richard Taylor drove Banks' force from Mansfield to Pleasant Hill and then to Alexandria. Here Banks found the Red River so low that his gunboats could not navigate the rapids. The situation seemed hopeless until Colonel Joseph Bailey conceived the idea of building wing dams to raise the water level. The scheme worked and the vessels were saved.

When the war ended Bailey was a general in command of a brigade of engineers at Mobile, Alabama. In his final report on the work of his engineers he wrote:

"No troops during this war have labored more severely or more arduously but those to whom most credit is due are the 96th and 97th U. S. Colored Engineer Regiments. Night and day without complaint those regiments worked, and it is difficult to comprehend how they endured through it."

## BATON ROUGE

*Southern University* is the outgrowth of an institute in New Orleans established by the legislature in 1880 to provide education for Negroes. It has been located in Baton Rouge since 1914, but has branches in New Orleans and Shreveport, with a combined enrollment in the Southern University System of nearly twelve thousand. The fifty-million-dollar physical plant is on a beautifully landscaped site that includes a ten-acre lake.

## DONALDSONVILLE

*Oak Alley* is one of the best-known of the huge Greek Revival mansions of the Old South. This plantation home is distinguished by the twenty-eight huge oaks that border the drive leading to it. They are matched by an equal number of huge Doric columns that support the roof of the veranda surrounding the house.

Negro slave labor was vital in the construction of homes such as this, and indispensable to their operation. It has been estimated that at the start of the Civil War, of 120,000 skilled artisans in the South, one hundred thousand were Negroes. They supplied virtually every need of the planter and his family, including the production of textiles and leather, and the fashioning of many of the garments worn by the very social white aristocracy of the day.

The highly vaunted "southern hospitality" owed its existence to the elaborate staffs of well-trained "house Negroes" maintained on every plantation. The wealth to sustain such luxury came from the dawn-to-dark labors of other Negroes who worked in the cotton, tobacco, and sugar cane fields.

## MANSFIELD

*Mansfield Battle Park,* four miles south on U. S. 84. Federal hopes of taking Shreveport ended when General N. P. Banks' Red River campaign was halted by Confederate troops under General Richard Taylor. The Federal troops, which included six Negro units, withdrew to the south after the battle. The park museum contains Civil War materials and maps describing the battle.

MANSURA

Battle of Mansura Marker on Louisiana 1 notes the unsuccessful effort of Confederate troops to prevent withdrawal of
Banks' Federal force after their defeat at Mansfield.

NEW ORLEANS

Chalmette National Historical Park, six miles south on
Louisiana 39. A fourteen-year-old Negro drummer boy was one of
the heroes of the last battle of the War of 1812, fought here on
January 8, 1815. Hundreds of other Negroes were among General
Andrew Jackson's troops. It was the last engagement in which Americans and British fought, except as allies, and ironically, it took place
after the signing of the Treaty of Ghent.

The battle actually began on December 23, 1814, when Jackson
learned that the British had landed near New Orleans, and attacked
them with fifteen hundred men. About two hundred of his soldiers
were free Negroes commanded by Colonel Joseph Savary. Jackson
attacked at night, and in the heavy fog it was the constant rattle of
a drum carried by Noble Jordan that kept the Americans together.

The Americans were poorly armed, and many of Savary's men
soon found their weapons useless, but they kept fighting, using their
guns as clubs. In his report, Jackson noted that "Savary's men manifested great bravery."

After the battle Jackson withdrew his men to Chalmette, where
they built a mile-long defensive breastwork, much of which can still
be seen. Behind it he gathered a force of four thousand, many of
them Negroes. When General Sir Edward M. Pakenham arrived on
Christmas Day 1814, he had a command of fifty-four hundred seasoned soldiers, against a smaller force of Creole aristocrats, free Negroes, Choctaw Indians, Kentucky backwoodsmen, and even pirates
of Jean Lafitte. He ordered attacks on December 28 and on January 1, 1815, both of which were repulsed.

By January 8, when Pakenham launched his final, suicidal attack
on the American line, there had gathered on Chalmette Plain the
largest group of Negro American soldiers ever assembled. They fought
in some of the hottest action of the day.

The engagement ended in disaster for the British, and death for
General Pakenham. Historians dispute who killed him, but a credible
witness, General Jackson himself, later gave this report to President
Monroe:

1. Booker T. Washington Memorial on site of shanty where the noted black educator founded Tuskegee Institute, July 4, 1881. *(Tuskegee Institute)*

2. Contemporary artist's sketch of soldier in the Tenth Cavalry, an all-black regiment that fought Indians in the West from the close of the Civil War to the late nineteenth century. *(U.S. Signal Corps)*

3. Diorama shows pioneer settlers arriving in Los Angeles in 1781. Twenty-eight of the original forty-four settlers were black. (*Los Angeles County Museum of Natural History*)

4. One of many memorials to the brilliant and fearless black abolitionist, Frederick Douglass. (*Morgan State College*)

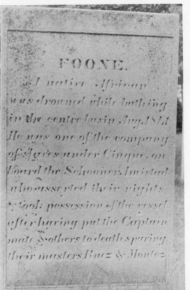

5. Memorial in Farmington, Connecticut, to one of the Africans who mutinied on the slave ship *Amistad* in 1839. Led by Joseph Cinque, Foone and other slaves seized control of the ship. *(Farmington Public Library)*

6. Black professor and students in chemistry laboratory at U.S. Coast Guard Academy, New London, Connecticut. *(U.S. Coast Guard Photo)*

7. Home of abolitionist Frederick Douglass in Washington, D.C., now a museum. (*American Oil Company*)

8. Administration Building at Georgetown University, named for black president of the university, Patrick Francis Healy. (*Georgetown University*)

9. Marker on grave in Jesuit cemetery at Georgetown University, Washington, D.C., burial place of black Georgetown president credited with establishing the university as a great institution. (*Georgetown University*)

10. "The Westwood Children," by Joshua Johnston, the first American Negro portrait artist, is in the collection of the National Gallery of Art in Washington, D.C. (*National Gallery of Art*)

11. State marker honoring a Georgia hero, Bragg Smith, who died trying to save the life of the Columbus city engineer after a cave-in. (*American Oil Company*)

12. The Lewis and Clark expedition's black guide, York, is shown at lower right in a mural in the rotunda of the Oregon State Capitol. Scene is at Delilo Falls on the Columbia River. (*Oregon State Highway Department*)

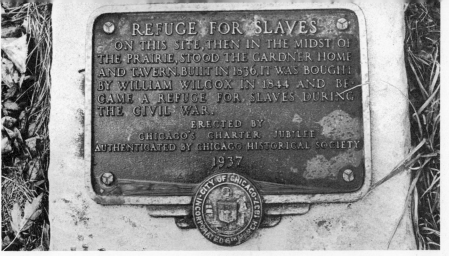

13. Underground railroad marker in Chicago. *(Ted Williams)*

14. Victory monument erected to honor Chicago's black soldiers and sailors who served in World War I. *(Chicago Park District)*

15. Memorial to George Washington Carver, distinguished black scientist and educator, in lobby of Simpson College science building, named in his honor. *(Simpson College)*

"Honour and shame from no condition rise; Act well your part, there all the honour lies"

(THE THOROUGHBRED RECORD—1896)

HERE LIES
ISAAC BURNS MURPHY
1860 —— 1896
FAMOUS NEGRO JOCKEY
FROM LEXINGTON, KY.
HE RODE 628 WINNERS IN 1412 RACES (44%)
HE WON THREE KENTUCKY DERBIES
BUCHANAN 1884 — RILEY 1890
KINGMAN 1891
HE WON FOUR AMERICAN DERBIES
HE WON FIVE LATONIA DERBIES
NAMED TO JOCKEY HALL OF FAME
AT
SARATOGA, N.Y., AND PIMLICO, MD.
REMOVED IN MAY 1967
FROM "OLD NO. 2 CEMETERY"
ON EAST 7TH STREET
THIS MEMORIAL PRESENTED TO
THE PEOPLE OF KENTUCKY
AND THE SPORT OF RACING
BY THE KENTUCKY CLUB TOBACCO COMPANY

All Colored Peop
THAT WANT TO
GO TO KANSA
On September 5th, 1877,
Can do so for $5.0

IMMIGRATION.

WHEREAS, We, the colored people of Lexington, Ky. knowing that there abundance of choice lands now belonging to the Government, have assembled and together for the purpose of locating on said lands. Therefore,

BE IT RESOLVED, That we do now organize ourselves into a Colony, as foll Any person wishing to become a member of this Colony can do so by paying the one dollar ($1.00), and this money is to be paid by the first of September, 1877, in ments of twenty-five cents at a time, or otherwise as may be desired.

RESOLVED. That this Colony has agreed to consolidate itself with the Nic Towns, Solomon Valley, Graham County, Kansas, and can only do so by entering cant lands now in their midst, which costs $5.00.

RESOLVED, That this Colony shall consist of seven officers—President, Vic dent, Secretary, Treasurer, and three Trustees. President—M. M. Bell; Vice-P —Isaac Talbott; Secretary—W. J. Niles; Treasurer—Daniel Clarke; Trustee Lee, William Jones, and Abner Webster.

RESOLVED, That this Colony shall have from one to two hundred militia, less, as the case may require, to keep peace and order, and any member failing to his dues, as aforesaid, or failing to comply with the above rules in any particular, be recognized or protected by the Colony.

16. Handbills such as this lured blacks to western homesteads such as the colony at Nicodemus, Kansas. Today the town is virtually deserted. (*Kansas State Historical Society*)

17. Burial place of Isaac Burns Murphy, famed black jockey who won 628 of 1412 races, including three Kentucky Derbies. His remains were transferred to this park, near the great horse Man o' War, at Derby time in 1967. (*Ted Warner Associates*)

18. First Negro American bishop of the Roman Catholic Church, James Augustine Healy, was consecrated at Portland, Maine, Cathedral on June 2, 1875. (*Georgetown University*)

"I heard a single rifle shot from a group of country carts we had been using, and a moment thereafter I saw Pakenham reel and pitch out of his saddle. I have always believed he fell from the bullet of a free man of color, who was a famous rifle shot and came from the Attakapas region of Louisiana."

When the battle ended the inexperienced American volunteers —Negro and white—had overwhelmed the British force, despite its superiority in numbers and experience. Incredibly, the Americans had only seven killed and six wounded. The British losses exceeded two thousand.

A drum, believed to be the one used by Noble Jordan, may be seen in the Louisiana State Museum.

*The Haunted House,* in the French Quarter at Bourbon and Hospital Streets, won its reputation more than a century ago when a fire broke out in the house. The cook, who was found chained in the kitchen, said she started the fire in preference to being tortured by her mistress, a Mme. Lalaurie.

When neighbors broke into locked doors on the third floor, they found other Negro slaves chained, mutilated, and half-starved. According to a newspaper of the day; "We saw where the collar and manacles had cut their way into quivering flesh. For several months they had been confined in those dismal dungeons with no other nutriment than a handful of gruel and insufficient quantity of water, suffering the tortures of the damned and longingly awaiting death as a relief of their sufferings."

There were seven slaves in all, some chained in collars and leg irons. Infuriated by the horrible activities of Mme. Lalaurie, a mob gutted the house. She escaped and fled to France, but the tradition is that the spirits of the tortured slaves still haunt the house.

*Jackson Square.* Laid out in 1720 as the public square by Bienville, founder of New Orleans, this has been the scene of historic events for more than two hundred years. General Jackson was welcomed here after the victory of his Negro and white forces in the Battle of Chalmette Plains in the War of 1812. A monument has been erected in his honor.

Negroes were active in the military history of the city almost a century before the War of 1812. They were involved in the Natchez Massacre of 1729 and under Bienville in the French and Indian Wars. When Bienville attacked the English and Indians in the Chickasaw War, he was accompanied by a free Negro named Simon, who led a company of nearly fifty other free Negroes. Some two hundred Negro wagon drivers were also involved.

Governor de Vaudreil had between two hundred and three hundred Negro troops in 1746. In 1779 Governor Bernardo de Galvez attacked the British at Baton Rouge, Manchac, and Natchez, with a force that included eighty free Negroes. They behaved, he said, "with as much valor and generosity as the whites." Under Spanish rule of New Orleans many Negroes served in the colonial militia, which also served as the local police force.

When Galvez moved against Pensacola, many free Negro soldiers helped him capture that city from the British, returning all of Florida to Spanish rule until it was purchased by the United States.

*Louisiana State Museum,* 751 Chartres Street, contains a plaque placed in 1934 by the world's sugar industries to honor Norbert Rillieux, a New Orleans Negro. In 1846 Rillieux invented a vacuum evaporating pan that reduced labor and costs in sugar refining, revolutionizing the industry.

Rillieux was born in 1806 to Vincent Rillieux and Constance Vivant, a slave on the wealthy engineer's plantation. He was educated in France and also died there in 1894.

Rillieux is only one of many Negro inventors whose work has been recognized. During the slavery era there were undoubtedly many others whose names will never be known. They were not permitted to obtain patents. An invention by one of his own slaves prompted Jefferson Davis to obtain passage of a law permitting slaves to obtain patents in the Confederacy.

Other Negroes who did get credit for their patents include Andrew J. Beard, who invented the "Jenny Coupler," greatly reducing accidents in the coupling of railroad cars; Henry Blair, who in 1834 was granted a patent for a corn-planting machine, probably the first patent granted to a Negro; Lewis Howard Latimer, who helped Alexander Graham Bell make the patent drawings for the first telephone and later became chief draftsman for both General Electric and Westinghouse; and Granville T. Woods, whose fifty patents ranged from the prototype of the modern egg incubator to a telegraph system which informed engineers about the location of other trains on the track.

The work of one Negro inventor, Elijah McCoy, also contributed to the American idiom. McCoy was born in Canada of former slave parents who escaped from Kentucky via the underground railroad.

He grew up on a farm outside of Ypsilanti, Michigan, and later moved to Detroit.

His major patent, of nearly sixty that he held, was one for a lubricating drip cup which was the basis for lubricating systems for moving parts. It was so successful that salesmen pointed out the device on their equipment, asserting that "It's the real McCoy." The phrase survives as a favorite description of the genuine article.

*Old State Capitol,* on the site of the Roosevelt Hotel. During the Reconstruction period following the Civil War the state government was quartered here. Heading it, in 1872, was the nation's first Negro governor, Pinckney Benton Stewart Pinchback. He succeeded to the office when Governor Henry C. Warmoth was impeached.

*Ursuline Convent,* 1114 Chartres Street, is said to be the oldest surviving building in the Mississippi Valley. It was built in 1745 by the Ursuline nuns, who began providing education for women, including many Negroes. As was the case with most of the old structures here and elsewhere in the South, Negroes were largely responsible for the construction. The metalwork affords an excellent example of the artistry of enslaved Negro artisans.

*Vieux Carré,* the Old Quarter, is also known as the French Quarter. This historic section is today a world-famous tourist attraction, but Negroes have long figured in its history. The quarter is renowned for its gracious architecture, much of which features elaborate use of iron grillwork in balconies, gates, and fences. The most delicate is the wrought iron, much of which was fashioned by Negro craftsmen during the early days of the city.

During the years when New Orleans was under Spanish rule, Negroes—slave and free—made great progress. They became skilled artisans in almost every field. One man, named Jacoba, was a master silversmith whose work was so exquisite that his services were demanded by members of the Cabildo.

It is not surprising that Negroes had so important a role in fashioning the gracious homes and buildings that still delight New Orleans visitors, for there were many Negroes in the city. In a census taken in 1805, considerably more than half of the 8475 residents of New Orleans were Negroes, and 1526 of them were free.

In later years, the French Quarter became the birthplace of American jazz, and it was the musically inclined Negroes of the city who were largely responsible for this.

*Xavier University*. This is the oldest Negro Catholic university in the nation. It began operation in September 1915 as a high school, became a two-year normal school in 1917, and a four-year college in 1925. The first five degrees were conferred in 1928.

Xavier has the only college of pharmacy among the eight colleges and universities in New Orleans, and also has a graduate school. Both the white and non-Catholic enrollment at the school are growing steadily, and during the 1965–66 school year students came from twenty-nine states and nine foreign countries. The modern library building houses the South's most complete collection of books about the Negro in history and literature.

*Opelousas*. Two of the oldest homes in Opelousas Parish are the Frilot and Lemelle houses, both built by free Negroes about 1800. The Estarge Mansion, at Market and Block Streets in Opelousas, was also built by Negroes in the 1820s, but in this case they were the slaves of Pierre Labyche, the owner.

## PORT HUDSON

*Port Hudson Siege Marker* on U. S. 61. The capture of Port Hudson began with the shelling of the city by the U.S.S. *Hartford* and other vessels between March 7 and 27, 1863. A siege followed that lasted until July, when the city fell.

It was in one of the first actions of the siege, on May 27, 1863, that Negroes were involved in one of their first actions of the Civil War. These were men of the 1st and 3rd Louisiana Native Guards—free Negroes who had been recruited in New Orleans by General Benjamin Butler.

During the half century before the Civil War the nation had forgotten the valorous participation of Negroes in the American Revolution and the War of 1812. A national debate over the arming of Negro soldiers was still in progress at the time of the Port Hudson siege, and most of the white officers involved commented on the performance of the Louisiana Negroes. General Ullman described the battle in these words: "[The Negro troops] made six or seven charges . . . against the enemy's works. They were exposed to a terrible fire and were dreadfully slaughtered . . . their conduct was such as would do honor to any soldiers."

In a letter home, a white engineer officer wrote, "You have no idea how my prejudices with regard to Negro troops have been dispelled by the battle. . . . The brigade of Negroes behaved magnificently and fought splendidly; could not have done better."

The New York *Times,* commenting on an official report of the battle, said: "This official testimony settles the question that the Negro race can fight with great prowess. Those black soldiers had never before been in any severe engagement. They were comparatively raw troops, and were yet subjected to the most awful ordeal . . . the charging upon fortifications through the crash of belching batteries. The men, white or black, who will not flinch from that, will flinch from nothing. It is no longer possible to doubt the bravery and steadiness of the colored race, when rightly led."

The *Times,* in that last reference, apparently assumed that all of the officers leading the Negro units were white. Actually, nearly two-thirds were Negroes. One of them, Captain André Gailloux, lost his life in the encounter, and was given a state funeral in New Orleans. The band of the all-white 42nd Massachusetts Regiment led the parade through the city. It was described as "the funeral pageant of a dead hero, the like of which was never before seen in that, nor, perhaps, in any other American city, in honor of a dead Negro."

The Federal troops entered Port Hudson on July 9, 1863. Eight Negro regiments had participated in the successful siege. This, along with the fall of Vicksburg, gave the Union control of the Mississippi River, and cut the Confederacy in two.

The National Cemetery in the area has the graves of three thousand Union dead, among them Negroes who fell here. The actual battlefield site is privately owned.

---

# MAINE

---

BRUNSWICK

*Bowdoin College* was the alma mater of John Brown Russwurm who, with Samuel E. Cornish, established the first newspaper edited by Negroes. The first issue appeared in New York City in March 1827. The paper, called *Freedom's Journal,* was published until 1829. In 1829 Russwurm got an M.A. degree here, the first one earned by a Negro. He later became superintendent of schools in Liberia in 1829; colonial secretary from 1830 to 1834; and was governor of Maryland, Liberia, Africa, from 1836 to 1851, when he died.

Bowdoin also graduated, in its class of 1850, General Otis Howard, who was instrumental in the founding of Howard University in Washington, D.C., in 1867. He was president of Howard from 1869 to 1874. Robert E. Peary, of the Class of 1877, is remembered for his expedition of discovery to the North Pole. His aide on that journey was Matthew Henson, a Negro, who reached the pole before him.

PORTLAND

*Portland Cathedral.* Here, on June 2, 1875, James Augustine Healy was consecrated as the first Negro American bishop of the Roman Catholic Church.

Bishop Healy was born in Macon, Georgia, in 1830, and graduated from Holy Cross College in 1849. He studied in Canada and France, and was ordained in the Cathedral of Notre Dame, in Paris, in 1854. On returning to the United States he served in Boston in various capacities, including that of pastor of St. James, and was active in developing a number of charitable institutions in Boston.

Two of Bishop Healy's brothers also rose to significant positions in the Catholic Church. One, Patrick Francis Healy, S.J., was president of Georgetown University, in Washington, D.C. Another, Sherwood Healy, was rector of the Boston Cathedral. Three sisters, Josephine, Eliza, and Martha, became nuns.

Harold Robert Perry, consecrated Auxiliary Bishop of New Orleans in January 1966, was the first Negro to achieve this high position in the Catholic Church in this century.

# MARYLAND

The State Capitol contains the Matthew Henson Plaque, dedicated in memory of the Negro who was the only man to accompany Admiral Peary on all of his polar expeditions, and the first to reach the North Pole. Peary, unable to walk, arrived less than an hour later to confirm Henson's reading of their position.

A convention was held in this building in 1864 to draw a state constitution. The twenty-fourth article provided for the abolition of slavery. The voters ratified it by a margin of only four hundred votes out of more than one hundred thousand cast, with the vote of soldiers who had fought beside Negroes during the Civil War believed to be responsible for the margin of victory.

United States Naval Academy. The Academy, established in 1845 for the training of career officers in the United States Navy, began operations with eighty-seven midshipmen on ten acres of land at the Army's old Fort Severn. Today, with more than four thousand midshipmen, it has 219 major buildings spread over 309 acres.

Bancroft Hall, residence for the entire student body, is the largest dormitory in the world. Within it is an impressive rotunda, decorated with murals depicting historic naval engagements. Stairs ascend from the rotunda to Memorial Hall, which honors the heroic deeds of naval personnel. A highlight is Admiral Perry's Lake Erie battle flag honoring the War of 1812 engagement in which the men of the United States fleet, about one-fourth of them Negroes, defeated the British.

James Conyers, of South Carolina, was the first Negro midshipman. He attended from September 21, 1872, to November 11, 1873, but did not graduate. The first Negro graduate was Wesley Anthony Brown, of Washington, D.C., on June 3, 1949. He was commissioned an ensign. There have been many others since.

The remains of John Paul Jones, who died in France at the age of forty-five, were returned here for reburial in a crypt. Many Negro sailors served under this naval hero.

### BALTIMORE COUNTY

*Banneker Marker*, on Westchester Avenue at Benjamin Banneker Junior High School, is named for the Negro mathematician, astronomer, and inventor. In 1792, the self-educated Banneker produced an almanac that was among the most accurate of his time. It gained for him an international reputation, which was later enhanced when he helped Pierre L'Enfant lay out the District of Columbia.

Banneker was the grandson of an English bondswoman who was transported to the colonies, earned her freedom, purchased a slave, married and freed him, and later purchased slaves as husbands for her daughters. He built the first clock made in America, using only what he had once learned from inspecting the inside of a watch.

Banneker is buried in an unmarked grave on his old farm near Ellicott City.

### BALTIMORE

*Basilica-Cathedral of the Assumption*, Cathedral Street. Here, before the acknowledged masterpiece of the great architect, Latrobe, America's first Negro Catholic priest was ordained on December 19, 1891. He was Charles Randolph Uncles, born in Baltimore, baptized at St. Francis Xavier Church, the nation's oldest Negro Catholic parish, in 1875, and confirmed in 1878.

After studying in Baltimore Catholic and public schools, Uncles entered St. Hyacinthe College, in Canada, and then returned to Baltimore to study theology at St. Joseph Seminary and St. Mary's Seminary. He was ordained by the late James Cardinal Gibbons, Archbishop of Baltimore.

Father Uncles became a teacher, first at Epiphany College, in Walbrook, Maryland, and later at the new Epiphany Apostolic College, in Newburgh, New York. He died there in 1933, and is buried in the cemetery of the Society of St. Joseph at the college.

*Coppin State College.* This is the youngest of the colleges founded in Maryland to provide higher education for Negroes. At its founding in 1900, it was named for Fannie Jackson Coppin, a slave who purchased her freedom and became the first Negro woman in the United States to earn a college degree. She also introduced teacher-training in the educational system of Philadelphia.

The Administration Building is named in honor of Miles Washington Connor, the first president of the college.

*Morgan State College,* organized under private auspices in 1867 to provide higher education for Negroes, became a state college in 1939 and today has an integrated faculty and student body.

On the campus are artifacts of Benjamin Banneker, the Negro astronomer and surveyor, and Matthew Henson, who preceded Admiral Peary to the North Pole. A women's residence hall is named in honor of the tireless abolitionist, Harriet Tubman, and there is also an eight-foot bronze statue of the abolitionist and Negro leader, Frederick Douglass.

*St. Francis Xavier's Catholic Church,* 1007 North Caroline Street, is the oldest Catholic church for Negroes in the United States.

Although the church was not established until 1863, its roots go back to 1798 when the Reverend Louis W. DuBourg, a future Bishop of New Orleans, began giving cathechetical instruction to Negroes. He was the first priest to give continuing attention to a Negro congregation.

In later years St. Francis Xavier's became the mother parish of the Josephite Missions in the United States. Priests of the English Society of St. Joseph left here to establish Negro missions in Louisville, Richmond, Washington, and Charleston, South Carolina.

On December 19, 1891, a native son of the parish, Father Charles Randolph Uncles, became the first Negro priest to be ordained in the United States. He celebrated his first solemn high mass here at 5 A.M. on Christmas Day in 1891 before a congregation that overflowed into the street outside the church.

After more than a century of service, St. Francis Xavier's is still a thriving inner-city parish, but the original church has long since been replaced.

BUCKTOWN

*Birthplace of Harriet Tubman,* eight miles south of U. S. 50, in Dorchester County, on Maryland 397. Often called "The Moses of Her People," Harriet Tubman was born in 1820 of slave parents, and later married John Tubman, a free Negro. A Quaker,

Thomas Garrett, of Wilmington, Delaware, helped her escape to freedom. Much of the remainder of her life was devoted to helping other slaves reach freedom.

In 1857, Mrs. Tubman led her parents from Dorchester County to Auburn, New York, where she had purchased a small farm from William H. Seward. She made nineteen trips back to Maryland's eastern shore and successfully led away some three hundred slaves. During the Civil War she served as a cook, nurse, scout, and spy, some of the time in South Carolina. Later she worked for programs designed to improve the lot of the Negro.

### HAGERSTOWN

*Kennedy Farm,* U. S. 340 near Maryland entrance to Old Harpers Ferry Bridge. In 1859 a bearded stranger who called himself Isaac Smith came here to rent the farm. Soon he had gathered a score of followers, and a collection of arms. On Sunday evening, October 16, 1859, Smith revealed his true identity when, as John Brown, he led his followers in an attack on the arsenal at Harpers Ferry. His effort to establish a fortress for escaping Negro slaves failed. He was captured and later hanged.

Ironically, one of those who helped hang Brown was Private John Wilkes Booth, who would later go down in history for the assassination of an even more famous abolitionist, Abraham Lincoln. The Kennedy home still stands, and there is a state marker at the site of the Maryland entrance to Old Harpers Ferry Bridge.

### PRINCESS ANNE

*Maryland State College* was founded September 13, 1886, by the Reverend Joseph R. Waters, a Methodist minister. It was originally known as the Delaware Conference Academy. Benjamin O. Bird, the first principal, is buried on the campus. The John Bailey Negro collection contains over seventeen hundred books and material about, or by, Negroes.

### ROCKVILLE

*Uncle Tom's Cabin.* A log cabin attached to a Montgomery county farmhouse is presumed to be the birthplace of Josiah Henson, the escaped slave who inspired the character Uncle Tom in Harriet Beecher Stowe's book. His own life, however, scarcely fits the stereotyped image of Uncle Tom.

Henson, born in 1789, was sold at auction and passed from master to master at an early age. In 1830, he escaped and set up a community for fugitive slaves at Dawn, Canada. He made several trips south to rescue slaves, bringing 118 to freedom in Canada.

Henson later became a Methodist minister and mill owner; his products won a bronze medal at the 1851 World's Fair in London. On this trip he met the Archbishop of Canterbury, who asked him from which university he was graduated. Henson replied, "The University of Adversity."

It was on a trip to Boston, in 1849, that he met Mrs. Stowe, and gave her the outline of his life as a slave. Three years later, *Uncle Tom's Cabin* was published, and Mrs. Stowe later wrote a preface to Henson's autobiography in which she acknowledged that his memories of slavery had been the basis of much of the material in her book.

## ST. MARYS COUNTY

*St. Clements Island* was the landing site of Maryland's first settlers in March 1635. They came on the *Ark* and the *Dove*, as part of an expedition sponsored by the Englishman Cecil Calvert, the second Lord Baltimore.

Among the passengers were two Negroes, Francisco Peres and Mathias DeSousa. DeSousa spent his first years in the new colony paying for his passage as the indentured servant of two Jesuit priests. Later he was freed, given fifty acres of land, tools, and three suits of clothes. He served in the General Assembly that met on March 23, 1641, the first Negro to do so.

DeSousa was licensed to trade with the Indians, and became pilot of a pinnace that traded with the Susquehanna Indians. Records of the time judge him an Indian trader of great tact and common sense who did not arouse hostility among the Indians as Virginia traders often did.

DeSousa's last known employer, John Lewger, apparently did not share this opinion, for he found DeSousa's work unsatisfactory and brought a court action against him. That is the last record of DeSousa in Maryland. No estate was ever filed for probate, so he may have been lost at sea.

# MASSACHUSETTS

## ARLINGTON

*Captain Benjamin Locke's Home,* 21 Appleton Street, was the residence of a Revolutionary officer who commanded a company at Lexington and Concord on April 19, 1775. Among his Minutemen were at least two Negroes, Cuff Whittemore, of Menotomy, and Cato Wood, of Charlestown.

Two months after the battle at Lexington, Whittemore was fighting at Bunker Hill, where a musket ball pierced his hat. An account of his service notes that he found a British officer's sword on the battlefield. Like countless enterprising American soldiers in subsequent wars, Whittemore soon converted the trophy into cash.

The flintlock musket carried by Captain Locke is owned by the Arlington Historical Society.

## BEDFORD

*Old Veterans' Cemetery.* A single stone, inscribed with their names and the dates 1775–1883, honors three escaped slaves who fought in the Battle of Concord.

Cambridge Moore, Caesar Prescott, and Caesar Jones were among the seventy-seven Minutemen from Bedford who helped defend "the bridge that arched the flood" against the British in 1775. Although little is known about them, they are not forgotten, and Bedford annually observes the traditional "Patriots' Day" by placing flowers on their graves.

## BOSTON

*Bunker Hill Monument.* The historic title will never be changed, but the Battle of Bunker Hill actually was fought on Breed's Hill. The monument commemorating the battle stands on the site where General Warren fell, June 17, 1775.

A number of Negroes fought with the Revolutionary troops on Breed's Hill, among them Peter Salem, Salem Poor, Titus Coburn, Cato Howe, Pomp Fiske, and Prince Hall, founder of the Negro Masonic Order. A Negro, Prince Estabrook, of West Lexington, was among the American casualties.

One of the most remarkable records of service in the Revolutionary War was that of Barzillai Lew, a Negro cooper from Chelmsford. Lew enlisted on May 6, 1775, as the fifer for Captain John Ford's company of the 27th Massachusetts Regiment, and served from Bunker Hill to Ticonderoga.

Lew could well have had two roles in the famous painting, "The Spirit of '76," for he also played the drum. Most members of the Continental Army served relatively short enlistments, but Lew was still fighting—or playing the fife or drum—when the war ended six years later.

Unlike most of those who fought in the Revolution, Lew was already an experienced soldier when he enlisted. In 1760, during the French and Indian Wars, he had served for thirty-eight weeks in Thomas Farrington's Massachusetts Company.

The cornerstone for this monument was laid by Lafayette in 1825; Daniel Webster was a featured speaker at that ceremony, and at the 1843 event that celebrated completion of the monument. His two speeches have become known as the Bunker Hill orations.

*Crispus Attucks Monument,* Boston Common, dedicated in 1888 in honor of the victims of the Boston Massacre.

The first man killed here on March 5, 1770, was not a Bostonian. Crispus Attucks, instead, is generally believed to have been a runaway slave from Framingham, Massachusetts.

Attucks was the leader of the group of men who converged on the British garrison on King Street (now State Street). Their march was the climax of a week of high tension and minor quarrels between the citizens and the soldiers sent to enforce the Townshend Acts. In spite of orders to the contrary, one of the soldiers panicked and fired. The first shot hit Crispus Attucks.

Four white men were also victims. Samuel Gray and James Caldwell were killed on the spot. Samuel Maverick and Patrick Carr died later of wounds received in the fighting.

The British soldiers and their captain were later tried for murder and acquitted. One of their defense attorneys was John Adams, who later wrote of the incident on King Street, "On that night the foundation of American independence was laid." His words are inscribed on the plaque set in the face of the monument.

A plaque on State Street, near the Old State House, marks the spot where Crispus Attucks fell.

*Granary Burying Ground* contains the graves of three who signed the Declaration of Independence; also the bodies of Paul Revere, Crispus Attucks, and the others who lost their lives in the Boston Massacre.

*Old Peoples Baptist Church,* Smith Court. This church was founded by Negroes in 1805. The building now houses a synagogue; the church's congregation, since 1898, has worshiped in a church at Camden and Columbus Avenues, in Roxbury. On its 160th anniversary, the congregation returned to the old church for a special service, with the present Hebrew congregation as hosts, and with the Cardinal Cushing Band playing a salute.

*Park Street Church,* Park and Tremont Streets. Henry Ward Beecher, the abolitionist, preached here, and Garrison delivered his first anti-slavery speech here in 1829.

*Shaw Monument,* on Beacon Street facing the State House, is a group statue of Colonel Robert Gould Shaw and the 54th Massachusetts Volunteers. Augustus Saint-Gaudens did the bronze memorial to the all-Negro regiment which distinguished itself with the Union forces in the Civil War.

Colonel Shaw was killed in battle at Fort Wagner, South Carolina in 1863. In the same engagement Sergeant William H. Carney of the 54th became the first of his race to earn the Congressional Medal of Honor for bravery.

Carney was born in Norfolk, and at fourteen attended a secret school supervised by a minister. When he was fifteen he ran away to become a seaman and settled in New Bedford, Massachusetts. He was twenty-three when he enlisted, in February 1863.

He won the medal for his role on July 18 of that year at Fort Wagner, one of the outer defenses of Charleston. During the battle the color-bearer, Sergeant John Wall, was wounded. Carney seized the colors and dashed to the head of the column. He was wounded in the action.

CAMBRIDGE

*Harvard University* has in its library a folio edition of "Paradise Lost" that was presented to Phillis Wheatley in 1773 during her triumphal trip to England. Miss Wheatley was the first Negro woman—and the second American woman—to write a book.

The poet was a frail child of seven or eight when she arrived in America in 1761 and was purchased by John Wheatley as a servant for his wife. In less than two years she was able to speak, read, and write fluent English. She wrote her first poem when she was only fourteen.

Harvard has educated many distinguished Negroes, among them Robert Weaver, who earned his Ph.D. here. He was the first Negro in the presidential cabinet. His grandfather, Dr. Robert Tanner Freeman, had previously been the first American Negro granted a doctor's degree in dentistry at Harvard.

Whitney M. Young, Jr., Executive Director of the National Association for the Advancement of Colored People, was once a visiting scholar here under a Rockefeller Foundation grant. William E. B. DuBois, a founder of the N.A.A.C.P., was awarded a Ph.D. at Harvard.

Dr. John Hope Franklin, the distinguished University of Chicago historian, won his M.A. and Ph.D. degrees and also taught history here. The Law School produced William H. Hastie, first U.S. federal judge and first Negro governor of the Virgin Islands. Dr. John C. Norman, eminent Negro surgeon and pioneer in organ transplant techniques, is a product of the Medical School.

The first Negro to win a Rhodes scholarship, author-critic Alain Leroy Locke, was educated at Harvard and subsequently stimulated the so-called "Harlem Renaissance" among Negro writers.

The John F. Kennedy Memorial Library, to be built at Harvard, will contain many documents related to the civil rights struggle during the slain President's career in government.

CENTRAL VILLAGE

*Memorial to Paul Cuffee,* Friends Meeting House. Born in 1759, the son of a freed Negro slave, Captain Cuffee amassed a fortune at sea and carried out a lifelong struggle in behalf of his race. He won important civil rights for Negroes by refusing to pay the personal property tax because he was denied the full rights of citizenship. He was the first Negro to be granted all the legal privileges that white citizens of Massachusetts enjoyed.

In 1815, in a colonization effort, he transported thirty-eight Negroes to Sierra Leone at his own expense. Today, his name is more often spelled "Cuffe."

## CONCORD

*Antiquarian Society Building*. Exhibited here is a statuette of Uncle Tom and Little Eva, given to Henry David Thoreau by an escaped slave who walked eighteen miles from Boston to Concord to deliver it. Thoreau was an active participant in the underground railroad, and the Negro was one he had helped escape from bondage.

*Hill Burying Ground*, next to St. Bernard's Church. One of Concord's early settlers was John Jack, a slave who earned his freedom and became a successful farmer and respected citizen. His death prompted Daniel Bliss, a great-uncle of Ralph Waldo Emerson, to write the epitaph on his gravestone. Oft-quoted, it reads:

> God wills us free, man wills us slaves.
> I will as God wills, God's will be done.
> Here lies the body of
> John Jack
> A native of Africa who died
> March 1773, aged about sixty years.
> Tho' born in a land of slavery
> He was born free.
> Though he lived in a land of liberty
> He lived a slave.
> Till by his honest, tho' stolen labors,
> He acquired the source of slavery,
> Which gave him his freedom,
> Tho' not long before
> Death the grand tyrant,
> Gave him his final emancipation,
> And set him on a footing with kings.
> Tho' a slave to vice,
> He practiced those virtues
> Without which kings are but slaves.

*The Minuteman*, the first statue executed by Daniel Chester French, guards the site of the battleground where white and

Negro Colonial volunteers defended Concord Bridge from the British. A concrete reproduction of the original wooden bridge has been erected.

*Walden State Reservation*, two miles out on State 126. Visitors here add stones to a cairn on the north shore of Walden Pond, the spot where Thoreau built his cabin, hewing trees with a borrowed ax. It cost him only twenty-eight dollars, but the cabin meant freedom to many escaped slaves who used it as a hiding place on the underground railroad.

## FRAMINGHAM

*Minuteman Monument*, in Buckminster Square, honors the local patriots who fought in the Revolutionary War. Among them were two Negroes, Crispus Attucks and Peter Salem.

Crispus Attucks was born a slave about 1723. He lived on what is now State Route 9, across the street from the present State Police headquarters. In 1750 Attucks escaped from his master and went to Boston, presumably after first going to sea. He became a familiar figure on the Boston docks. He also became the first man to die for his country in the war for American independence.

Peter Salem lived on Pleasant Street here at the time he joined Captain Simeon Edgell's company of militiamen and went off to fight at Lexington and Concord. He had already fought at Bunker Hill, where he was credited with killing the British commander, Major Pitcairn.

Salem is buried among Framingham's leading former citizens in the Old Burying Ground less than one hundred yards from this monument. There is a marker and a flag on his grave, maintained by the local Daughters of the American Revolution. His name is also inscribed on a bronze tablet in the town's Memorial Municipal Building.

## GREAT BARRINGTON

*James Weldon Johnson Cabin* is maintained as a memorial to the poet, civil rights advocate, and diplomat. This was the workshop of Johnson, who was the author of several volumes of poetry, including *God's Trombones*. With his brother, J. Rosamund Johnson, he also composed the hymn, "Lift Every Voice and Sing," which is sometimes called the Negro national anthem.

LEICESTER

*Site of the Shack of Peter Salem,* near the village off Rochdale Road. Salem, who killed British Major Pitcairn in the Battle of Bunker Hill, came to Leicester after the war and built a crude hut. He lived here in poverty until his late years when he was taken to the poorhouse in Framingham, where he died.

LINCOLN

*Scipio Brister Grave,* Lexington Road Cemetery, near center of town on the road to Lexington, is the burial place of an ex-slave who lived in the town of Lincoln until his death in 1820.

Scipio lived with the family of John Hoar, who later fought at Concord bridge. According to family legend, Mrs. Hoar, on a trip to Boston, passed a cabin where a Negro woman asked her to take her baby because she feared it would be sold as a slave. Mrs. Hoar put the baby and a little bundle of clothing into her saddlebag and took him home with her to Lincoln.

When Scipio grew up he was given his freedom, but he remained with the Hoar family for the rest of his life. The Massachusetts archives reveal that he served with two different companies raised in Lincoln during 1776 and 1777 for service in the Revolutionary War. Each April 19, when Lincoln residents honor their Revolutionary heroes with simple ceremonies, Scipio's grave is among those decorated with flowers.

A spring, since disappeared, was named for him, as was a nearby hill on what is now Brister's Hill Road. Emerson and Thoreau often drank from the spring. In later years Thoreau came upon Brister's grave in the cemetery and read the marker:

> In Memory of
> Scipio Brister
> A Man of Colour
> who died
> Nov. 1, 1820

Thoreau said of the epitaph, with its missing birthdate: "Scipio Brister, man of color, as if he were discolored. It also told me with staring emphasis when he *died* which was an indirect way of informing me he ever lived."

LYNN

*Jan Ernst Matzeliger Statue.* This memorial honors a Negro inventor who revolutionized the shoe industry. Born in Dutch New Guinea, he came to the United States in 1876. In 1883 he patented a shoe-lasting machine that solved the problem of attaching the soles to the uppers of a shoe.

The patent was purchased by the United Shoe Machinery Company of Boston. After Matzeliger's death he was awarded a gold medal by the Pan-American Exposition of 1901.

NEW BEDFORD

*Liberty Bell Tablet,* on east wall of Merchant's National Bank, recalls that:

"News of the passage of the Fugitive Slave Law was brought from Boston in 1851 by an express messenger who rode all night, and the bell on the old Hall was rung to give warning to fugitive slaves that U.S. Marshalls were coming."

*Rodney French Memorial Tablet,* entrance to Hazelwood Park, was erected by the Negroes of the city in honor of an abolitionist mayor in 1853–54.

*Whaling Museum,* 18 Johnny Cake Hill. After the War of 1812, New Bedford surpassed Nantucket as the leading whaling port. At the peak, in 1845, New Bedford's whaling fleet brought in 158,000 barrels of sperm oil, 272,000 barrels of whale oil, and 3,000,000 pounds of whalebone. Ten thousand seamen, many of them Negro, manned the ships.

A Negro blacksmith, Lewis Temple, invented a harpoon, called the Temple toggle iron, that was almost universally used because it permitted the secure fastening of lines to the whale. Born in Virginia in 1800, Temple had no formal education and did not patent his invention. He was destitute when he died in 1854.

Several examples of the Temple iron, ship models, whaling equipment, ships' logs, and other memorabilia are on display at the museum, which is operated by the Old Dartsmouth Historical Society.

Paul Cuffee, a freed slave who amassed a fortune as a shipmaster, was in the whaling trade here. Another Negro named Mashow operated a successful shipyard in the whaling days.

Many of Robert Gould Shaw's Negro troops of the Massachusetts 54th U. S. Colored Infantry were recruited in New Bedford. Sergeant William H. Carney, a member of the 54th, was the first Negro to win the Congressional Medal of Honor. In the years before the Civil War New Bedford had been a center of abolitionist activity and an important Underground Railroad station. During the Civil War it was the headquarters for privateers which raided Confederate shipping.

PITTSFIELD

*The Berkshire Museum.* On exhibit here is one of the five sledges with which Admiral Peary's expedition reached the North Pole. It may be the one in which Matthew Henson became the first man at the top of the world. Henson's suit is also mounted in a case in an exhibit which was completely renovated in 1967.

These items were donated by Zenas Crane, who founded the museum in 1903, was vice president of the Peary Arctic Club, and also made a substantial personal contribution toward the expedition.

SALEM

*The Witch House,* 310½ Essex Street, was the residence of Judge Corwin, who presided over many of Salem's notorious witchcraft trials. The witch-hunting epidemic began when the daughters of the Reverend Samuel Parris became frightened at the scary tales their Negro nurse, a West Indian slave, told them at bedtime. The village physician declared that they were bewitched, and the girls accused the nurse, Tituba, and two unpopular old women.

All three were sentenced to death for witchcraft in 1692. For a year thereafter the witchcraft epidemic persisted in the area, with nineteen persons hanged on Gallows Hill; at least two others died in prison.

SOMERSET

*Jorathmeal Bowers House,* on South Street, was built in 1770 by the founder of Somerset. His son, Henry, purchased the son of an African chief as a slave. Bowers was unable to control the slave and finally sent him to sea. The Negro escaped at Haiti, local legend has it, where he participated in the successful slave uprising and became Emperor under the name of Toussaint L'Ouverture.

WORCESTER

*Worcester Art Museum,* 55 Salisbury Street. Included in the collection is a gouache entitled "They Live in Fire Traps," by Jacob Lawrence.

In Worcester, in 1845, Macon B. Allen became the first Negro admitted to the American bar.

# MICHIGAN

ADDISON

*Site of Woodstock Manual Labor Institute.* Prior Foster founded this school in 1852. Although it was probably the earliest school in the country founded and run by Negroes, it was integrated, and at one time served more than one hundred students, both Negro and white. Foster's grandson, Dr. Laurence C. Jones, subsequently founded the famous Piney Woods School in Mississippi.

BATTLE CREEK

*Sojourner Truth Grave,* Oak Hill Cemetery. Like Harriet Tubman, Sojourner Truth was a former slave who became a leader in the battle against slavery; but there the similarity ends.

Harriet Tubman was a small woman; Sojourner Truth stood over six feet tall. Harriet escaped to freedom; Sojourner was freed under New York's gradual emancipation act. Harriet attacked slavery directly, going back into the South repeatedly to lead others to freedom; Sojourner fought her battles from the lecture platform and in the courts.

Sojourner may have helped slaves escaping on the Underground Railroad, but the only slave she actually freed herself was her son. He was freed through court action.

Although she was illiterate, Sojourner had the power to captivate her audience. Her withering replies to hecklers became legendary, though in one famous instance she became a heckler herself and stopped Frederick Douglass cold. In the last days before the Civil War, Douglass, disillusioned with the slow progress of the anti-slavery cause, called for slave uprisings. Sojourner, sitting in the back of the hall, rose and shouted: "Frederick, is God dead?"

Douglass later wrote that he replied, "No. And that is why slavery must end in bloodshed," but William Lloyd Garrison, who was present, insisted that Douglass could make no answer at all.

After the Civil War, Sojourner Truth raised funds to assist the freedmen, and campaigned for women's suffrage. She settled in Battle Creek, but continued traveling on lecture tours until a few years before her death in 1883. She was then about eighty-five years old.

CASSOPOLIS

*Underground Railroad Marker,* 2.5 miles east of Cassopolis on M-60, notes another point on the route of escaping slaves.

DEARBORN

*Greenfield Village,* established by Henry Ford, has the air of a country village, but contains the homes or workshops of many famous Americans. Some of these structures were transported here from their original locations; others are reproductions.

The George Washington Carver Memorial was built at Greenfield Village in 1942, in honor of the Negro agricultural scientist. Mr. Ford knew and admired him, and shared a keen interest in his work.

The memorial, designed by Village Architect Edward J. Cutler, resembles the log cabin in which Carver was born at Diamond Grove, Missouri. When he visited Mr. Ford in 1942, Dr. Carver spent a few days in the three-room cabin.

DETROIT

*Detroit Institute of Arts,* 5200 Woodward Avenue, has an excellent collection of African art, much of it the gift of former Governor G. Mennen Williams, also formerly Assistant Secretary of State for African Affairs, and Mrs. Williams. In the permanent collection are paintings and other works by three Negro artists: Robert S. Duncanson, Jacob Lawrence, and Hughie Lee-Smith.

*Detroit Public Library*, 5201 Woodward Avenue. The Azalia Hackley Memorial Collection is a treasure trove of material related to Negroes in music and the performing arts. It was named for a Detroit pioneer who worked tirelessly to promote concert performances of works by Negro composers. With the proceeds she created scholarships for talented young Negro musicians—among them Kemper Harreld, Clarence Cameron White, Nathaniel Dett, and many others.

The collection has its own room and exhibition area. There are six hundred books on Negroes in the performing arts and a large collection of clippings, programs, and photos. Also included is a remarkable collection of popular songs by Negro composers and lyricists, including special collections of Duke Ellington and Bert Williams tunes. Negro writers, including Langston Hughes, have been generous donors of material to the collection.

*Douglass-Brown Marker*, East Congress Street at St. Antoine, marks the site of the William Webb house, where John Brown, Frederick Douglass, and others met in March 1859 to plan abolitionist strategy.

Although Brown and Douglass were equally determined to end slavery, Brown chose the route of violent insurrection, while Douglass advocated the use of legal and political means. Brown soon went to his death at Harpers Ferry, on a venture Douglass strongly opposed. Douglass continued to work in behalf of his race for many years during and after the Civil War.

*Second Baptist Church*, 441 Monroe Street. A marker identifies the site of the first observance of the Emancipation Proclamation on January 6, 1863. The marker was dedicated a century later by President Lyndon B. Johnson.

MARSHALL

*Crosswhite Boulder*, in Triangle Park, Michigan Avenue and Mansion Street, marks the site where Marshall citizens, in 1847, prevented four Kentuckians from taking Adam Crosswhite and his family, all fugitive slaves, back to Kentucky. They were later taken to safety in Canada. Henry Clay of Kentucky used the Crosswhite case as one of his arguments in favor of the Fugitive Slave Law, which was adopted in 1850.

MUSKEGON

*Jonathan Walker Grave,* in Evergreen Cemetery, Pine and Irwin Streets, is the last resting place of an abolitionist who was arrested for helping fugitive slaves before the Civil War. After his conviction in Federal Court the letters SS—Slave Stealer—were branded on his hand. This prompted John Greenleaf Whittier to write the poem, "The Man with the Branded Hand." The gravestone was placed by another abolitionist, Photius Fisk.

VANDALIA

*Underground Railroad Marker,* on M-60, one-half mile west, notes that "Vandalia, prior to the Civil War, was the junction of two important 'lines' of the Underground Railroad. Slaves fleeing through Indiana and Illinois came to Cass County, where Quakers and others gave them shelter. Fugitives seeking a refuge in Canada were guided to 'stations' in the east. Many stayed here and built a unique Negro rural colony. Slave-hunting by Kentuckians in 1847 led to legal action and increased North-South tensions."

# MINNESOTA

MINNEAPOLIS

*Phillis Wheatley Community Center,* 809 Aldrich Avenue North, was named in honor of the famed Negro girl who was one of the first women writers in America, and a famed poet of the Colonial era.

The center was founded in 1924 as a settlement house to serve Negro girls. During the period after World War I Minneapolis began to experience its first major influx of Negro residents, but was ill-equipped to provide social or recreational facilities for them. The center was established to partially fill this need, and its services were soon broadened to fill a wide variety of needs.

For many years the center was the home away from home for some of the nation's most distinguished Negro personalities, who found the city's places of public accommodation closed to them. It is perhaps a symbol of interracial progress that this is no longer the case, and that meanwhile the Phillis Wheatley Center has undertaken to serve the young and the old of all races, white as well as black.

The center has operated a day nursery since 1929, but today many of those who use its services are elderly, retired persons who live in the urban renewal area that it serves. Individual and group counseling services are provided. Athletic activities are stressed, and the center operates a summer camp.

ST. PAUL

*Fort Snelling State Park.* Although Negroes were engaged in fur trading in Minnesota in the early nineteenth century, their number was small, and much of their early history revolved around this fort.

The first Negro born in the state probably was George Bonga, who was born near the present site of Duluth about 1802. His grandfather was Jean Bonga, who had migrated west to Michilimackinac as the servant of a British Army officer in 1782.

George Bonga, who was regarded by others of his day as an intelligent, gracious, and charming host, is also recorded as having been a "man of wealth and consequence." He is believed to have been interpreter when the Chippewa Treaty was signed at Fort Snelling in 1837.

The records indicate that at least two slaves were sold at Fort Snelling in the 1820s and 1830s. One, James Thompson, was purchased by a Methodist missionary named Alfred Brunson, freed, and then served as Brunson's interpreter among the Sioux. When a Methodist Church building was built on Market Street in St. Paul, the ex-slave interpreter contributed two thousand feet of lumber, fifteen hundred shingles, and an unknown amount of cash. Thompson referred to himself as "one of the first white settlers" in Minnesota.

Best known of the Negroes at Fort Snelling was Dred Scott, who was brought here from Illinois in 1836. He met and married Harriet Robinson, and the first of their children was born here. When Dred's master returned with him to Missouri, the stage was set for the trial that made Dred the most famous slave of his time. (See St. Louis, Missouri.)

Fort Snelling was established in 1819, and several Negro military units have served here. A portion of the 25th U. S. Colored Infantry Regiment was stationed here between 1880 and 1885, and Negro units from this post were among those dispatched to Cuba, where they distinguished themselves in the Spanish-American War.

# MISSISSIPPI

**BALDWYN**

*Brice's Crossroads National Battlefield Site*, State 370, six miles west. The superb Confederate tactician, General N. B. Forrest, defeated Union forces commanded by General S. D. Sturgis in a bitter and bloody contest here on June 10, 1864. Even in defeat, Negro units demonstrated their courage as they covered the retreat of Sturgis' artillery and ammunition train. Their role was recorded in the diary of Lieutenant John Merrilies, who served with a battery of Illinois light artillery during the encounter. He wrote:

"The Cavalry . . . were formed in line on one flank and the Colored Brigade on the other, checking the onward rush of the enemy until the artillery had passed and then covering the rear of that and the ammunition train. . . . The 59th U. S. Colored Troops was also detailed (with some cavalry) to cover the rear and altho the first fighting they had seen, they behaved, under very trying circumstances, with a coolness and confidence worthy of old troops."

The white officer noted that he had seen "numbers shot in the arms, hands, legs, their clothing soaked with blood, marching along with the rest, without a sign of pain."

The battlefield is marked with texts and maps, and is maintained by the National Park Service.

CORINTH

*Corinth National Cemetery*, 1551 Horton Street. Mississippi was the scene of countless military engagements during the Civil War. Frequently, after the battle, the dead were separated according to the color of their uniform and buried in trenches. In later years, many soldiers who fought and died in engagements in Mississippi, Alabama, and Tennessee were reburied here. Among them were men of the Federal 14th, 40th, 106th, 108th, and 111th Colored Infantry Regiments. A marker at the junction of U. S. 45 and State 2 describes the Battle of Corinth.

JACKSON

*Greenwood Cemetery*, North West Street at Davis Street. John R. Lynch, Negro Secretary of State after the Civil War, is buried here. He was one of many Negroes who served in the state government during the Reconstruction period.

*Jackson State College* had only twenty Negro students in 1877 when it was founded at Natchez by the American Baptist Home Mission Society. It was moved to Jackson in 1882, and taken over by the state in 1930.

The program was expanded in 1942, and members of the first four-year class under state support received their degrees in 1944. In 1953 the college began offering a liberal arts program and established a Division of Graduate Studies. It has had only six presidents in ninety years of existence. Portraits and a rare book collection are in the Founder's Room of the library.

NATCHEZ

*Natchez National Cemetery*, 61 Cemetery Road. At the close of the Civil War, 2484 Negro soldiers were buried here. Negro dead from the Spanish-American War, World Wars I and II, Korea, and Vietnam have since joined their Civil War comrades-in-arms.

Among the heroes buried here is landsman Wilson Brown, of Natchez. He and another Negro landsman, John Lawson, of Pennsylvania, won the Medal of Honor for courage aboard the Union vessel *Hartford* in Mobile Bay on August 5, 1864. Both men were wounded by shellfire, and Brown was knocked through a hatch to a lower deck. When he recovered consciousness he returned to duty, although wounded, supplying powder to the gunners. So did

Lawson. Brown's citation read, in part: "Brown . . . zealously continued to perform his duties although four of the six men at his station had been either killed or wounded by the enemy's terrific fire."

Natchez was the home of Hiram R. Revels, the first Negro elected to the United States Senate. He won the seat previously occupied by Jefferson Davis, the President of the Confederacy. Four years later another Negro, Blanche K. Bruce, was also elected to the Senate from Mississippi.

Revels, a Methodist minister, recruited Negroes for the Union Army during the war, founded a school for freed slaves in St. Louis, and served as chaplain of a Union regiment from Mississippi.

## OKOLONA

*Civil War Marker* on U. S. 45W at the southern city limits describes the actions here. The town was raided three times by Federal troops, and recaptured once by Confederate General Forrest. Portions of the city were damaged in each engagement, and it was virtually destroyed in the final Union raid in December 1864. Among the units involved was the 3rd Colored Cavalry Regiment, one of six Negro cavalry units that served in the Civil War.

## OXFORD

*Battle of Oxford Marker* on State 6 recalls the destruction of the city by Federal forces in 1864. The Union troops, including the 55th Colored Infantry Regiment, destroyed the town but spared the buildings of the University of Mississippi. They were used as a Civil War hospital.

## PORT GIBSON

*Grant's March through Claiborne County Marker* on U. S. 61 is the first of ten describing the route taken by Grant after he landed twenty-two thousand men and sixty guns at nearby Bruinsburg. His march through the county led to the siege of Vicksburg. Many Negro units were involved.

## RODNEY

*Alcorn Agricultural and Mechanical College.* Established by the state in 1871, this school was originally called Alcorn

University. It was the first Negro land-grant college established under the Morrill Act of 1872.

## TOUGALOO

*Tougaloo College,* founded by the American Missionary Association in 1869, began as a small school for Negroes. It was more than thirty years before it awarded its first A.B. degree to the sole member of the Class of 1901. Today it is a fully accredited liberal arts college with an enrollment of over six hundred.

## TUPELO

*Tupelo National Battlefield,* on State 6, one mile west of U. S. 45. Negro and white units commanded by Union Generals A. J. Smith and Joseph A. Mowrer moved into the outskirts of Tupelo on July 14, 1865. They were met by troops commanded by the brilliant Confederate General Nathan Bedford Forrest, fresh from a June victory over General Sturgis at Brices Cross Roads.

The battle was confused, disorderly, and a sort of standoff. Smith saved the railroad for the Union forces, but Forrest's forces could claim that they had halted the Union drive. Markers and maps at the site, which is maintained by the National Park Service, describe the actions.

## VICKSBURG

*Vicksburg National Military Park,* on U. S. 80 Historical. In the early spring of 1863 Major General Lorenzo Thomas began recruiting Negroes for service in the Union Army. By late May, Negro regiments had been organized and were in training at Helena, Arkansas, and also at Goodrich's Landing and Milliken's Bend, Louisiana, as part of General U. S. Grant's Department of the Tennessee.

Many Negro regiments participated in the Vicksburg campaign. The 9th, 11th, and 13th Louisiana and the 1st Mississippi fought at Milliken's Bend. In that desperate fight these four Negro regiments and the 23rd Iowa suffered 101 killed, 285 wounded, and 266 missing. The Negroes of the 9th Louisiana had the greatest number of casualties on a single day of any Union unit in the Vicksburg campaign.

The Milliken's Bend encounter included the longest hand-to-hand bayonet fight of the war. After it was over, Union General Dennis reported that "It is impossible for men to show greater gallantry than the Negro troops in this fight." Grant, in his *Memoirs,* wrote, "These men were very raw, but they behaved well."

Another Negro unit, the 1st Arkansas (African Descent), engaged the Confederates near Goodrich's Landing on June 29, 1863. After the fall of Vicksburg on July 4, 1863, many Negro units were included in the occupying garrison.

The park visitors' center has exhibits, electric maps, and a recorded lecture describing the Vicksburg campaign. In the park, also, is a national cemetery where more than sixteen thousand Federal soldiers were reburied after its establishment in 1866. There are more than twelve hundred markers and monuments in the park.

# MISSOURI

## DIAMOND

*Carver National Monument,* west on Alternate U. S. 71, is located on the land where the great scientist spent his childhood, and includes the site of the cabin where he was born.

Carver was born a slave in 1864 and, with his mother, was kidnaped when he was six weeks old. Their owner, Moses Carver, ransomed the boy for a horse valued at three hundred dollars, but the mother was never found.

Moses Carver and his family raised George until he was ten, when he made his way to Minneapolis, Kansas, and worked his way through school. From Kansas, young Carver went to Iowa, where he again supported himself while he earned his degree and gained a place on the faculty. Booker T. Washington discovered him there in 1896, and persuaded him to join the faculty at Tuskegee Institute.

The park was the first national monument to honor a Negro. There is a statue of Carver as a boy, and several trails lead to views and places of which he was especially fond.

Also in the park are a visitors' center, and a museum that displays many of the scientist's discoveries, personal belongings, and objects related to the area at the time he lived there.

## INDEPENDENCE

*Harry S. Truman Library.* A large mural, "Independence and the Winning of the West," dominates the lobby of this building, which houses the White House papers of President Truman and those of some of his principal aides. The artist, Thomas Hart Benton, has included many figures representative of people who lived and worked in early-day Independence.

Almost in the center of the mural is a Negro blacksmith at his forge preparing horseshoes for a wagon train. Although not his likeness, the figure represents Hiram Young, who worked in Independence during its early days. At one time he operated a wagon factory and employed some fifty men on twenty-five forges, helping to equip the westbound pioneers for their journey.

There are many documents here associated with the nation's progress in civil rights. Among them are papers relating to President Truman's 1946 Executive Order forming the Committee on Civil Rights. The committee, in 1947, condemned racial injustices in a formal report. Others pertain to a Truman Executive Order of 1948 directing "equality of treatment and opportunity" in the Armed Forces, and his 1951 appointment of a committee to supervise compliance with provisions against discrimination by government contractors.

President Truman has an office here, and occasionally a lucky visitor encounters him.

## JEFFERSON CITY

*Lincoln University* was born in the hopes and dreams of Civil War soldiers of the 62nd U. S. Colored Infantry. During their service they and their officers talked of the need for education "for the benefit of freed blacks." After their discharge the men contributed about five thousand dollars, and raised another $1324.50 among the men of the 65th U. S. Colored Infantry. Assisting them was James Milton Turner, who later became the first Negro American diplomat in a foreign post when President Grant sent him as minister to the Republic of Liberia.

Although the amount raised was small, it represented great sacrifice on the part of the Negro soldiers. One soldier in the 65th, whose monthly earnings were only thirteen dollars, gave one hundred dollars. The total raised was enough to enable the newly formed board of trustees to buy a two-room building, twenty-two feet square, and to begin classes on September 17, 1866.

The original structure has long since disappeared. The nucleus of the present campus, a lot facing on Atchison Street, was bought for six hundred dollars in 1870, and was gradually expanded. In that same year Lincoln Institute, as it was then known, received its first aid from the state for teacher training. In 1879 the school became a state institution, and work at the college level was added to the curriculum in 1887. The name was changed to Lincoln University in 1921, and graduate instruction was begun in 1940.

During a century of vigorous growth, Lincoln's first class of two elementary students has grown to a student body of more than two thousand. In the words of university librarian A. P. Marshall, "Lincoln University itself is a living memorial to the members of the 62nd and 65th Regiments who, having just emerged from slavery, gave of their meager savings so that a school could be established . . ."

## KANSAS CITY

*William Rockhill Nelson Gallery of Art.* In addition to a drawing by Julien Binford, a Negro, titled "Preaching Deacon," this gallery has some fine pieces of African sculpture.

## ST. LOUIS

*City Art Museum of St. Louis* has an oil painting by Negro artist Robert S. Duncanson entitled "View of the St. Anne's River, Canada."

*Jefferson Barracks National Cemetery.* The marker on Grave 15009 in Section 57 here recalls a hazard of nineteenth-century warfare that was even more costly than bullets. It is dedicated "To the memory of 175 Non-Com Officers and privates" of the 56th U. S. Colored Infantry who died of cholera in August 1866.

The remains of these soldiers were brought here from Quarantine Station, Missouri, and the probability is that the men were sent there from Helena, Arkansas, where their unit was stationed from March 1864 to September 1866. Much of their service was in garrison duty, although they saw action at other points in Arkansas and Mississippi on several occasions.

During two-and-one-half years of service, the 56th Infantry lost

674 men: twenty-five were killed or mortally wounded in action, and 649 died from disease.

*Old Courthouse.* Jefferson National Expansion Memorial. Construction of the Old Courthouse began in 1839, and it is an interesting example of government buildings of its era. Its great historical significance goes back to 1847, when a slave named Dred Scott appeared in a courtroom in the west wing to bring suit for his freedom.

The Dred Scott case was in the state and federal courts for ten years. It became a raging political and social issue throughout the country, and made Dred Scott the most famous slave of his time.

The chief issue was whether Scott was, in fact, a slave, since his master had taken him into Illinois, where slavery was forbidden by the state constitution, and to the Wisconsin Territory, where it was banned under the Missouri Compromise.

Ultimately the case went to the U. S. Supreme Court, where Chief Justice Taney ruled that slaves could not become free by escaping or being taken into free territory, and Negroes could not become citizens.

The decision started a furor which was not settled until passage of the Fourteenth Amendment at the close of the Civil War. By that time it made no difference to Dred Scott. His owner freed him as soon as the case was settled. Scott died a year later, in 1858.

# MONTANA

## BIG HORN STATION

*Site of Fort Manuel Marker* on U. S. 10, one mile west. One of the first Negroes here was York, who camped at this site with Captain William Clark and his party on July 26, 1806. A year later Manuel Lisa established a fur trading post here, the first in Montana, which eventually employed 350 men.

It was also at this site on the Yellowstone River, at the mouth of the Big Horn, that Major Andrew Henry built the Rocky Mountain Fur Company's first post in 1822. This expedition was guided by a Negro, Edward Rose.

## BRIDGER

*Jim Bridger, Mountain Man Marker* on U. S. 310, two miles south, tells the story of Bridger's arrival in Montana in 1822. Bridger came as a member of a party of fur traders headed by William H. Ashley, a general in the War of 1812, and his partner, Major Andrew Henry.

The interpreter and guide for this expedition was Edward Rose, whose ancestry was Negro, Indian, and white. The party lost a boat and some equipment in an encounter with hostile Indians at the Aricara Villages, and Ashley decided to return to St. Louis. History records that his defeat was due to his failure to take advice given by Rose.

Henry, Bridger, and the others pushed on to found Fort Henry, at the mouth of the Yellowstone River. This was the beginning of the Rocky Mountain Fur Company, which was active in fur trading for many years.

## CASCADE

*Hillside Cemetery.* This pleasant little town was once the home of Charles M. Russell, a white artist who painted western history, and Mary Fields, a Negro woman who made it.

At one point Mary Fields was a nurse for the Ursuline nuns at St. Peter's Mission, but she moved from that to a more active life. The Negro woman ran a restaurant, hauled freight, drove a stagecoach, and finally, in her seventies, settled down to a career as the village laundress.

Mary Fields knew how to use a gun, and fought at least one gun duel. She could hold her own with any man in an era when law was scarce, and self-defense the rule.

On one occasion, when a pack of wolves frightened her horses and they overturned the wagon, Mary stood guard all night to protect the load of supplies. On another, she got lost in a blizzard and walked back and forth all night to keep from freezing to death.

Even when she was past seventy, she collected a laundry bill from a deadbeat customer by overtaking him on the street and knocking him down with one blow of her sturdy fist.

Mary became highly respected in Cascade, but not only for

courage and strength. She befriended many local people. School children were her special friends, and she treated all of them to fruit or candy on her birthday.

One who recalled her from childhood was movie star Gary Cooper, who visited relatives here as a boy. Charley Russell, who gained international fame as an artist, sketched Mary in ink, and the result hangs in the lobby of the Cascade bank.

In 1912 disaster struck Mary—her home burned to the ground. The community reacted swiftly, contributing the lumber and labor to replace it.

Mary had two years to enjoy the home, and the flower gardens she prized so highly, before her death in 1914. She lies in the Hillside Cemetery, with a cross marking her grave.

## CROW AGENCY

*Custer Battlefield National Monument and Reno-Benteen Battlefield National Monument.* These monuments commemorate the Battle of the Little Big Horn, in which three battalions led by General George Armstrong Custer were wiped out by a party of Sioux, Cheyenne, and other Indian tribes led by Sitting Bull, June 25, 1876.

There were three battles that day, the first of them involving an advance party led by Major Marcus Reno. One of those who died in the first fighting was Isaiah Dorman, a Negro who had lived among the Sioux and joined Custer as a Sioux interpreter. The Indians sometimes called him the "black white man."

Dorman's was one of the few bodies that were not scalped or otherwise mutilated. According to one account, Sitting Bull found Dorman wounded and dying, gave him water, and ordered that his body was not to be harmed. Dioramas at the battlefield tell the full story of the action of the day.

Reburied in the Custer Battlefield National Cemetery here are the remains of many soldiers who served at the various forts that protected the countryside during the Indian wars. Included are those who died at Negro cavalry posts such as Fort Custer, Fort Keogh, and others.

## FORT SHAW

*Site of Fort Shaw,* a military post established in 1867, and named for Colonel Robert Gould Shaw, who died while commanding the heroic 54th Massachusetts Regiment during the Civil

War. Another all-Negro unit, the 25th Infantry Regiment, was stationed here to protect miners and settlers from hostile Indians.

A major role of the soldiers stationed here was that of guarding the stage and wagon trail from Fort Benton, the head of navigation on the Missouri River, to the mines of Last Chance Gulch, at Helena.

## GREAT FALLS

*Lewis and Clark Expedition Markers* in and near the city. Captain Meriwether Lewis first saw the Great Falls of the Missouri River on June 13, 1805. The Negro, York, and other members of the party spent a month making the difficult portage around them. Today's visitor can cover the eighteen miles in a few minutes.

It was during this period that Captain William Clark almost lost his life. He had left camp with York, Sacajawea, and her husband to make topographical notes of the low ground along the river. A sudden thunderstorm flooded a normally dry gully, and Clark almost drowned while escaping a fifteen-foot wall of water that swept down the ravine.

York, who had left the others to hunt buffalo, rejoined them to discover that Clark had lost the expedition's only compass in escaping the flood. It was later recovered from the mud of the river bottom.

One of the attractions of Great Falls is Giant Springs, discovered by the Lewis and Clark expedition. It discharges nearly four hundred million gallons of water every twenty-four hours, at a constant temperature of fifty-two degrees.

## HARDIN

*Site of Fort Custer,* two miles west of town off U. S. 87. This fort was built the year after Custer and his men died in their encounter with the Sioux Indians led by Sitting Bull. It was garrisoned by a unit of Negro troopers of the 10th Cavalry Regiment from 1893 to 1898.

They had a quiet time here. In fact, the only recorded excitement in the history of the fort was a visit in 1880 by John Maguire, an Irish minstrel from Butte who became an impresario. He staged a theatrical performance here one night with a cast of Crow Indians. While they were onstage a band of Sioux made off with the Crows' horses.

The performance was interrupted while the actors joined the cavalrymen in pursuit of the horse thieves.

HAVRE

*Fort Assiniboine Marker* off U. S. 87, five to seven miles south, marks the site of the home of units of the 10th Cavalry Regiment from 1893 to 1898. General Pershing served here as a lieutenant during part of that period. The fort was established in 1879 to prevent uprisings among the Blackfeet, and to guard against the return from Canada of Sitting Bull and his warriors. The post was abandoned in 1911, but some buildings remain.

HELENA

*State Capitol Building.* The exploits of the famous Negro servant, guide, and interpreter of the Lewis and Clark expedition—Captain William Clark's man, York—are well represented in paintings and exhibits here.

York spoke fluent Sioux and was an expert hunter and woodsman —traits that were invaluable to a pioneer expedition in the West. He is pictured in a forty- by twenty-five-foot painting that dominates the entire front wall of the House of Representatives. The work of famed western artist Charles M. Russell, it is priceless. The scene depicts Lewis and Clark conferring with the Flathead Indian tribe in the search for a route over the Lolo Pass in the Rocky Mountains near Missoula.

In the State Historical Society Museum is another Russell painting of York among Mandan Indian friends near the Missouri River. His black skin was a source of great wonder to the Indians, and their curiosity about him was often helpful to members of the expedition. York is also featured in two diorama displays in the museum.

Many Negroes came to Helena after gold was discovered here in the summer of 1864, in what is still known as Last Chance Gulch. They were involved in a variety of enterprises; one owned a hotel on the narrow, winding main street. When the Placer Hotel was built, enough gold was removed from the excavation to pay for it.

MISSOULA

*Fort Missoula.* The 25th U. S. Infantry was stationed here when it was ordered to duty on Easter Sunday, April 10, 1898. Easter services were postponed so that the townspeople could see the

Negro troops off for Cuba, and what was to be a heroic role in the Spanish-American War.

## VIRGINIA CITY

*Thompson's Museum* here contains many relics of the days when this was a typically wild and wooly western mining camp. Once almost a ghost town, the village has been greatly restored and is a popular tourist attraction.

Gold was discovered in Alder Gulch here in May 1863, and Virginia City became Montana's first incorporated town in 1864. It was also the first territorial capital.

By 1870 it was a metropolis, by the standards of the time. Nearly nine hundred people lived here, nineteen of them Negroes. At one time the local waterworks was owned by Negroes.

The city was long a symbol of lawlessness in the West, and much of the gold mined here was a source of profit only for outlaws. A vigilante committee finally cleaned up the town; the local boot hill cemetery remains as testimony to their efforts.

---

# NEBRASKA

---

## BAYARD

*Chimney Rock National Historic Site*, near U. S. 26, was a major landmark and campsite on the Oregon Trail.

State and local historical organizations have erected scores of markers noting points on the many pioneer trails that passed through Nebraska. These included, in addition to the Oregon Trail, the Mormon Trail, the Ox Bow Trail, the Texas-Ogallala Cattle Trail, the Sidney-Black Hills Trail and, of course, the route of the famed Pony Express and the Lewis and Clark expedition.

Negroes and whites together broke all of these old trails, and rode the Pony Express and stagecoach lines. The incredible hardships they endured as they journeyed westward on horseback, or in covered wagons, are emphasized by occasional isolated graves along the various routes.

BEATRICE

Homestead National Monument, U. S. 77, 3½ miles northwest, marks the homestead of Daniel Freeman, probably the first claim filed under the Act of Congress, May 20, 1862. Among the Negro homesteaders was a woman, Jenny Morgan, who faced the hardships of the plains alone on a homestead near Wellfleet in 1883.

FORT ROBINSON

Fort Robinson, near Crawford, became the home of the 9th Cavalry Regiment in the summer of 1885, and of the 10th in the early 1900s. In addition to the routine of preserving law and order, the 9th saw action against the Sioux in the Ghost Dance uprising in 1890, which resulted in the Battle of Wounded Knee.

The 9th, under Major Henry, fought a skirmish a few days after the Wounded Knee battle, rescuing men of another regiment who were surrounded and under attack by the Sioux. Corporal William O. Wilson, who risked his life to ride through the enemy forces and bring a relief force to the rescue, was awarded the Medal of Honor. He was one of thirteen Negroes of the 9th and 10th Regiments who won the Medal of Honor during half a century of action in the Indian wars.

Wounded Knee was the last battle with the Sioux, but in 1906 the 10th Cavalry was involved in what was probably the last trouble with any of the Indian tribes. Troops from the Fort Robinson garrison were ordered to the field when three hundred Ute Indians fled their reservation in an effort to relocate in the Big Horn country of Montana. The Fort Robinson troops intercepted them and escorted them to Fort Meade, South Dakota.

The 9th Cavalry was stationed here when it was ordered to Chicamauga Park, Georgia, in 1898, enroute to distinguished service in Cuba in the Spanish-American War.

Fort Robinson is now a state historical park, maintained by the Nebraska Historical Society and by the Nebraska Game, Forestation and Parks Commission. The headquarters building has been converted into a museum by the Society.

NEBRASKA CITY

*Allen B. Mayhew Cabin,* near the city on State Highway 2, is a small log cabin in which fugitive slaves were sheltered
overnight, or longer, until they could be smuggled across the Missouri River to Tabor, Iowa. Some were concealed in an underground
passage connected with the cabin.

Although there were slaves in the Territory prior to the Civil
War, most Negroes arrived after the Civil War and, like their white
neighbors, worked at various trades to earn a living.

Early Negro settlers included Tom Cunningham, who was the
first Negro police officer in Lincoln in 1880; Eliza Galloway, an
ex-slave who came to Kearney in 1888 and lived there until her
death in 1936, at the age of one hundred; Jules Miles, an ex-slave
Civil War veteran, who settled in Omaha in 1892; and Jubilee Johnson, an ex-slave who died at Schuyler in 1894.

# NEVADA

GOLDFIELD

*Site of Joe Gans Fight.* Goldfield did not exist until
1902, when the first mining claim was staked here. It became a
metropolis, by local standards, in 1910, and was already fading into
obscurity in 1912 when the mines began giving out. A disastrous fire
in 1923, which destroyed fifty-two city blocks, virtually wiped out
the town.

At the peak of its boom, lots in Goldfield sold for as much as forty-
five thousand dollars apiece. Residents had such confidence in the
future of their city that they even promoted a world championship
boxing event here in 1906.

The principal promoter of the fight was the fabulous Tex Rickard.
He had piled up a fortune running a saloon in the Klondike of
Alaska, during the gold rush there. He lost it in California, and

when gold was found here, Rickard hastened to Goldfield to recoup. His new venture, the Northern Saloon, was such a success that at one time he had eighty men tending bar.

At the time of the championship fight Goldfield had a population of twenty thousand, which swelled to several times that size during the week in which Joe Gans, a Negro, met "Battling Nelson" for the lightweight championship of the world. Gans was the victor, but the fight went forty-two rounds.

Today, the remaining residents—a bare five hundred of them—live among the ruins, and memories, of Goldfield's days of glory.

RENO

*Jim Beckwourth's Trail.* The route of U. S. 395, west of Reno to the California line, is one that ox-drawn covered wagons followed in the days when Nevada was a seemingly endless stretch of desert and mountains that had to be endured en route to the "Golden West." The original trail, used by tens of thousands of migrant pioneers, was laid out by Jim Beckwourth, a Negro explorer, trapper, and guide who was one of the legendary Mountain Men.

Beckwourth didn't know it, but his discovery of the pass in the Sierra Nevada Mountains that is now named for him put Reno on the map. His route was used by the railroad that was built through the Territory in 1868, and Reno was born when the railroad company picked it as the site for a town and began selling lots.

Reno enjoyed its first boom as the rail center for Goldfield and Tonopah, when the mines were opened there. More people came in later years when the city became a divorce mecca, and when gambling was legalized in 1931.

Nearly a century after Beckwourth first came here, another Negro also helped put Reno on the map. In 1910, because of the worldwide publicity given the Gans-Nelson fight in Goldfield, Reno decided to promote a boxing event of its own. The great Jim Jeffries was persuaded to come from retirement to try to regain his heavyweight crown. Reno saw him lose it to a great Negro champion, Jack Johnson, who had won the world title in Sydney, Australia in 1908.

Johnson remained the champion until 1915, when he fought Jess Willard in Havana and was knocked out in the twenty-sixth round. He was the last Negro heavyweight champion until Joe Louis captured the title in 1937.

# NEW HAMPSHIRE

## CORNISH

*Saint-Gaudens National Historic Site,* on State 12A, two miles from town. Here are the home, gardens, and study of the renowned American sculptor who created the moving memorial to Robert Gould Shaw that stands in Boston Common. The museum has a full-size plaster cast of the memorial honoring the colonel and men of the celebrated 54th Regiment of Massachusetts Volunteers.

Shaw and many of his Negro soldiers died in the assault on Fort Wagner, in South Carolina, during the Civil War. Saint-Gaudens, before completing the final sculpture, did preliminary models of forty heads, of which sixteen are visible in the final relief. The original models are on display here.

Tradition has it that Saint-Gaudens moved here while working on a Lincoln statue for a Chicago park. A friend told him that he would find "plenty of Lincoln-shaped men up there" among the lean New Hampshire Yankees.

## DEERFIELD

*Captain Jonathan Longfellow Marker* is at the site of "The Garrison," which he erected in 1743 as a defense against the Indians.

When Longfellow bought the property he paid for it with Negro slaves. Although slaves were few in number in pre-Revolutionary New England, ships from these colonies carried on an active trade in Negroes. They carried New England rum to Africa, exchanged it for slaves, and then either sold the slaves in the United States or exchanged them for sugar and molasses in the West Indies.

The property of Longfellow, who was a distant relative of the poet, Henry Wadsworth Longfellow, was purchased by Major Simon Marston in 1765 and is still owned by his descendants.

## HANOVER

*Dartmouth College* was chartered by King George III in 1769 and began operations in a single log cabin in 1770. Prior to the Civil War Hanover became a center of anti-slavery sentiment in New Hampshire. By 1863 opposition to slavery had become so strong that a Dartmouth president with thirty years' tenure was compelled to resign because he had written several pamphlets defending slavery as a divine right.

## JAFFREY CENTER

*Amos Fortune Grave,* in the Old Burying Ground, on Route 124, is the last resting place of a former slave whose incredible spirit and determination could not be subdued during a near-lifetime of servitude.

Amos Fortune was still a boy when he was brought to the United States as a slave. He served a succession of masters until 1770. Finally, when he was sixty, he had saved enough money to purchase his freedom.

At an age when most men would begin thinking of retirement, Fortune began a new life. He established a homestead in Woburn, Massachusetts, purchased one wife out of slavery, who died in 1775, and another who died within a year of their marriage in 1778. In 1779 he bought freedom for a third wife, Violet Baldwin, and her daughter, Celyndia.

In 1781, Fortune moved to Jaffrey Center and established a tanning business. Although he was already past seventy, he soon became one of the town's leading citizens, and his reputation as a tanner brought business from a large surrounding area and even from his old home in Woburn. He was chosen as attorney for some of his townsmen; both Negro and white apprentices served under him. He was founder of the Jaffrey Social Library in 1795.

When he died in 1801, Fortune left a will directing that gifts be made to the church and the local school district. A silver communion service was purchased for the church, and his other gift was used by School District No. 8. When the district went out of existence in 1927, the Fortune fund was set aside to provide annual prizes in public speaking for students at the Jaffrey high school. The Amos Fortune Forum, a memorial to the former slave, is held Friday evenings in July and August in the Old Meeting House where he attended church, now the Town Hall.

Fortune also left funds to provide markers for his grave and that of his wife, which are in the burial ground behind the Old Meeting House. His gravestone reads:

> "Sacred to the memory of Amos Fortune, who was born free in Africa, a slave in America, he purchased liberty, professed Christianity, lived reputably, and died hopefully, Nov. 17, 1801. AEt91."

His wife's stone reads:

> "Sacred to the memory of Violate, by sale the slave of Amos Fortune, by marriage his wife; by her fidelity his friend and solace. She died his widow Sept. 13, 1802. AEt73."

Fortune's freedom papers and many receipts for the sale of leather are kept in the Amos Fortune Room at the Jaffrey Public Library. His house and barn are still standing.

PORTSMOUTH

*Portsmouth Navy Yard*, New Hampshire-Maine Turnpike. The U.S.S. *Kearsarge*, famous Union vessel of the Civil War, was built here in 1861. It destroyed the pride of the Confederate fleet, the cruiser *Alabama*, off Cherbourg, France, June 19, 1864. Among the fifteen Negroes on board the *Kearsarge* was Joachim Pease, loader of the no. 1 gun.

The *Alabama* had a record of sixty-nine ships sunk, burned, or captured, but the *Kearsarge* was not to be the seventieth. After a bitter ninety-minute duel, during which most of Pease's gun crew was killed or wounded, he sent off the shell that ended the engagement.

For "marked coolness, good conduct, and qualities even higher than courage and fortitude," Joachim Pease was awarded the Medal of Honor, the second earned by a Negro. But he probably took equal satisfaction in the personal congratulations he got from Acting Master David H. Sumner, who told him: "You sustained your reputation as one of the best men on the ship."

# NEW JERSEY

COLUMBUS

Old Columbus Cemetery. Several Negroes who fought with George Washington's Continental Army are buried here.

EAST ORANGE

Alpha Lodge No. 116, Free and Accepted Masons, 508 Main Street, was the first recognized Negro Masonic lodge in the United States. Its warrant was issued on January 19, 1871, at Newark, New Jersey. The original meeting place, Oriental Hall, no longer exists.

The first Negro Mason in the United States was Prince Hall, later a Revolutionary soldier. He was initiated in March 1775 into a British Army lodge at Boston, Massachusetts.

In July 1776 Hall and other Negroes formed African Lodge No. 1 in Boston. After the Revolution was ended, this lodge applied in 1784 for a warrant from the Grand Lodge of England. The charter was granted in 1787, but the lodge was not recognized by American Masonry.

Prince Hall fought at Bunker Hill, and later became an active abolitionist. A native of Barbados, he came to the American colonies in 1765.

FREEHOLD

Monmouth Battle Monument, at 70 Court Street, across from the Historical Association Museum, was unveiled in 1884. The 100-foot granite shaft has several bas-reliefs around the base that depict scenes in the battle. These are the work of Sculptor J. E. Kelly, of New York.

It has been estimated that seven hundred Negroes fought the

British in the Battle of Monmouth in June 1778. It was almost a disaster for the Americans because of a retreat ordered by the ranking American general, Charles Lee. The British, under Lord Clinton, came from New York to attack the American forces. Lee retreated from Freehold, but was intercepted by General Washington near Tennent. Washington promptly ordered a counterattack, pausing only long enough to express some uncomplimentary opinions to General Lee.

It took the talent and daring of Washington, Anthony Wayne, Von Steuben, and Lafayette to turn the tide and send the defeated British back toward New York. Many American patriots, white and black, contributed to the victory. Among the latter was Private John Harris, who had seen service with two Virginia regiments before entering the action at Monmouth. He so impressed young Major James Monroe that he was made orderly to the officer who later became the fifth President of the United States.

One of the best-remembered figures in the Battle of Monmouth was Molly Pitcher, who reportedly brought water to the American soldiers and then manned a gun herself when her husband fell. One of the attractions here is the well from which she is said to have drawn the water, but some believe that she got it from a nearby stream.

Molly Pitcher gained fame for a day of spontaneous service with the Continental Army. Another American woman put on the Colonial uniform and served for more than seventeen months, but she is scarcely remembered. She was a Negro lady, Deborah Gannett, who enlisted as a regular soldier in the Fourth Massachusetts Regiment under the name of Robert Shurtliff.

This intrepid woman served undetected from May 20, 1782, to October 23, 1783. How her masquerade was finally uncovered is not known, but that it occurred is beyond question. In fact, on January 20, 1792, the State of Massachusetts recognized her service as "an extraordinary instance of female heroism," and gave her a reward of £34.

The museum across the street from the monument has two floors of exhibits related to the battle and the Colonial and Revolutionary periods. Included is the painting, "Washington Rallying His Troops at the Battle of Monmouth," by Emanuel Leutze.

### LAWNSIDE

*Mount Pisgah AME Church*, Warwick Road and Mouldy Road, traces its history to 1792, when Negroes and whites from the area began holding religious services in shaded groves, private homes, and tenant houses. In 1801 a plot of land was purchased for thirty dollars, and a thirty-six- by twenty-five-foot church was built, with benches for seats and a dry goods box for a pulpit.

In 1813 the white members withdrew and formed their own congregation. Three other churches also sprung from the original congregation, but Mount Pisgah Church continued to grow, and in 1868 a second church was built. It was replaced by the present structure in 1912.

Negro veterans of many of the nation's wars are buried in the church cemetery. One old marker, still legible, bears the name of Elisha Gaiter, who died May 21, 1858, at the age of seventy. He was a member of the crew on the U.S.S. *Constitution* during the War of 1812.

Lawnside, originally known as Free Haven, derived that name from its role as an underground railroad station. Later it was also known as Snow Hill. Many fugitive slaves remained here to create one of the nation's oldest predominately Negro communities.

*Mount Zion Methodist Church,* White Horse Pike and Charleston Avenue, was organized in 1797 and is the oldest church on White Horse Pike. Its first meeting house was built at another site in 1808. The land for the present church was purchased in March 1828, by the African Wesleyan Methodist Episcopal Church, and services have been held here continuously since that time. The name became Mount Zion Methodist Church when the church was incorporated in 1892.

NEWARK

*The Newark Museum,* 43–49 Washington Street, has the paintings "The Good Shepherd," by Henry Ossawa Tanner; "Sojourner Truth and Booker T. Washington," by Charles W. White; and "Poor Man's Cotton," by Hale A. Woodruff.

Tanner's father was a bishop of the African Methodist Church. The son was born in Pittsburgh in 1859, was a pupil of Thomas Eakins at the Pennsylvania Academy, and later studied and painted in France. In his later years he painted religious subjects, traveling frequently to Palestine for inspiration. White and Woodruff are contemporary Negro artists.

PERTH AMBOY

*Grave of First Negro Voter.* A marker on the south inside wall of St. Peter's Church is in memory of Thomas Mundy

Peterson, the first Negro to vote in the United States under the 15th Amendment. Mr. Peterson was buried in the churchyard at St. Peter's, and the mayor was on hand in August 1959, when a large stone monument was placed on the grave.

Peterson's life is an excellent example of the truth that prominence and prosperity are not essential elements of good citizenship. He exercised his franchise on March 31, 1870—the first time he was given the opportunity. The issue was revision of the Perth Amboy charter. The vote went for revision, and Thomas Mundy Peterson—custodian in a local public school—was appointed to the seven-member commission that carried it out.

Later Peterson became a delegate to the Republican County Convention. His fellow citizens thought so highly of him that on Memorial Day 1884, they gathered at the City Hall and presented him with a medal that he wore proudly until his death in 1904.

### TRENTON

*Trenton Battle Monument* stands at the site of the main gun emplacement in the Revolutionary War Battle of Trenton, fought in December 1776. The engagement took place after General Washington and his men had made their hazardous crossing of the Delaware River. The Continental Army, which included Negroes from many New England states, captured nearly one thousand Hessian mercenaries.

# NEW MEXICO

### BAYARD

*Site of Fort Bayard.* The 24th Infantry Regiment, stationed here in the 1870s, participated in many actions against hostile Indians. One of them inspired a local legend.

The Indians were causing trouble in Grant County; the Negro

soldiers pursued them to a point near Victorio Park, and then made camp near a waterfall.

The Indians raided the camp at dusk and killed the entire military detail, except for one soldier who took refuge under the waterfall. There he discovered nuggets of gold, and collected several. When the Indians left, he began making his way back to the fort, got lost, and lived for days on herbs and the small animals he could kill. He finally arrived at the fort with the gold, but was never able to find his way back to the place where he found it.

People are still looking.

## COLUMBUS

*Raid by Pancho Villa.* A force of nearly one thousand Mexicans, of the notorious Pancho Villa's band, attacked here in March 1916, burning half the town and killing and wounding many soldiers and civilians. There had been many previous incidents along the Mexican border, but this one prompted the government to send a punitive expedition into Mexico to deal with Villa.

General "Black Jack" Pershing, who later won fame as commander of the American Expeditionary Forces in World War I, was placed in charge of the expedition. The Negro troops of the 10th Cavalry Division were among those assigned to the fruitless pursuit. The cavalrymen had only two days' rations for themselves and their horses when they rode off from Culberson's Ranch in New Mexico, across the Mexican border. For thirty days they literally lived off the land, and very barren land at that.

Ten men of the 10th died in an encounter with Villistas at Carrizal, Mexico, on the return journey. Villa later retired to an estate in Chihuahua, and was assassinated in 1923. The men of the 10th went back to their station at Fort Huachuca, where they tried to collect subsistence money for all of the meals they had missed on their long, hard ride. They didn't get it.

## FOLSOM

*Folsom Cemetery* is the burial place of George Mc-Junkin, a Negro cowboy who came to New Mexico after he was freed from slavery in 1863, and who became known throughout the territory for his skill, courage, and integrity.

George once worked for a cattle company called the "Pitchforks," west of Folsom. He and fourteen other cowboys were holding a herd of cattle about two miles north of Mineral, on Cottonwood Arroyo, when the bitter Blizzard of 1889 descended upon them.

For two days, blinded by the snow, tired, and half frozen, the cowboys tried to hold the herd together. Finally, they were forced to drift with it, lost it, and lost all sense of direction themselves. They had abandoned hope of finding shelter when George urged them to follow him. He led them, with some unerring sense of direction that even he could not explain, to the Harvey Bramblet ranch, where they remained under shelter until the blizzard ended after raging for thirteen days.

The cowboy later began riding for W. H. Jack, manager of the XYZ Ranch, and when Jack died in 1913 his widow made George the ranch foreman. He built up a herd of his own, built a home in Folsom, and died there in April 1927. Mrs. Jack cared for him during his final illness.

He is buried here among many of his cowboy comrades.

There were many other Negro cowboys in New Mexico. One named Frank, who took the name of his employer, John Chisum, is believed to have been the first Negro in southeastern New Mexico. He arrived in the Pecos River country, in 1867, and assisted in planting the first orchard in the Pecos Valley in 1872.

A respected New Mexico pioneer, Frank Chisum was a familiar figure at the forefront of the annual Cotton Carnival parade in Roswell until he died in 1930.

FORT STANTON

*Fort Stanton*, south of State 48, off U. S. 380 at Capitan. Negro troops of the 9th Cavalry operated from Fort Stanton in pursuit of Apache chief Victorio and his warriors throughout 1879. Sergeants Thomas Boyne of Maryland and John Denny of Big Flats, New York were each awarded the Medal of Honor for heroism in these engagements. Boyne's award came for gallantry on two separate occasions; Denny's for dashing three hundred yards under the fire of Victorio's guns to rescue a fallen comrade.

The old fort buildings now house a state institution.

Negro cavalrymen also served at many other frontier military posts in New Mexico, but even the ruins have long since been obliterated at many of them. An example is Fort Tularosa where, in May 1880, Sergeant George Jordan and a small detachment of twenty-five cavalrymen defeated a band of one hundred Apaches, headed by Chief Victorio, who attacked the fort. For this and other displays of gallantry during thirty years of Indian fighting, Jordan was awarded the Congressional Medal of Honor. The remainder of his life was spent in the Soldiers' Home at Washington, D.C., on a pension of twelve dollars a month.

## LAS CRUCES

*Amador Hotel*, Amador Street, now caters to business-men and tourists, but for many years it was a favorite rendezvous for United States troops who were stationed in or passing through the area.

The structure is built around a two-story central court, with the second-floor rooms opening onto a balcony. It is probably the only hotel in the world with rooms that are named instead of numbered —Esperanza, Natalia, Dorotea, Maria—twenty-three names in all. Many of the rooms are furnished with massive four-poster beds and other antiques transported by oxcart over the plains more than a century ago.

## LINCOLN

*Old Courthouse*. Every year, on the first weekend of August, residents of Lincoln re-enact the jailbreak of Billy the Kid. He escaped from the Old Courthouse, now a frontier museum.

The Kid (William H. Bonney) was a key figure in the bloody Lincoln County cattle war that began in 1876. Negro cowhands fought and died on both sides of the war, and Negro cavalrymen surrounded him in one of the war's bloodiest episodes. The Kid escaped. Later it was a Negro, George Washington, who found and returned him to Governor Lew Wallace.

The Kid was held in jail as a witness, testified in a murder case, and was then released. He became a fugitive again.

The Kid's career finally ended in 1881 in northern New Mexico when he was shot by one of the state's toughest sheriffs, Pat F. Garrett.

## ZUNI

*Zuni Pueblo* was discovered by Estevanico, a slave of a Spanish expedition that originally landed in Florida in 1528 (see St. Marks, Florida).

When the four survivors of the Narvaez expedition reached Mexico in 1536 the Viceroy of New Spain, Antonio de Mendoza, purchased Estevanico from Dorantes and sent him on an expedition across the Rio Grande as guide for Fray Marcos de Niza. Their object was the fabled Seven Cities of Cibola, which legend said were paved with gold.

Estevanico ranged far ahead of the expedition, sending back reports with friendly Indians as he traveled. His last message was a huge wooden cross indicating a major discovery. When the expedition neared the Zuni pueblo, they learned that Estevanico had been murdered by the Indians, and Fray Marcos turned back, taking with him greatly embroidered tales of the wealth of a pueblo that he had actually never seen. A disappointed Coronado discovered his deception when he visited the area during the years that followed.

History records Fray Marcos as the first white man to set eyes on New Mexico. Actually, the first non-Indian explorer here was a Negro.

# NEW YORK

ALBANY

*Emancipation Proclamation.* The New York State Library here has the original draft in Lincoln's own hand of the preliminary proclamation issued in September 1862. Gerrit Smith, a wealthy abolitionist and friend of John Brown, purchased it at auction. Lincoln's draft of the January 1, 1863 proclamation was destroyed in the Great Chicago Fire of 1871, but a true copy is in the National Archives, in Washington, D.C.

One of the earliest Negro newspapers, the *African Sentinel and Journal of Liberty,* was published in Albany in 1831 and 1832. No copies of the paper have been found.

AUBURN

*Harriet Tubman Home,* 108 South Street, was the last home of the heroic figure of underground railroad days. It has been preserved in memory of the woman who led some three hundred slaves to freedom.

Harriet Tubman escaped from Maryland, where she had been born in slavery, when she was about twenty-five years old. She was not content simply with freeing herself, and returned to the South at least nineteen times to lead others to freedom in the North and in Canada. Although rewards of up to forty thousand dollars were offered, she was never captured, nor did she ever lose a "passenger" on her underground railroad.

During the Civil War, Miss Tubman performed valuable service as a Union Army scout. When the war ended she settled in this home, converting what had been an underground railroad station into a home for old people. It is maintained by the African Methodist Episcopal Zion Church. A memorial plaque to Miss Tubman has been installed in the Auburn courthouse, and she is buried in Underwood Memorial Cemetery.

### BROOKLYN

*The Brooklyn Museum,* Eastern Parkway, has several works by Negro artists. The paintings include "Funeral Sermon," by Jacob Lawrence; "Speracedes France," by Lois Mailoux Jones; "Before the Storm," by Richard Mayhew; and "Shoe Shine," by Ernest Crichlow.

### BUFFALO

*Albright-Knox Art Gallery* has a gouache by Jacob Lawrence titled "Going to Work." Also in the collection is "Self Portrait," by Horace Pippin.

Pippin has made a distinguished place for himself among American primitive artists. Born in West Chester, Pennsylvania and brought up in Goshen, New York, he began drawing at ten, and left school at fifteen to help support his family as a hotel porter, warehouse helper, and junk dealer.

When World War I began, Pippin promptly enlisted in the Army, and when he returned from France a year later, it was with a shoulder wound that denied him the independent use of his right arm. Unable to work, he finally began painting, guiding his right hand with his left. He worked on his first canvas from 1930 to 1933, but by 1938 had four paintings on display in a Museum of Modern Arts exhibit. He has had many shows since, and many admirers, including the great actor, the late Charles Laughton.

*Front Park* contains a memorial to Oliver Hazard Perry's victory in the Battle of Lake Erie during the War of 1812. Executed by sculptor Charles H. Niehaus, it was dedicated in 1915. About one-fourth of the sailors in Perry's victorious fleet were Negroes. (See Put-in-Bay, Ohio.)

CHAMPLAIN

*Jehudi Ashmun Birthplace Marker* at site. Ashmun was the first colonization agent in Liberia, Africa, from 1822 to 1828. During one period in the evolution of the American Negro as a free citizen, many advocated colonization programs to rescue Negroes from the yoke of slavery. Jefferson favored this approach, as did Lincoln at one point in his career.

The attitude of most Negroes toward colonization was summed up in the statement of one Negro convention: "This is our home and this is our country. Beneath its soil lies the bones of our fathers; for it, some of them fought, bled, and died. Here we were born, and here we will die."

COOPERSTOWN

*National Baseball Hall of Fame and Museum.* Although Negroes did not become deeply involved in major league baseball until 1947, when Branch Rickey brought Jackie Robinson to the Brooklyn Dodgers, this museum is crowded with memorabilia of Negro achievements in the nation's "national pastime."

There is a bronze plaque for Robinson, of course, as the first Negro player in contemporary big league ball, and as Rookie of the Year in 1947. It is a tribute to Negro athletic prowess that less than twenty years later, when the Los Angeles Dodgers played the World Series with the Minnesota Twins, half of the players were Negroes.

Robinson won the National League's Most Valuable Player Award in 1949. Negro players have won it in eleven of the subsequent sixteen years. In 1966 the Most Valuable Players in both leagues, Roberto Clemente and Frank Robinson, were Negroes.

The museum has too much material on Negro ballplayers to list, but included are the bat with which Willie Mays set a new National League record by hitting his 512th home run; his 535th home run ball is there, too—the one that placed him second only to Babe Ruth in lifetime home runs. A special case on Mays includes copies of the contract he signed in 1951 for five thousand dollars and the one he signed twelve years later for one hundred thousand dollars.

The museum even has a uniform worn by Satchel Paige, one of the greatest Negro pitchers of all time. He was still playing at the age of sixty-four.

## ELMIRA

*Woodlawn National Cemetery,* 1825 Davis Street. Confederate prisoners were kept here between July 1864 and August 1865. Of twelve thousand prisoners, about 2952 died, partly because of the poor condition in which they arrived, and partly because of an unusually severe winter. The Federal government had made no provision for the burial of prisoners, so city officials authorized use of space in the city cemetery. Before the camp closed, two and a half acres of Woodlawn had been used.

In most Civil War cemeteries vast numbers of burials are unknown, but not at Woodlawn. At the time of the Confederate burials, the sexton was John Jones, an escaped slave who found freedom in Elmira. Jones kept so meticulous a record of each Confederate burial that when the Federal government, in 1907, decided to mark the graves, it was possible to mark each stone with the soldier's name, company, regiment, date of death, and grave number.

One of those whom Jones had so tenderly buried was from the household in which he had lived as a slave in Virginia.

## KINGS POINT

*United States Merchant Marine Academy* educates young Americans, regardless of creed or color, to become officers in the Merchant Marine.

The Memorial Chapel here was dedicated in 1961 "in memory of the American Seamen of all faiths who gave their lives at sea."

Says Rear Admiral Gordon McLintock, the superintendent: "Included among the almost seven thousand men of the American Merchant Marine who died at sea in wartime are some gallant Negroes. Therefore this chapel can be said to be another monument to our citizens regardless of color or creed."

NEW YORK

*Cooper Union,* Cooper Square. One of Lincoln's most effective and significant statements on slavery was made here on February 27, 1860. Many abolitionist leaders also occupied the rostrum during the slavery era, among them William Lloyd Garrison, Henry Ward Beecher, and Harriet Beecher Stowe. More than a century later, the lectern at which Lincoln stood is still in use.

*Countee Cullen Branch,* New York Public Library, 104 West 136th Street, was named in honor of a Negro poet who was an important figure in the renaissance of Negro literature that followed World War I. Cullen was a Phi Beta Kappa at New York University, and while there wrote the book, *Color,* that later won the first Gold Medal for Literature of the Harmon Foundation.

Cullen received his masters degree at Harvard University and won a Guggenheim fellowship in France during which he wrote *The Black Christ.* He died in 1946.

The library has an extensive collection of Negro materials which are circulated. On display are four murals by Negro artist Aaron Douglas depicting stages in the history of the Negro in America. Douglas was born in Topeka, Kansas, in 1899, and graduated from the University of Kansas. He has illustrated a number of important books by Negro authors.

*Grace Episcopal Church,* 802 Broadway. The first Negro bishop of the American Protestant Episcopal Church was the Reverend Samuel David Ferguson, who was elected to the House of Bishops in 1884. He was consecrated in this church June 24, 1885, as the successor of the Missionary Bishop of Liberia.

*Hall of Fame for Great Americans,* New York University, University Avenue at 181st Street. Among the busts of famous Americans displayed here is one of Booker T. Washington, done by Negro sculptor Richmond Barthe in 1946. Barthe has received critical acclaim for a series of busts of famous actors and actresses, including Katherine Cornell, John Gielgud, and Phillips Holmes, and for other works such as "Shoe Shine Boy" and "The Boxer."

*Madison Square Garden* has presented many of the nation's championship boxing events.

Negroes have been prominent in boxing since the United States began world competition. The first American heavyweight contender was Tom Molineaux, a Negro slave from Virginia who fought in England in 1810 and 1811. He lost both fights.

The first United States Negro heavyweight champion was Jack Johnson, who held the title from 1908 to 1915. In 1937 the great Joe Louis became the second Negro to capture the crown and held it for twelve years. Subsequent Negro heavyweight champions have been Ezzard Charles, Jersey Joe Wolcott, Floyd Patterson, Sonny Liston, and Cassius Clay (Muhammad Ali).

The first Negro titleholders in other weight classes were: Battling Siki, light-heavyweight, 1922; Tiger Flowers, middleweight, 1926; Joe Walcott, welterweight, 1901; Joe Gans, lightweight, 1901; George Dixon, featherweight and bantamweight, 1890.

Two of the greatest Negro boxers were Henry Armstrong and "Sugar Ray" Robinson. During most of the period between 1946 and 1960 Robinson held either the welterweight or middleweight titles, defending them on twenty-five occasions.

*Metropolitan Museum of Art,* Fifth Avenue at 82nd Street, has the painting "Victorian Interior" by Horace Pippin. Born in 1888, this self-taught Negro artist drew for many years before he began to paint at the age of forty-two. This primitive painting was done in the year of his death, 1946.

*The Museum of Modern Art,* 11 West 53rd Street, has drawings, prints, paintings, and sculpture by a great many Negro American artists. Included in its collections are works by William Majors, Jacob Lawrence, Romare Bearden, Junius Redwood, Selma Johnson Street, Norma Morgan, Richard Hunt, Thomas Sills, Daniel LaRue Johnson, and Mildred Thompson. It also has photographs by Gordon Parks and Roy DeCaraba.

Among the most interesting items are thirty panels from Jacob Lawrence's series, *The Migration of the Negro.* The other thirty panels of the series are in the Phillips Collection in Washington, D.C. Not all of the paintings are on display, but photographs of all of them are available.

*Museum of the City of New York,* Fifth Avenue and 103rd Street, has a theater and music collection that includes many portraits, photographs, playbills, scene designs, and costumes dealing with the Negro on the New York stage.

Many of the major "firsts" for Negroes in the musical and theater arts were achieved in New York. Today, Negroes have attained such prominence in the field of entertainment that individual accomplishments are too numerous to list. The trailblazers, often in New York, included Paul Robeson, in *Othello*; Hilda Simms, in *Anna Lucasta*; Gordon Heath, in *Deep Are the Roots*; Canada Lee, in *On Whitman Avenue*; and Richard B. Harrison as De Lawd in *Green Pastures*.

Count Basie, Louis Jordan, Cab Calloway, and Louis Armstrong established great popularity in the field of jazz music, while Duke Ellington, Jimmie Lunceford, Noble Sissle, and many others achieved success in the more sophisticated fields of popular music. William Grant Still won critical acclaim for the composition of more serious music, including a work done for the 1939–40 New York World's Fair.

Dean Dixon and Rudolph Dunbar won recognition as conductors; Paul Robeson, Roland Hayes, Edward Matthews, Aubrey Pankey, Kenneth Spencer, and William Warfield charmed concert audiences. Marian Anderson was acclaimed by Sibelius and Toscanini as one of the most gifted singers of the world; singers Dorothy Maynor and Carol Brice won the praise of Serge Koussevitsky; and Ann Brown and Todd Duncan triumphed in the title roles of George Gershwin's *Porgy and Bess*.

By the mid-fifties, the Metropolitan Opera Association had signed contracts with many Negro singers, including Marian Anderson, Robert McFerrin, and Mattiwilda Dobbs. In 1951 Janet Collins, featured in *Aïda*, became the first Negro to dance at the Metropolitan Opera House. Meanwhile, Leontyne Price and Lawrence Winters were singing opera on television and with the New York City Opera Company.

Materials related to the careers of many of these great Negro entertainers, as well as others, may be found in this museum.

*St. George's Episcopal Church*, 207 East 16th Street. For more than twenty-five years prior to his death in 1949, the great Negro baritone, Harry T. Burleigh, was soloist at this church. He also sang at Temple Emanuel, in New York, and appeared before King Edward VII of England, and in concert throughout the world.

Born in Erie, Pennsylvania, Burleigh was also a composer and arranger. In addition to countless compositions and arrangements of his own—most of them Negro spirituals—he assisted Anton Dvorak in the composition of *New World Symphony*.

*The Schomburg Collection*, New York Public Library, 103 West 135th Street, is a collection of Negro art, literature, and history built around the private collection of Arthur A. Schomburg, a Puerto Rican of African descent. The Carnegie Corporation purchased the collection in 1926, presented it to the New York Public Library, and its holdings have grown rapidly ever since.

Today, the collection is a major resource in the study of Negro history. Included are books, pamphlets, manuscripts, photographs, art objects, and recordings that cover virtually every aspect of Negro life from ancient Africa to the present.

The materials in the Schomburg Collection are not circulated, but can be used or viewed at the library. Among the manuscripts are those of Claude McKay, the Jamaica-born poet who came to America in 1913, and in the 1920s was one of those who led what has become known as the "Harlem Renaissance" in Negro literary effort. One of his first major works, published in 1922, was *Harlem Shadows*. His novels included *Home to Harlem*, in 1928, and *Banjo*, in 1929.

The library has, on microfilm, copies of the nation's first Negro newspaper, *Freedom's Journal*, which began publication in New York on March 16, 1827. The originals are held by several different libraries. The editors of the newspaper, which survived for about two years, were Samuel E. Cornish, a Presbyterian minister, and John Brown Russwurm. (See Brunswick, Maine.) The collection also includes the field notes and memoranda used by Gunnar Myrdal in writing *An American Dilemma*.

*369th Regiment Armory*, Fifth Avenue and 143rd Street. All-Negro in World War I, this entire unit was awarded the Croix de Guerre by the French government. One of its members, Henry Johnson, received one of the first two such medals awarded to Americans for individual bravery. Johnson fought off an entire German patrol single-handedly to rescue a wounded comrade. He killed four of the enemy and wounded several more although he was severely wounded himself.

A former commanding officer of the 369th, Colonel Benjamin O. Davis, in 1940 became the first Negro to be promoted to the rank of brigadier general.

*Union League Club*, 38 East 37th Street, was organized in 1863 by Professor Wolcott Gibbs as the Union League of America, to combat secession sentiment. The club aided in recruiting a regiment of Negro troops in 1864.

*United Nations Building.* One of the United States' most distinguished representatives in this body is Dr. Ralph J. Bunche, a scholar-diplomat who left a post in the Library of Congress to join the State Department. He served there as Chief of the Division of Dependent Territories, and became a member of the United Nations Trusteeship Council and its director, and is now undersecretary general of Special Political Affairs. He won the 1950 Nobel Peace Prize for his brilliant negotiation of the Arab-Israeli dispute in Palestine.

Other high-ranking Negro Americans who have served with the United States delegations in the General Assembly include:

Ambassador James M. Nabrit, Jr., Deputy Representative of the United States to the United Nations, and Deputy Representative on the Security Council; Ambassador Franklin H. Williams, United States representative on the Economic and Social Council; Marjorie McKenzie Lawson, United States representative on the Social Commission of the Economic and Social Council; Carmel Carrington Marr, adviser, Legal and International Organization Affairs; Frank C. Montero and Hugh H. Smythe, advisers on Economic and Social Affairs.

Two other Negroes, Charles H. Mahoney and Samuel C. Adams, have served as United States representatives, and a dozen others have served as alternate representatives. They are Archibald J. Carey, Jr., Robert Lee Brokenburr, Richard Lee Jones, Genoa S. Washington, Marian Anderson, Charles W. Anderson, Jr., Zelma Watson George, John W. Morrow, Clifton R. Wharton, Carl T. Rowan, Mercer Cook, and Patricia R. Harris.

NORTH ELBA

*John Brown Grave.* Six miles south of Lake Placid on State 73 is the farm where "John Brown's body lies a'mouldering in its grave." Brown purchased the farm after he left Ohio, and lived here until he joined the Kansas Free Soil fight.

The land was part of one hundred thousand acres set aside by Gerrit Smith, an abolitionist and philanthropist, for freed and fugitive slaves. He planned to teach the ex-slaves farming and trades, and establish an independent community. Brown came to help build the colony, but the idea did not meet with success, and was abandoned.

Other Browns buried here include his sons, Watson and Oliver, who were killed in the raid at Harpers Ferry. Brown's widow is said to have returned the abolitionist's body here in secret, so it would not be molested. She sent an empty hearse by another route to delude emotional crowds along the way.

## OGDENSBURG

*Remington Art Memorial.* Negroes, particularly the men of the 9th and 10th U. S. Cavalry Regiments who fought in the Indian wars in the West, and in Cuba, were the subjects of many sketches and paintings by Frederic Remington.

This museum has a painting, "The Charge of the Rough Riders at San Juan Hill." It shows one Negro cavalryman. Remington could have shown many more, for troops of the all-Negro 9th and 10th Regiments, riding on the Rough Riders' flanks, were in the forefront in this and other battles of the Spanish-American War. The museum also has portraits of two white officers from these cavalry regiments.

## ROCHESTER

*Frederick Douglass Monument,* Central Avenue and St. Paul Street, was dedicated by Governor Theodore Roosevelt in 1899. Douglass, a noted Negro abolitionist, helped organize Negro troops in the Civil War and was appointed minister to Haiti.

*Mount Hope Cemetery,* 791 Mount Hope Avenue, is the burial place of Douglass, who moved to Rochester in 1847.

## STONY POINT

*Stony Point Battlefield Reservation.* Negroes fought on both sides of the encounter on July 15, 1779, in which American General "Mad" Anthony Wayne defeated the British. His Negro and white Revolutionaries killed or captured more than six hundred British troops. Among the captives were three Negroes.

During the Revolution the British made repeated efforts to enlist Negro slaves to their cause, promising them freedom. Meanwhile, after the opening stages of the war, Washington and his generals went through a long period of indecision regarding the use of Negro troops in the Continental Army.

Inevitably, some Negroes turned up on both sides of the conflict, but at war's end the overwhelming majority had cast their lot with Washington. Ironically, many of those who fought with the British departed with them as free men, while countless Negroes

who fought for America's freedom waited another half century for
their own.

The most famous Negro of this conflict was a slave named Pom-
pey, who contributed significantly to the victory. As a spy for
Wayne, he secured the British password, enabling the Americans
to surprise the enemy troops.

## TICONDEROGA

*Fort Ticonderoga.* This restored Colonial fort was used
by French, British, and American forces during the Colonial and
Revolutionary period. A military museum is maintained for visitors.

The fort was captured by American forces on May 10, 1775. In
the assault were Ethan Allen and his famed Green Mountain Boys,
many of whom were black. Among the Negroes in the battle were
Lemuel Haynes (who was later to win greater recognition preaching to white congregations in New England), Primas Black, and
Epheram Blackman.

After the American victory some of the cannons captured here
were hauled to Boston, where they helped Washington capture that
city from the British.

The loyalty of American Negroes is one of the remarkable aspects
of the Revolutionary War. White Americans were strongly moti-
vated to fight for the freedom they had won in the colonies, but
even the free Negroes, who were a minority, had found little freedom here.

Some Negroes yielded to temptation; Israel Newport went "over
the hill" from Ticonderoga to the British on June 8, 1877. The
wonder is that more Negroes, many of them slaves sent to fight in
place of their masters, did not do the same.

## WARSAW

*Warsaw Presbyterian Church.* The first anti-slavery
party, called the Liberty Party, was organized here at a meeting
of the Western New York Anti-Slavery Society on November 13,
1839. James G. Birney was nominated as a candidate for President
and Francis J. Lemoyne of Pennsylvania as the vice-presidential
candidate.

The Liberty Party was actually named at a larger convention in
Albany in 1840. It never became a significant political force, al-
though in the 1844 campaign, had its support been thrown to Henry
Clay, it would have brought about his election. In that year a

Liberty Party convention was held in the Congregational church in nearby Arcade.

Negro abolitionists Samuel Ringgold Ward and Henry Highland Garnet were among the founders of the new party.

## WEST POINT

*United States Military Academy.* There are no memorials to individual Negroes at this famous training post for Army officers, but there are many class memorials honoring graduates, both Negro and white.

The Class of 1936 Memorial, located near the Cadet Chapel, honors—among others—Lieutenant General Benjamin O. Davis, Jr. Davis commanded the all-Negro 332nd Fighter Group in the Mediterranean Theater in World War II. The unit's pilots destroyed 111 enemy planes in the air and 150 on the ground and won more than 80 Distinguished Flying Crosses. Davis later became Chief of Staff, United States Forces, Korea, and Chief of Staff, United Nations Command, Korea.

Another Negro graduate, Major Hugh G. Robinson, Class of 1954, was appointed military aide to President Johnson in July 1965.

## WHITE PLAINS

*Washington's Headquarters,* Virginia Road, was built about 1680 and used by General Washington during the Battle of White Plains in 1776. It has its original furniture.

When Baron von Closen visited here on July 4, 1781, he noted that more than a quarter of the troops were black. One of them was Salem Poor, who had already made a name for himself at Bunker Hill. His superiors in that battle said he "behaved like an experienced officer as well as an excellent soldier."

# NORTH CAROLINA

### ANSONVILLE

*Bethlehem Cemetery.* A grove of tall pines towers over the markers here, one of which honors Ralph Freeman, also known as Elder Ralph. Born a slave, Freeman joined the Baptist Church and was authorized to preach by the church of which he was a member.

Eventually, the members of the Bear Creek Association bought his freedom and he became an ordained minister, preaching to white congregations in several surrounding counties. He often substituted for the Reverend John Culpepper when the latter was representing the district in Congress. Freeman died in 1831.

### DURHAM

*The Bennett Place State Historic Site,* two miles west on U. S. 70, includes the farmhouse of James Bennett, where Confederate General Joseph E. Johnston surrendered his army to Union General William T. Sherman, April 26, 1865. General Johnston's surrender followed Lee's at Appomattox by seventeen days. It ended the Civil War in the Carolinas, Georgia, and Florida.

Exhausted but jubilant Negro Union troops were on hand for the historic event. Many northerners felt the surrender terms were not sufficiently harsh, but it is probable that they were determined before his death by President Lincoln, who was looking ahead to the restoration of the Union, and not by his successor, President Andrew Johnson.

### FAYETTEVILLE

*Evans Metropolitan Methodist Church,* Cool Spring Street, stands on the site of the first Methodist church in the city, built about 1803 by a Negro minister, the Reverend Henry Evans.

Evans, a shoemaker, was converted to Methodism at an early age and licensed to preach by the Methodists in Virginia. He came to North Carolina and began preaching prior to 1800, to both Negroes and whites. The town council's objections to his ministry forced him to preach surreptitiously for a time, but eventually citizens of the community intervened and Evans was authorized to preach with the blessings of town officials as well as his parishioners.

When Methodist Bishop Asbury visited the city in 1803, he found that Evans had built a twenty- by thirty-foot church of rough-sawn lumber on a leased lot. He preached to both races, and soon added another ten feet to the church to accommodate his growing flock.

Evans died in 1810 and is buried under this church, which stands on the site of the one he built.

*Fayetteville State Teachers' College* was established in 1867 by seven local Negroes seeking educational opportunity for their children. They bought a lot and persuaded General O. O. Howard of the Freedmen's Bureau to build Howard School. In 1877 the state acquired the school for the education of Negro teachers, creating what is today the oldest normal school for any race in the South. In 1908, the school was located permanently on a ninety-two-acre campus.

On the grounds is a marble tablet honoring Dr. E. E. Smith, principal of the school from 1883 to 1933, minister to Liberia, and an adjutant in the Spanish-American War. The library building is named for another former principal, Charles W. Chesnutt, who was also an author of short stories and novels, and winner of the 1928 Spingarn Medal for pioneer literary work.

GREENSBORO

*Agricultural and Technical College of North Carolina* began operations in 1890 as an "annex" of Shaw University in Raleigh. It was known as the Agricultural and Mechanical College for the Colored Race.

The college was moved to Greensboro after local citizens contributed fourteen acres of land and eleven thousand dollars to assist in the construction of buildings. The General Assembly added another twenty-five hundred dollars for construction, and the college began operations when the first building was completed in 1893.

The name was changed in 1951, and the course offerings have been broadened to include degrees in education and the liberal arts.

Many of the buildings are memorials to former administrators or faculty members. The Richard B. Harrison Auditorium was named for the famous Negro dramatic artist who taught dramatics here for several years before achieving international fame as De Lawd in *Green Pastures*.

### GUILFORD COLLEGE STATION

*Coffin Birthplace Marker* on U. S. 421 identifies the nearby birthplace, in 1789, of Levi Coffin, often called the President of the Underground Railway. A white abolitionist, Coffin helped organize the escape of countless Negroes from slavery.

### KINGS MOUNTAIN

*Kings Mountain National Military Park* is the site of a victorious battle of American frontiersmen in the Carolina foothills. The mountain men and colonial troops from Virginia met a Cornwallis scouting force commanded by Major Patrick Ferguson. Regarded as the best shot in the British Army, Ferguson had invented the first breech-loading rifle used by the military forces of any nation.

It is believed that more than a dozen Negroes were under arms in the battle but the name of only one, John Braddy, is known. He was employed by one of the four senior officers in the engagement, Colonel William Campbell of Virginia, and fought at his side.

### MILTON

*The Yellow Tavern,* presumed to be the oldest building in Milton, was once an overnight stop on the stagecoach road through the Piedmont country from northern Virginia to southern Georgia. It vied with the Red Brick Tavern in the competition for trade by boasting that George Washington often dined here while his postillions changed horses in Milton.

More significant was the Yellow Tavern's use for more than thirty years as the workshop of one of the greatest Negro artisans of the ante-bellum South. His name was Tom Day, and his hand-wrought mahogany furniture is even more prized today than it was by the wealthy southern aristocrats who furnished their mansions with it more than a century ago.

Day made his first mahogany furniture for sale in 1818, and in 1823 bought the old Yellow Tavern and converted it into a factory. He employed and trained white apprentices and Negro slaves to help him with his work—the latter because, in that era, it was the only way he could secure permanent help. All of them, apprentice and slave, were taught the craftsmanship that enabled the production of masterpieces of furniture art to be continued for many generations.

Day furniture became *the* style throughout the southern states, and Tom Day became a prosperous and respected citizen of Milton. Many homes in Milton display examples of his artistry today, as do those of collectors all over the East. But Day was remarkable in many other ways, as well.

He earned the respect of his white neighbors in an era when the social system was designed to prevent it. More than that, he resisted the indignities that were imposed on Negroes—slave or free. While his origins are in doubt, his adult life is revealed in official records that can still be found.

In 1829 Day married Acquilla Wilson, a free Negro of Halifax County, Virginia—a woman with beauty to match Day's own magnificent physique and Chesterfieldian manners. Only after the marriage did he discover that the North Carolina assembly, in 1827, had passed an act that prohibited the migration of any free Negro or mulatto into the state. Landowners feared the influence of free Negroes on their slaves.

When Day discovered that he could not bring his new wife to Milton, he announced that he would leave the state. Immediately, sixty Miltonians sprang to his defense, traveling to the state capitol in Raleigh to petition for an amendment to the Act of 1827 that would grant a special exemption to Acquilla Wilson Day.

The North Carolina archives hold the words of praise heaped upon the Negro furniture maker by his fellow townsmen. He was described as a "first-rate workman, a remarkably sober and steady and industrious man, a high-minded good and valuable citizen, possessing a handsome property." The legislature responded with a bill that permitted Tom's wife to move into North Carolina and live there "free from the fines and the penalties of the Act of 1827."

Tom also won some moral victories in his hometown. In his day, the Presbyterian church was attended by all of the local aristocracy.

Tom attended, too, but because of his color was required to sit in the gallery with the slaves.

Tom chafed over the demeaning situation in which he and other Negroes were required to worship, and one day conceived a solution, for himself, at least. He went to the officials of the church and offered to make a set of mahogany pews to replace the existing ones, which were showing signs of wear. The officials were delighted with the offer, but then Tom added a qualification. In exchange for the pews, he wanted the privilege of sitting in one of them, on the main floor of the church.

The church officials pondered the bargain a bit, and there was some resistance, but avarice overcame prejudice and the deal was made. Tom would make new mahogany pews and in return would be allowed to sit in their midst, in the front pew on the left of the church.

The new pews were magnificent, adding much to the grandeur of the church—even with Tom Day sitting in them—and the parishioners were delighted. Not until many years later did they discover that Tom, in a subtle gesture of defiance that must have given him many moments of quiet satisfaction, had enjoyed the last word. As one contemporary Miltonian puts it, the pews "turned out to be not a bit of mahogany at all. The old fellow outfoxed those Presbyterians" and gave them maple pews.

The church and the pews may still be seen today. The Yellow Tavern also stands, but is now a private home. And Tom Day's grave is there, on his farm just outside of town.

NEWTON GROVE

*Bentonville Battleground State Historic Site*, three miles off U. S. 701, north of the city. This is a magnificent restoration of one of the most significant battlegrounds of the late stages of the Civil War. It was here, in a three-day encounter in March 1865, that a Confederate force of thirty thousand men under General Joseph E. Johnston tried valiantly to halt General William T. Sherman's determined march.

Sherman's force of sixty thousand, which included many Negro regiments, was split into two wings, marching on parallel routes. Their objective was Goldsboro, where they would be reinforced by forty thousand fresh troops and obtain supplies.

Johnston, with an army headed by twenty officers with the rank of major general or above, was more than a match for Sherman's left wing on the first day of the battle, but could not cope with the additional force of thirty thousand when the right wing joined the battle on the following day. Johnston withdrew, and Sherman, eager to reach Goldsboro, did not pursue.

The engagement was the only significant all-out Confederate attempt to stop Sherman after the Battle of Atlanta in August 1864. It was also the largest battle fought on North Carolina soil, and the last major Confederate offensive in the war in which the South chose the ground and launched the initial attack.

RALEIGH

*John Chavis Memorial Park,* E. Lenoir at Worth Street, dedicated to John Chavis, a freeborn Negro, educator, and preacher. Chavis is believed to have been educated at Princeton. He founded a school in Raleigh, teaching both whites and Negroes, and some of his pupils went on to become senators, congressmen, and governors.

In 1831, as a result of the Nat Turner slave rebellion, Negroes were banned from preaching in North Carolina; Chavis retired from the ministry. He also was compelled to restrict his teaching to white children. He died in 1838.

*St. Augustine's College* was founded by the Protestant Episcopal Church for work among Negroes following the Civil War. Since its founding in 1867 it has concentrated on the training of teachers, and 75 percent of its graduates still enter the educational field. Unlike the many southern Negro colleges which eventually were turned over to the state, this is still a church-sponsored institution.

*Shaw University.* The founder of Shaw, the Reverend H. M. Tupper, of Massachusetts, received his commission to undertake a program of education for freed slaves here while still a soldier in the Civil War. He began teaching a single class on December 1, 1865. In later years Shaw began a unique program of education for Negro women.

During the last twenty years of the nineteenth century Shaw expanded into fields of professional service, and trained many of the region's first professional men in education, medicine, pharmacy, law, and theology. Today it is in the midst of an ambitious expansion and construction program, and offers a broad liberal arts education.

*Surrender Site Marker,* on old U. S. 70, south of city, marks the spot where city commissioners surrendered the city to the white and Negro forces of General Sherman's army on April 13, 1865.

## ROCKY MOUNT

*Dred Wimberly Marker* honors a former slave who "voted for better roads, schools, and colleges as a State Representative, 1879, 1887; and State Senator, 1889. His home stands here."

## SALISBURY

*Livingstone College* was founded in 1879 at Concord, North Carolina, as Zion Wesley Institute. Two years later it was moved to its present site and renamed Livingstone College in memory of David Livingstone, Scottish missionary, explorer, and humanitarian. The change was prompted by the fact that Robert Livingstone, David's son, had enlisted in the Union Army during the Civil War under an assumed name, died in nearby Salisbury Prison, and was buried in Salisbury National Cemetery.

This fully accredited four-year liberal arts college was founded by Dr. Joseph Charles Price, an eloquent orator, noted platform speaker, and internationally known leader of his race. The state has erected a historical marker near his birthplace at Elizabeth City. The most widely known graduate of Livingstone was Dr. James E. K. Aggrey, often called "Aggrey of Africa," who taught here and at Columbia University and became co-founder of Achimota College in West Africa. He is buried in the city cemetery.

*Salisbury National Cemetery,* 202 Government Road. Many Negro soldiers are buried here. Salisbury was the site of a large Confederate prison which held ten thousand Union soldiers in a space suited for two thousand. When Union General George Stoneman captured Salisbury in April 1865, he used the prison briefly for a stockade and then burned most of the area. A marker on U. S. 52 notes the site.

## TOWNSVILLE

*Nutbush Presbyterian Church.* Organized in 1754, this church frequently heard sermons by John Chavis during the period 1809–32. Chavis, who also taught school, produced many accomplished students, including Charles Manly, who was governor of North Carolina from 1849–51. The church burned in 1941.

## WILMINGTON

*Fort Fisher State Historic Site*, at southern terminus of U. S. 421. Assaults by Negro and white troops of Union General Paine's division, coupled with naval bombardment, led to the fall of this fort on January 15, 1865. It was probably the greatest land-sea battle of the war, with Federal casualties totaling thirteen hundred. This was the price of closing the last important port used by the South for blockade-running during the Civil War.

*Fort Anderson* is identified by two markers, on State 133 and on U. S. 17 west of the city. It was evacuated after a strong attack by white and Negro Union regiments on February 18, 1865, preliminary to the fall of Wilmington.

# NORTH DAKOTA

## BISMARCK

*The State Capitol.* North Dakota is one of the newer states. It had just become a territory when Fort Sumter fell, and did not achieve statehood until 1889. There have never been many Negro citizens; there were only 617 in 1910, and fifty years later, in 1960, there were only 677. However, many Negroes visited here in the days when riverboats were still operating. Late in the nineteenth century a Negro named Cassius Clay is said to have worked at the boat landing.

The first territorial governor, William Jayne, was an abolitionist and onetime neighbor of Abraham Lincoln in Springfield, Illinois. He tried to persuade the first legislature to prohibit slavery in the territory, but the predominately Democratic members refused.

There is no monument to the woman who is the most famous

former Negro citizen of Bismarck, but she doesn't really need a monument because she helps create one of her own every month. Era Bell Thompson, the international editor of *Ebony*, grew up here.

## DICKINSON

*St. Joseph's Cemetery.* John Tyler, a Negro cowboy on Teddy Roosevelt's ranch, is buried here. Tyler was well known as a cook at "roundup" time and as a musician. His fiddle was much in demand at country dances in the area. Tyler had a colorful career as a rancher about forty miles south of Medora for about forty years after he left Roosevelt's employ.

The cowboy-rancher died in 1928 and was buried in January of that year by Monsignor George P. Aberle, pastor of St. Joseph's Church. Monsignor Aberle still recalls the cross-country trip through deep snow to the cemetery. The entire funeral party consisted of the priest, the sleigh driver, and two helpers.

## MEDORA

*Theodore Roosevelt National Memorial Park.* The heart of this park is the ranch operated by the former President and hero of the Spanish-American War.

Just as Roosevelt placed confidence in the Negro cavalrymen who fought under him at San Juan Hill in the Spanish-American War, he also admired their horsemanship in less military pursuits. He was particularly impressed with the skill of a horsebreaker named Williams, who worked for his neighbors, the Langs.

Negro cowboys were less numerous here than in the Southwest, where there were thousands of them, but they also contributed to the lore of this part of the "Wild West."

There are several entrances to the park, which covers 110 square miles. The one at Medora is close to the visitors' center and park headquarters.

## STANTON

*Fort Mandan Marker,* on the eastern bank of the Missouri River, southeast of town. Lewis and Clark spent the first winter of their westward expedition among the Mandan Indians here. In March, as they were preparing to depart, a fierce Minnetaree chief arrived, obviously upset. He finally revealed that he had been told

19. Matthew Henson, the only man to accompany Admiral Peary on all of his polar expeditions, and first man to reach the North Pole. *(Portrait by Vince Cullers for American Oil Company)*

20. Harriet Tubman, the "Moses of Her People." *(Portrait by Vince Cullers for American Oil Company)*

21. Father Charles Randolph Uncles, first black priest ordained in United States, on December 19, 1891, in Baltimore, Maryland. *(St. Francis Xavier's Catholic Church)*

22. Crispus Attucks monument in Boston Common, commemorating the first American killed in the American Revolution. *(American Oil Company)*

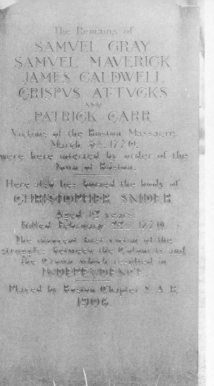

23. Marker on grave of Crispus Attucks and other Americans who were killed in the Boston Massacre, March 5, 1770. (*American Oil Company*)

24. "They Live in Fire Traps," by Jacob Lawrence, in Worcester Art Museum. (*Worcester Art Museum*)

25. Memorial on grave of Sojourner Truth in Battle Creek, Michigan. Black woman was a fiery and persuasive foe of slavery. (*American Oil Company*)

26. An early western pioneer was Mary Fields, who gained fame driving stagecoaches and freight wagons over rugged mountain trails. In her seventies she settled down to a more placid existence in Cascade, Montana, where she was an avid supporter and mascot of the local baseball team. *(Photo courtesy of Mayor Cecil R. Kirk)*

27. This self-portrait is the work of Horace Pippin, black artist who lost the use of his right arm in World War I. *(Albright-Knox Art Gallery)*

28. "Shoe Shine," by black artist Ernest Crichlow, in the Brooklyn Museum. *(The Brooklyn Museum)*

29. Dr. James E. K. Aggrey, "Aggrey of Africa," who founded Achimota College in West Africa. (*Livingstone College*)

30. Marker in Oberlin City Cemetery on graves of three blacks killed in John Brown's raid on Harpers Ferry. Inscription reads: These colored citizens of Oberlin, The Historic Associates of the Immortal John Brown, gave their lives for The Slave. (*Oberlin College*)

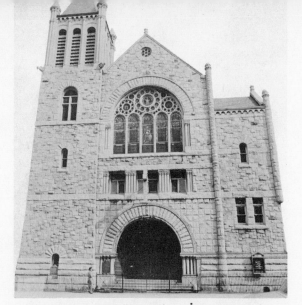

31. Mother Bethel AME church, founded by Richard Allen and Absalom Jones in 1793, is the oldest African Methodist Episcopal Church in the nation. This property in Philadelphia has been owned continuously by blacks longer than any other in the country. *(American Oil Company)*

32. Negro Soldiers Monument in Philadelphia, a memorial to the black soldiers and sailors who have fought in all of the nation's wars since the American Revolution. *(American Oil Company)*

33. Headquarters band and four companies of the black 25th Infantry Regiment drilling at Fort Randall, Dakota Territory, where they guarded Sioux Indian prisoners. *(Nebraska State Historical Society)*

34. Statue in Memphis park overlooking Beale Street, dedicated to William Christopher Handy, "Father of the Blues." *(Ebony* Magazine)

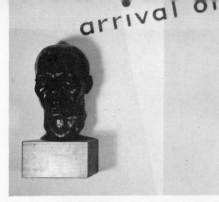

**NEGRO**

Twenty Negroes landed here in 1619 —
the first in British North America.
Like white indentured servants,
they became free citizens after
several years of labor.

They probably had been slaves in the Spanish
West Indies. A Dutch raider captured and brought
them to Jamestown to sell. English law prohibited
holding Christians as slaves, and these people had
names such as Anthony, Isabella and John, showing
they had been baptized.

After 1667 the baptism of a slave did not
alter his condition of bondage because of
a Virginia law adopted that year.

35. Display at Jamestown Historical Park where first twenty Africans were put ashore by a Dutch frigate in August 1619. *(Jamestown Historical Park)*

36. Workshop at Walnut Grove, where Cyrus Hall McCormick and a black assistant, Jo Anderson, perfected the mechanized grain reaper in 1831. *(State Historical Society of Wisconsin)*

37. Fire engine house of the U.S. armory at Harpers Ferry, West Virginia, where abolitionist John Brown and a handful of black and white supporters battled federal troops in October 1859. *(National Park Service)*

38. Father Patrick Healy, S.J., first black president of an American University. (*Georgetown University*)

39. Black soldiers of the 9th and 10th Cavalry regiments played a major role in the Spanish-American War. Here they support the Rough Riders near Santiago, Cuba, in 1898. (*New York Public Library*)

by "some foolish young men" that one of those with the expedition was black.

York, the lone Negro in the party, was summoned. The chief stared at him in disbelief and finally even moistened his finger and tried to rub the color off. When York removed his hat he further astonished the chief with his kinky black hair. Greatly awed by the Negro, the Indian finally left, ending another tense moment for the explorers.

# OHIO

### ALBANY

*Enterprise Academy*, Route 50, was probably the first educational institution in the United States conceived, owned, and operated by Negroes, many of whom were former slaves. Until the late 1850s the Albany Manual Labor University permitted Negroes to enroll, although some citizens objected and established the Citizen's Academy, an all-white school which operated only briefly.

When the Manual Labor University came under the control of denominational churches, Negroes were excluded. This led the Negroes to establish a school of their own. It opened in 1863 and closed in 1886 after one of its dormitories was destroyed by fire. The original building is now a private residence. Students could attend Enterprise Academy for three dollars for each twelve-week term. Furnished rooms cost a dollar a week, and unfurnished rooms were free for those who had paid their tuition.

### ASHTABULA

*The Hubbard House*, Lake Avenue and Walnut Boulevard, was an underground railroad station from which escaped slaves left for Ashtabula Harbor, where boats took them to Canada. State Highway 45, from Warren, was called Freedom Road.

CINCINNATI

*Cincinnati Art Museum.* The permanent collection here includes two paintings by the nation's pioneer Negro studio artist, Robert Duncanson, and one by the greatest of Negro primitive artists, Horace Pippin.

Duncanson, born in New York and educated in Canada, was sent to Scotland to study by the Freedman's Aid Society of Cincinnati in 1840. One of the paintings that made him famous, a landscape done in 1851, is on display here. It is called "Blue Hole, Flood Waters, Little Miami." The museum also owns "Portrait of Nicholas Longworth." Duncanson died in Detroit in 1871.

Pippin is represented with "Christmas Morning." Born in West Chester, Pennsylvania, in 1888, he was "discovered" in the late 1930s after he had been painting for nearly twenty years. Before his death in 1946, he won a Carnegie Exhibition Award.

*Civil War Fortifications,* in Mount Adams, along Fort View Place overlooking the Ohio River, remain from the defense of the city against attacks that never came. Nevertheless, the city's preparations for an expected attack by Morgan's Raiders in September 1862 marked the first appearance of Negroes in military operation in the Civil War. Nearly sixteen thousand civilians, black and white, enlisted in the defense of the city, but the defenses they built were so strong that the Confederate troops did not challenge them.

*Harriet Beecher Stowe House,* 2950 Gilbert Avenue, is now "A State Memorial honoring both the people for whom she showed so much sympathy and understanding and her own contribution to American life. Dedicated to the history of the Negro in the United States and particularly in Ohio, the home has been converted into a museum of exhibits on Mrs. Stowe and the American Negro."

Mrs. Stowe lived here with her father, an abolitionist minister and educator, Dr. Lyman Beecher. Her association with underground railroad activities exposed her to the brutality of slavery and helped inspire *Uncle Tom's Cabin.*

CLEVELAND

*Case-Western Reserve University.* Western Reserve, originally located at Hudson, was deeply involved in abolitionist activity during its early years. The Western Reserve Historical Society Museum and Library, at 10825 East Boulevard, has exhibits and document collections. The present institution was formed in a merger with Case Institute.

Cleveland was an important station on the underground railroad. It sent lawyers to the defense of John Brown after the raid on Harpers Ferry. On September 6, 1848, the first national Negro convention opened here.

One of Cleveland's outstanding pioneer Negroes was John Melvin, who came to the city from Virginia in 1830. Although the son of a slave, he accumulated enough money to buy a lake vessel, helped organize the first Negro school in Cleveland, and as an organizer of the First Baptist Church opposed segregation of Negroes so vigorously that the principle of free seating was adopted.

Another Cleveland Negro, Garrett A. Morgan, invented a belt fastener for sewing machines in 1901 and later won a gold medal award for inventing a smoke inhalator. He also got a gold medal from the City of Cleveland in 1916 when he donned his own invention and entered a tunnel under Lake Erie to rescue some trapped workmen. His invention of the first automatic "Stop" signal probably won no appreciation from impatient motorists, but the General Electric Company bought it for forty thousand dollars.

COLUMBUS

*Poindexter Barber Shop,* 61 High Street, was the political headquarters of James Preston Poindexter, central Ohio's leading Negro politician and clergyman in the last half of the nineteenth century. Poindexter was a confidant of President Hayes and several Ohio governors, and was elected the first Negro city councilman of Columbus.

*Paul Lawrence Dunbar Home,* 219 North Summit Street, was the residence of a Negro poet who was not quite thirty-four, and at the height of his fame, when he died in 1906. His home, furnished with his personal belongings and manuscripts, is much as he left it. Dunbar's poetry was highly praised during his lifetime but recently has been little read. Yet he was the first Negro poet after Phillis Wheatley to achieve anything approaching a national or international reputation; he was the first to concentrate on Negro themes. His poems and stories give an accurate, if limited, picture of his era.

Dunbar started writing poems when he was seven, and his first collection, *Oak and Ivy,* was published in 1892. He became a national figure in 1896 when William Dean Howells praised his book "Majors and Minors" in a review in *Harper's Weekly.* Although he achieved considerable fame, he earned little money. He died February 9, 1906, and is buried in Woodland Cemetery.

## MOUNT PLEASANT

*Friends Meeting House* near State 150 is maintained by the Ohio Historical Society as a state memorial. The Quaker settlers here sheltered fugitive slaves and published an anti-slavery newspaper. In 1848 they established the Free Labor Store, which refused to sell products made with slave labor.

## OBERLIN

*Oberlin City Cemetery,* Morgan Street. A simple stone marker here reads: "These Colored Citizens of Oberlin, the heroic associates of the immortal John Brown, gave their lives for the slave." It marks the grave of three Negroes killed in John Brown's raid on Harpers Ferry.

*Oberlin College.* There are no monuments to the distinguished Negro graduates of Oberlin College, but the school itself is a monument to the ideal of equality of educational opportunity. Oberlin was not the first school to admit Negroes, but it became, in 1835, the first institution to adopt an official admissions policy of nondiscrimination.

The school was a well-known sanctuary on the underground railroad, and during the years immediately prior to the Civil War demonstrated its contempt for the Fugitive Slave Law. In the famous Oberlin-Wellington rescue some twenty villagers, both college and community, were jailed for seizing from Federal agents a Negro who was being returned to his Kentucky owner. Subsequently, when three of John Brown's party at Harpers Ferry were identified as Oberlin Negroes, Oberlin and abolition became synonymous.

Oberlin has produced distinguished Negro alumnae in a variety of fields, among them Blanche Kelso Bruce, a fugitive slave who graduated from Oberlin, became a Mississippi planter after the Civil War, and was the first Negro elected to the United States Senate, in 1875.

Oberlin also produced the first Negro player in major league baseball—not Jackie Robinson, but Moses Fleetwood "Fleet" Walker, of

Mount Pleasant, Ohio. Walker was born in 1857, the son of a Negro physician. He graduated, left Oberlin, and attended the University of Michigan Law School until 1883, when he joined the Toledo team of the Northwestern League.

Toledo joined the original American Association in 1884. It was an early rival of the National League, and was recognized as a major league. Walker caught forty-six games for a list of pitchers that included Hank O'Day, who later pitched, managed, and umpired in the National League.

## PUT-IN-BAY

*Battle of Lake Erie, Perry's Victory and International Peace Memorial National Monument.* This memorial commemorates the battle in the War of 1812 in which Captain Oliver Hazard Perry defeated and captured the British fleet. About one hundred men in Perry's fleet—about one-fourth of the total—were Negroes. In July 1813, Perry had complained to the Secretary of War about the men who were being sent to him—boys, old men, and Negroes. Commodore Isaac Chauncey replied on July 30 that "I have yet to learn that the color of the skin . . . can affect a man's qualifications or usefullness."

The Battle of Lake Erie was fought six weeks later, on September 10. When it was over, Perry sent his famous message, "We have met the enemy and they are ours." He also sent another one, of unstinted praise for the Negro members of his crew, saying that "They seemed absolutely insensible to danger."

Others confirmed his view. Commodore Chauncey, who commanded another vessel on the upper lakes, said the fifty Negroes aboard were among his best men. Nathaniel Shaler, who commanded the *Governor Tompkins* in the Battle of Lake Erie, was awed by the courage of his Negro sailors. He recalled that Seaman John Johnson, dying after being struck by a twenty-four-pound shot, shouted to his comrades to keep fighting and not haul the colors down. John Davis, with a similar injury, begged Shaler to throw him overboard because he was getting in the way of the others.

The monument and grounds here are administered by the National Park Service.

## RIPLEY

*John Rankin House Museum* was the home of a minister who began preaching in Tennessee in 1816 but moved to Ohio because of his hatred of slavery. In 1845 he founded the Free Presbyterian Church of America, which excluded slaveholders and actively opposed slavery. He also established an academy for Negro students, and wrote anti-slavery articles for Garrison's *Liberator*.

The Rankin House was an important station on the underground railroad, sometimes housing as many as twelve fugitive slaves at a time, until they could be sent on to stations farther north. Rankin had thirteen children who were also active participants in the underground railroad.

It was in this house that Harriet Beecher Stowe heard the story of Eliza, who became a character in *Uncle Tom's Cabin*. She had carried her child across thawing ice on the Ohio River to sanctuary in the Rankin house and was saved from capture when the river ice broke up behind her.

### UPPER SANDUSKY

*Wyandotte Indian Mission Church*. When the Wyandotte Indians signed the treaty that sent them to new homes in Kansas, they did it on the condition that this church be held forever by the Methodist Episcopal Church. It was their way of paying tribute to the mulatto missionary who is buried here. John Stewart was the first successful missionary to the Wyandottes, but he seemed an unlikely candidate for the job.

Of French-Negro-Indian stock, Stewart migrated to Ohio from Virginia. Until shortly before he appeared among the Wyandottes in 1816, he was known chiefly as a drunkard.

After his reformation he became a self-appointed missionary to the Wyandottes. Half-educated and unlicensed, Stewart had only two assets—a remarkable tenor voice and Jonathan Poynter, a Negro who had been raised by the Wyandottes and was persuaded to serve Stewart as an interpreter.

The fact that Stewart was able to win over the Wyandottes is also remarkable because previous missionaries had been driven off, and the Indians seemed to have a marked aversion to Christianity.

Stewart won the Wyandottes by singing to them the spirituals and hymns he had learned in Virginia. He died in 1823. The church was erected a year later. The 1960 Methodist General Conference named the grave and church one of the ten official shrines of American Methodism.

WESTERVILLE

*Benjamin R. Hanby House,* 160 West Main Street. Hanby's song, "Darling Nellie Gray," had an impact on slavery that made it a sort of musical *Uncle Tom's Cabin.*

The composer was a minister whose father had operated underground railroad stations at Rushville and Westerville, and he developed a strong sympathy for the fugitives. It is presumed that the story of an escaped slave named Joseph Selby, who died in Rushville while trying to reach Canada to earn money for the purchase of his sweetheart's freedom, inspired the song.

WILBERFORCE

*Central State University* was created by the General Assembly of the State of Ohio in 1887 and began operations in quarters supplied by Wilberforce University. This connection was severed in June 1947, and the state began developing a separate college, which achieved university status in 1965.

In its history the university has had only two presidents, the first of whom was Dr. Charles H. Wesley, a noted Negro historian who is now Director of the Association for the Study of Negro Life and History in Washington, D.C. A classroom building is named in his honor.

The science hall is named for Benjamin Banneker, who helped lay out Washington, D.C. A men's residence hall is named for Colonel Charles C. Young, a former professor of military science at Wilberforce University, who was the first Negro to achieve the rank of colonel in the U. S. Army, and the third Negro to graduate from West Point.

Among the graduates of the university are the world-famous opera star Leontyne Price, and popular singer Nancy Wilson.

*Wilberforce University* was the first college owned and operated by Negroes. It grew from the 1863 merger of the Union Seminary, founded by the African Methodist Episcopal Church, and a college founded by the Cincinnati Conference of the Methodist Episcopal Church. The university was the first predominately Negro college committed to the work-study program of cooperative education.

## XENIA

*Greene County Historical Society Museum,* 2nd and Monroe Streets. Among the Civil War memorabilia here is a flag sent by President Lincoln in 1864 to honor Ohio for leading all other states in Union enlistments. Greene County led the other counties in the state.

Many Negroes from Ohio enlisted before the state began accepting Negro recruits, even though they had to travel to other states to do it. Consequently, while over five thousand Negro troops were credited to Ohio—out of a population of about thirty-six thousand Negroes—many more actually served. A number of Negroes from Xenia enlisted in Colonel Robert Gould Shaw's 54th Massachusetts Regiment.

One of them wrote the local editor from Morris Island, South Carolina, in July 1864, that he had been in the Union Army for a year and two months and had yet to see his first pay. He had seen plenty of action, however, reporting that "Since I left home I have been in four fights, two on James Island with the assault on Fort Wagner and the Battle of Olustee. I have just come back to Morris Island from the fight that General Hatch had with the Johnnies and if I am not much mistaken, we whipped them out. The day was very hot. Several of the troops were sunstroked and died."

Ohio also supplied a large portion of the troops for the 55th Massachusetts, which fought in the engagement at Fort Pillow, where 250 of its men were killed or wounded. This was the battle of which Major General S. A. Hurlbut reported to General Sherman that "the rebels butchered Negro troops after resistance had ceased."

When Ohio finally began enlisting its own Negro troops, they, too, distinguished themselves. At the bitter Battle of Chaffin's Farm, Virginia, September 29, 1864, Ohio's 5th U. S. Colored Troops had 236 casualties, and four of its noncommissioned officers won the Medal of Honor for gallantry and initiative in leading their men into battle after the white officers had been put out of action.

# OKLAHOMA

## BIG CABIN

*Battle of Cabin Creek.* Two Civil War battles were fought here, at the point where the Old Texas Road crosses Cabin Creek. The cast of characters offers a classic example of the way history deceives when a casual reader assumes that all of the participants were white.

During the Civil War this was known as the Indian Territory, and five civilized tribes lived here—Cherokee, Chickasaw, Choctaw, Creek, and Seminole. They aligned themselves needlessly with the Confederacy and, led by Confederate General Stand Watie, waged a war that prevented Federal invasion of the Red River area.

In the encounters here, General Watie's Confederates (red) faced Union soldiers (many of them black) in what was far from a white man's war.

In the first encounter, on July 1 and 2, 1863, the Confederates attacked a wagon train and were repulsed. Little more than a year later, on September 19, 1864, they tried again at the same spot, and captured a train of supplies worth $1,500,000.

## CLAREMORE

*Will Rogers Memorial,* off U. S. 66, honors the half-Cherokee cowboy-humorist. The museum has a duplicate of the Jo Davidson statue that stands in Statuary Hall in the national Capitol building. Rogers got his start in the entertainment world with the Miller Brothers Rodeo, which included a number of Negro cowboys. One of them assisted Rogers in developing his fancy roping act.

DOAKSVILLE

*Site of Fort Towson, Marker* on U. S. 70. Negro soldiers were on hand when General Stand Watie surrendered here in June 1865. He was the last Confederate general to surrender. Some stone ruins remain at the site.

FORT GIBSON

*Fort Gibson State Monument,* on U. S. 62. The 1st Kansas Colored Regiment was en route here when its wagon trains were attacked in the engagements at Cabin Creek. There are now a museum and a state monument on the site of the old log fort.

LANGSTON

*All-Negro Town.* Organized in 1891, Langston was the first all-Negro town in Oklahoma. It was named for the Negro statesman and diplomat, John M. Langston. It is now the site of Langston University. Several such towns were established in Oklahoma during this period, and although Langston was the first, Boley, organized in 1903, was the largest.

LAWTON

*Fort Sill Military Reservation,* four miles north on U. S. 277. Many Negro soldiers served at Fort Sill in the years after the Civil War. Units of the 10th Cavalry and the 24th Infantry Regiments were once in the garrison.

All of their problems were not with hostile Indians. During seven years at this post, the 10th Cavalry spent much of its time suppressing horse and cattle thieves and chasing men who peddled whisky to the Indians. Often they were more dangerous than the Indians who bought the whisky.

It was to this fort that Negro cavalrymen escorted the notorious Apache warrier, Geronimo, after his capture. He ended his days here and is buried in the Apache cemetery, two miles northeast. There is a museum in the old guardhouse where he spent much of his time. The post is a National Historic Landmark.

OKTAHA

*Site of Battle of Honey Springs,* on U. S. 69, north of town. Any doubt about the military ability of the 1st Kansas Colored Regiment was dispelled here on July 17, 1863. After marching all night, Major General James G. Blunt's Negro troops encountered a strong Confederate force. The Negro unit held the center of the Union line, flanked by white and Indian cavalry and infantry regiments.

The Negroes charged under fire to less than fifty yards from the Confederates, halted, and exchanged bullets for twenty minutes until the Rebels broke and ran. The proud Kansas Negroes emerged from the fight with the colors of a Texas regiment.

If General Blunt had entertained any doubts about his Negro troops, they were gone when this fight was over. He wrote: "I never saw such fighting done as was done by the Negro regiment. They fought like veterans, with a coolness and valor that is unsurpassed. They preserved their line perfect throughout the whole engagement and, although in the hottest of the fight, they never once faltered. Too much praise cannot be awarded for their gallantry. The question that Negroes will fight is settled; besides, they make better soldiers in every respect than any troops I have ever had under my command."

PONCA CITY

*101 Ranch,* U. S. 77, twenty-three miles west, was the birthplace of the famous Miller Brothers Rodeo which thrilled audiences around the world. It was here that Will Rogers developed the rope-spinning act that ultimately led to less energetic and more spectacular successes in the entertainment world.

The man who helped him develop the act was a 101 Ranch cowhand named Henry Clay—a Negro. Clay was only one of many Negro cowboys at the 101. It was here that Bill Pickett, another Negro cowboy, invented the art of bulldogging steers. Pickett was still an active rider past the age of seventy. He was thrown while trying to break a horse and it kicked him in the head. He died with a fractured skull.

Another skilled cowhand at the 101 was Perry Britton, and Negro cowboy George Hooker was one of the best trick riders in the business.

The ranch finally went bankrupt and was broken up.

SAWYER

*"Uncle Wallace" Willis Marker,* on U. S. 70. Wallace Willis and his wife, Minerva, were Negro slaves hired out by their

master to work for the missionaries at the Old Spencer Academy. In the 1850s they composed and sang many songs for the Choctaw students and residents of the area. Among them were: "Swing Low, Sweet Chariot," "Steal Away to Jesus," and "Roll, Jordan, Roll." The songs survive, but "Uncle Wallace" lies in a Negro cemetery nearby, in an unmarked grave.

### SUPPLY

*Camp Supply*, east on U. S. 70, was a base camp for operations against the Plains Indians from 1868 to 1893. The 24th Infantry and 10th Cavalry Regiments both operated from here. Sometimes, as on June 11, 1871, when the fort was attacked by Comanche, the Negro soldiers had a fight without ever leaving their base.

Some of the original buildings are now part of Western State Hospital. A granite monument commemorates the officers and men who were stationed here.

# OREGON

### ASTORIA

*Fort Clatsop National Memorial*, on old U. S. 101, six miles south. The members of the Lewis and Clark expedition found themselves near here in the late fall of 1805. A vote was taken among the members of the party to decide on a winter campsite, and they selected this spot on the south side of the bay. In a remarkable expedient indicating the democracy of humans sharing adversity, Army protocol was abandoned and the Negro, York, and the Indian woman, Sacajawea, were each allowed to cast a vote.

The party set to work building a fort, and by Christmas Day the most substantial quarters yet built in the Pacific Northwest had been completed. There were eight log cabins, sixteen by thirty feet, with their doors facing inward and the outer walls joined by a stockade.

BAY CITY

*Murderer's Harbor*, Route 8o-N. This was the name given Tillamook Bay by Captain Robert Gray and the first party of civilized men to set foot in the state of Oregon. Gray, commanding the sloop *Lady Washington*, visited here on August 16, 1788. His was the consort vessel to the ship *Columbia Rediviva*, commanded by Captain John Kendrick.

When Gray's men went ashore to replenish the sloop's wood and water supplies they encountered hostile Indians. A young Negro crew member, known in different accounts as Markus Lopeus, Marcus Lopius, and Marcos Lopez, was killed trying to recover a knife the Indians had stolen. The exact spot of the landing is not known.

It was on this voyage that Gray, assuming command of the *Columbia Rediviva*, sailed back to Boston by way of China, carrying the U.S. flag around the world for the first time.

BOARDMAN

*Oregon Trail Marker*, Route 8o-N west of town. One of many historic markers at major points on the Oregon Trail, the marker reads:

> American settlement of the Pacific Northwest by way of the Old Oregon Trail is one of the great migrations of history. From 1843 to 1880 thousands of families, sometimes with no previous experience, undertook an expedition of 2000 miles over plains, deep rivers and lofty mountains—often beset by hostile Indians. The journey lasted from early spring until late fall for most of the wagons were drawn by slow-moving oxen and loose cattle accompanied the trains. The number of immigrants crossing to the Oregon country is estimated as follows:

| | | | |
|---|---|---|---|
| 1842 | 105–137 | 1847 | 4000–5000 |
| 1843 | 875–1000 | 1848 | 400 |
| 1844 | 700 | 1849 | 2000 |
| 1845 | 3000 | 1850 | 1500 |
| 1846 | 1350 | 1851 | 2500 |

Negro families were among the pioneers who undertook this hazardous journey. Their numbers were not great, but some achieved considerable stature in the Northwest (see Washington). There were only fifty-five Negroes in Oregon Territory in 1850 and about 125 in 1860; some, finding that they were not welcome in the "civilized" part of Oregon, had gone on north to settle in what is now the state of Washington. They believed the area north of the Columbia River would go to Great Britain when the boundary dispute was settled. Instead, their presence was a factor in making it part of the United States.

HUNTINGTON

*Farewell Bend State Park,* south of the city on Route 80-N. For pioneers on the Oregon Trail this was the last camp on the weary journey across the Snake River plains. Here the Oregon Trail left the Snake River and wound overland to the Columbia. Negro and white pioneers rested themselves and their oxen here. The Fremont expedition, with Kit Carson and the Negro scout, Jacob Dodson, also stopped here on October 13, 1843.

JACKSONVILLE

*Jacksonville Museum,* in Old County Courthouse, has relics of Oregon's Gold Rush days of the early 1850s. The city is being restored to its appearance during the heyday when gold seekers swarmed here in the hope of becoming wealthy overnight. There were not many Negroes, but early census records list a number of them as miners and mule packers who carried supplies to the miners. As in most gold camps the packers probably made more money, or kept more of what they made.

PORTLAND

*Oregon Historical Society Museum,* 1230 Southwest Park. On display here are Captain Robert Gray's sea chest, other relics and papers of the ship *Columbia Rediviva,* and many pioneer artifacts and materials related to the Oregon Trail.

SALEM

*State Capitol.* A mural here shows the Lewis and Clark expedition along the Columbia River, with the Negro member of the party, York, in the left foreground. Another mural depicts Captain Robert Gray and the discovery of the Columbia River in 1792. It was on Gray's first voyage four years earlier that a Negro member of his crew was killed by Indians.

## SUMMER LAKE

*Fremont Memorial,* on Oregon Route 31. On December 16, 1843, Captain John Fremont and his second expedition arrived here after struggling down from the snowy heights through a canyon that lies west of the memorial. The change in climate led them to name this "Summer Lake" from the mountain "Winter Ridge."

A marker lists the members of the party, including Jacob Dodson, a free Negro who had been a servant of Fremont's father-in-law; Kit Carson, and others. The party continued from here to Sutter's Fort on the Sacramento River in California.

On his return from the expedition Dodson became an attendant in the United States Senate, and at the outbreak of the Civil War volunteered three hundred Negroes in defense of the nation's capital. The offer was refused because Lincoln had not yet made the decision to arm Negroes.

## TROUTDALE INTERCHANGE

*Lewis and Clark State Park,* Route 80-N, east of Trout-dale, at the mouth of the Sandy River. Lewis and Clark, who called this the Quicksand River, arrived here in the fall of 1805 after shooting hazardous rapids and encountering difficult portages in their journey down the Columbia River. After navigating the Short Narrows of the Columbia one of the party, Cruzat, still had enough energy to play the violin while York danced, to the delight of the Indian natives.

# PENNSYLVANIA

## BALA-CYNWYD

*James A. Bland Grave.* State 23, at Conshohocken State Road and Manayunk Road. Buried in the cemetery here is the Negro minstrel comedian and composer, who wrote more than six hundred songs.

Bland was born in Flushing, New York in 1854, the son of one of the nation's first Negro college graduates, and was educated at Howard University. Among his compositions were "Oh, Dem Golden Slippers" and "In the Evening by the Moonlight."

Bland died in obscurity in Philadelphia in 1911. Few Americans knew that it was he, and not Stephen Foster, who had written the celebrated "Carry Me Back to Old Virginny." A quarter of a century later, when Virginia adopted the song as its official state anthem, most Virginians were also surprised to learn that it had been written by a Negro.

## CARLISLE

*Dickinson College* was founded by Dr. Benjamin Rush, pioneer pre-Revolutionary physician in Philadelphia. Rush was an admirer and friend of the first Negro doctor in America, James Derham, who had been the slave of a British Army surgeon.

Derham's master served as a Revolutionary soldier, and Derham engaged in the limited practice of medicine in his absence. After the war he was sold to a New Orleans physician, who paid him for working as his assistant.

Derham saved enough money to buy his freedom, went to Philadelphia, and entered medical practice on his own. By 1789 he had built a prosperous practice, and his skill had earned the respect and friendship of Rush.

After discussing medicine with Derham in three languages, Rush commented that "I had expected to have suggested some new medicines to him, but he suggested many more to me."

## CHADDS FORD

*Brandywine Battlefield,* north on U. S. 202 off U. S. 1. Here Washington's Continental Army failed to halt British General Howe's advance on Philadelphia in September 1777. This was also the headquarters of French General Lafayette, who was wounded in the action.

A rare display of courage at Brandywine was that of Edward Hector, a Negro soldier in the 3rd Pennsylvania Artillery. He was with the ammunition wagons when the order came to retreat. He disobeyed it and used discarded weapons to hold off the attacking British forces long enough to save the horses and wagons and return them to the American lines. His valor was recognized half a century later by the Pennsylvania legislature. It awarded him a forty-dollar "donation."

Less fortunate was John Francis, a Negro in Captain Epple's company of the 3rd Pennsylvania Regiment. He "had both legs much shattered by grape shot," according to the pension lists of the state of Pennsylvania.

## CHESTER COUNTY

*Lincoln University,* on U. S. 1, forty-five miles southwest of Philadelphia, is the oldest college in the United States established to provide higher education for Negro youth.

The school was founded in 1854 as Ashmun Institute by the Reverend John Miller Dickey. Dickey's family had a traditional interest in the welfare of Negroes. His maternal grandfather was a marble merchant who made contributions to the education of Negroes in Philadelphia as early as 1794. Mr. Dickey served as a missionary and preached to slaves in Georgia before he took over the Oxford Presbyterian Church, in Oxford, Pennsylvania, from his father.

In 1851, as a member of the American Colonization Society, the minister was active in court actions that freed a young Negro girl who had been abducted by slave raiders from Maryland. At about the same time he sought to obtain college admission for a young Negro, John Amos. Failing to persuade even the most liberal colleges to accept the young man, Dickey began preparing him for the ministry.

This experience led Dickey to persuade the Presbytery of New

Castle to establish "an institution to be called Ashmun Institute, for the scientific, classical and theological education of colored youth of the male sex." The name was changed and the educational program expanded in 1866, and white students were encouraged to enroll. The student body has been interracial ever since.

EASTON

*Lafayette College* held its first classes in a farmhouse on a sunny morning in 1832. It was integrated from the outset; in fact, the first class was assembled by Aaron Hoff. Lafayette's first Negro student had the honor of calling the forty-three students from nearby fields and shops by blowing a few blasts on a large horn.

In later years the college established the first Chair of Civil Rights in the United States. It was made possible by a gift, in 1919, from Fred Morgan Kirby, a member of the board of trustees. Kirby donated one thousand shares of stock in the F. W. Woolworth Company, of which he was vice president.

ERIE

*Flagship Niagara* is the restored brig which served as Commander Oliver Hazard Perry's flagship during the Battle of Lake Erie in the War of 1812, after the *Lawrence* was put out of action.

The battle occurred on September 10, 1813. One hundred years later the *Niagara* was raised from the bottom of Lake Erie, where it had sunk after falling into disrepair.

Today, visitors may board the restored vessel to observe the conditions under which Navy men fought and died more than 150 years ago. The *Niagara* was part of a nine-ship squadron that routed the British fleet on Lake Erie, removing the British threat in the Northwest and opening supply lines to American troops in Ohio. About one-fourth of the men who served on these ships were Negroes.

*Harry T. Burleigh Birthplace Marker* on East 6th Street notes that the "Eminent American baritone, composer, and arranger was born three blocks north in 1866. He arranged 'Deep River' and other spirituals, and set to music poems by Walt Whitman. Was a student and associate of Dvorak. He died in 1949."

GETTYSBURG

*Gettysburg National Military Park,* U. S. 15 Business, and U. S. 30. A great favorite of Civil War buffs, this is an excellent place to recapture the style of warfare fought in the days when men bet their lives on horses, rather than their money.

Here, in July 1863, more men died than in any other battle fought before or since on U.S. soil. Although they were theoretically non-combatants, some who died were black. The battle was fought before the Federal forces authorized enlistment of Negroes. They were, however, employed as teamsters, cooks, and laborers. The remaining earthworks are testimony to some of their labors.

*Wills House,* Center Square. Abraham Lincoln wrote the Gettysburg Address here, among other places, and the room has been preserved. There is also a collection of Lincolnia.

LAMOTT

*Site of Camp William Penn,* in LaMott Community Center grounds. The first eighty Negro recruits reported here for training on June 23, 1863, and were followed by thousands of others before the Civil War was brought to a close.

The men trained here fought and died in many of the major engagements of the war. They led the Union forces into Richmond, were present when General Robert E. Lee surrendered at Appomattox, and fought in the bloody battle at Olustee, Florida. In the drive on Richmond they helped establish the Negro as a superior soldier, winning high-level praise for their performance.

LANCASTER

*Thaddeus Stevens Grave,* Shreiner's Cemetery, Chestnut and Mulberry Streets. Pennsylvania Congressman Thaddeus Stevens was probably the most outspoken, tough-minded advocate of Negro rights during the Civil War. Along with Massachusetts Senator Charles Sumner, he waged a relentless campaign to force a change in the national attitude toward slavery and toward the course of the Reconstruction period after the war.

Stevens and a handful of others won legislation to forbid Union officers to return fugitive slaves to rebels, to emancipate District of Columbia slaves, to declare free the slaves of all rebels, and to give Lincoln discretionary power to use Negro troops. After the war, when Congress was debating what to do about the emancipated Negroes, Stevens urged that they each be given forty acres of land and treated as human beings.

Dissatisfied with President Andrew Johnson's attitude toward Reconstruction, Stevens led a drive to deprive him of control, and vested it in a congressional committee. The committee then put the South under military control and gave the vote to all males, regardless of color, which resulted in the election of many southern Negroes to high public office.

Stevens and Sumner prodded Congress to enact the 14th and 15th Amendments, and Stevens was one of the more vigorous advocates of the effort to impeach President Johnson. The attempt failed in May. Stevens died in August.

Even in death, Stevens did not abandon his cause. He selected this cemetery as his last resting place for reasons that are apparent in the words he wrote for the marker:

> I repose in this quiet and secluded spot,
> not from any natural preference for solitude,
> but finding other cemeteries
> limited by charter rules as to race,
> I have chosen this that I might illustrate in my
> death the principles which I advocated through a
> long life,
> Equality of Man before his Creator.

### NEW HOPE

*Washington Crossing State Park,* on State 32 south of the city. It was bitterly cold on Christmas Night 1776, when General Washington and twenty-four hundred men in boats crossed the ice-filled Delaware River. The maneuver led to victory over the British at Trenton and Princeton, New Jersey.

Among the many Negroes with Washington were Prince Whipple and Oliver Cromwell. Whipple was actually in Washington's own boat. Emanuel Leutze's noted painting of the crossing, owned by the Metropolitan Museum of Art in New York, hangs in the Memorial Amphitheater in this park.

### PHILADELPHIA

*The Academy of Music* is the home of the Philadelphia Symphony Orchestra, which has delighted lovers of good music the world over. Leopold Stokowski presented the first symphony based on Negro folk music here in 1934 when the orchestra played Symphony No. 1 by Negro conductor Levi Dawson.

The orchestra has also performed the works of William Grant Still, composer of a number of symphonies and the opera, *Troubled Island,* for which Negro poet Langston Hughes did the libretto. Among Still's successful musicals were *Running Wild* and *Dixie to Broadway.*

Born in Woodville, Mississippi, May 11, 1895, Still began his musical training in Little Rock, Arkansas, where his mother taught school. He later studied at Wilberforce University, Oberlin Conservatory of Music, and the New England Conservatory.

*Franklin Institute.* Benjamin Franklin is revered as Philadalphia's greatest citizen, and memorials to him are located throughout the city. In Memorial Hall here is a white marble statue of Franklin, done by Sculptor James Earle Fraser. It is the only permanent shrine in America honoring the great American.

Franklin was a slave owner in his youth, but had given up his slaves before the Revolution. He was prompted to do so by reading Quaker anti-slavery pamphlets that were brought to him for printing. His friendship with poet Phillis Wheatley and Anthony Benezet may also have crystallized his views. At any rate, Franklin became an active opponent of slavery, and in 1785 was elected president of the "Pennsylvania Society for Promoting the Abolition of Slavery and the Relief of Free Negroes Unlawfully held in Bondage."

His last public act, before his death in 1790, was the signing of a memorial to the first Congress urging the members "to countenance the restoration of liberty to those unhappy men, who alone, in this land of freedom are degraded into perpetual bondage."

Anthony Benezet, probably the leading Negro anti-slavery propagandist in the pre-Revolutionary period, apparently influenced Franklin greatly. Benezet founded a school for slaves in his home in 1770. On his death he left funds to establish a school for Negroes —Benezet House.

*Mother Bethel AME Church,* 419 South Sixth Street, founded in 1793, is the oldest African Methodist Episcopal Church. The land on which it stands has been owned continuously by Negroes longer than any other plot in the nation. The present church is the fourth on the site; the first was erected in 1794.

The AME church grew from the Free African Society, which was organized by Richard Allen and Absalom Jones after they had been jerked to their feet while praying in a white church, and ordered to the gallery.

Born a slave, Allen became a minister and circuit rider and was the denomination's first bishop. Throughout his life he was a leader of anti-slavery groups. In 1830 he led the first national Negro convention formally organized to oppose slavery.

The hazards of life as a free northern Negro in slavery times were demonstrated by one experience of Bishop Allen. Southern traders often came into the North, accused free Negroes of being fugitive slaves, and with the aid of corrupt magistrates carried them off to bondage. One trader had Allen arrested and swore in court that he had recently purchased him as a slave.

The trader was unaware that Allen, for more than twenty years, had been the most prominent Negro in Philadelphia. Countless citizens rushed to Allen's defense, and the trader was sentenced to jail for perjury. Many Negroes in the same situation, however, were less fortunate.

Allen is entombed in a basement vault at Mother Bethel. In a room adjoining the tomb is the pulpit used by Allen and Jones, and other memorabilia.

*Negro Soldiers Monument*, Lansdowne Drive, West Fairmount Park, was erected by the state in 1934 in memory of the Negro soldiers of Pennsylvania who fought in the nation's wars.

Pennsylvania became a haven for runaway slaves after 1780, when an act was passed providing that no child born in the state would be a slave. The Quaker influence in the abolitionist movement was also strong, and the Fugitive Slave Act was opposed by citizens and public officials alike.

As a consequence, when the city was threatened by the British in 1814, Bishop Richard Allen, James Forten, and Absalom Jones were able to rally a force of twenty-five hundred free Negroes to its defense. Forten served in the Revolutionary war, enlisting at fifteen as a powder boy aboard the Pennsylvania privateer *Royal Louis*. After the ship was captured, the British sent him to a floating prison, the *Jersey*, where he was imprisoned for seven months.

On his return to Philadelphia, Forten became a sail maker and one of Philadelphia's most influential Negroes. He amassed a fortune, much of which was devoted to abolitionist causes. Forten was one of the backers of the early anti-slavery societies, and one of the signers, in 1800, of a petition asking Congress to modify the Fugitive Slave Act of 1793. He loaned William Lloyd Garrison the money with which to found his abolitionist newspaper, *The Liberator,* and subsequently helped him out of numerous financial difficulties.

After his death, Forten's sons and daughters continued his work in the abolitionist cause. His granddaughter, Charlotte, taught in the first schools established for freed slaves in the Sea Islands off the Carolinas in 1862. She left a diary that is one of the best surviving descriptions of the life of the free Negro during and after the Civil War.

*The Pennsylvania Academy of the Fine Arts,* Broad and Cherry Streets, has several paintings by Negro artists, not all of which are on display at any one time.

The major work is "Nicodemus," painted by Henry Ossawa Tanner in the Holy Land. A native of Pittsburgh, Tanner received part of his education in the Academy schools. The collection also includes Horace Pippin's "John Brown Going to His Hanging." Pippin was born in West Chester in 1888.

*Philadelphia Museum of Art,* Benjamin Franklin Parkway and Twenty-sixth Street, has two paintings by Negro artist Horace Pippin: "The End of the War: Starting Home" and "A Chester County Art Critic," and Henry Ossawa Tanner's "The Annunciation."

## PITTSBURGH

*Avery College Marker* on East Ohio Street. Near here, at Nash and Avery Streets, stood Avery College. It was founded in 1849 by Charles Avery, a Methodist lay preacher, philanthropist, and abolitionist, to provide a classical education for Negroes. Avery provided three hundred thousand dollars to establish the school, which had an interracial faculty.

## VALLEY FORGE

*George Washington Carver Library* was established by the Freedoms Foundation at Valley Forge to bring together comprehensive information on the contribution of the Negro to American culture. Although the project is relatively new, the card index already contains the names of more than one thousand Negroes who have contributed significantly to the progress of America.

*Valley Forge State Park,* off Pennsylvania Turnpike on State 23 (Interchange 24). The hardships endured here during the winter of 1777–78 by the cold, ragged, and hungry men of the Continental Army earned for this campground a hallowed place in

American history. Many of the frozen fingers and shoeless feet were black, and so were many of the men who died.

One who met death here in 1778 was a Dutchess County, New York Negro named Phillip Field. He was a member of the 2nd New York Regiment. One of the great Negro heroes of the Revolution was also here during that bitter winter. He was Salem Poor, of Colonel Frye's Massachusetts Regiment, who fought at Bunker Hill and in many subsequent actions. He so distinguished himself that fourteen white Massachusetts officers petitioned the General Court of that state in his behalf.

The petition, dated December 5, 1775, said "that a Negro called Salem Poor . . . in the late battle at Charlestown, behaved like an experienced officer, as well as an excellent soldier." The officers said it would be tedious to supply the many details of Poor's courageous conduct, and concluded: "We only beg leave to say, in the person of this said Negro centers a brave and gallant soldier."

Adjoining the park is the Washington Memorial Chapel, and a museum maintained by the Valley Forge Historical Society.

*Washington's Headquarters* were here during part of the winter of 1777–78, in the home of Isaac Potts, son of the iron-master of the forge from which the area took its name. The house is now furnished with mementoes of his occupancy.

It was here that Washington first began to change his point of view regarding the arming of Negroes, including slaves. Following the initial hostilities of the Revolution, a controversy arose over the use of Negro soldiers. For a time, recruitment of Negroes was actually prohibited by law, but the commanders of many volunteer companies enlisted them in spite of it.

Washington vacillated considerably on the issue, but during the winter here he began to encourage greater use of Negroes, and they were eager to serve. An officer was sent to Rhode Island to urge the assembly to authorize the enlistment of Negroes, and that state promptly raised a regiment. Ultimately Negroes were recruited in all thirteen colonies. Some five thousand Negroes, both slave and free, served in the Continental Army by the end of the war. Most of them were integrated into predominately white units.

# RHODE ISLAND

COVENTRY

*General Nathanael Greene Homestead,* on Taft Avenue in the village of Anthony, was the home of Rhode Island's most famous soldier. He was one of Washington's most able generals, and second in command of the Revolutionary forces.

Greene's stature and influence helped persuade General Washington to arm slaves and free Negroes for service in the Revolutionary War. Although many individual Negroes served with volunteer companies from the outset, official approval for the enlistment of Negroes had not been given as late as 1781.

Greene maintained an unrelenting pressure on the government to permit Negroes to fight. His efforts, reinforced by the valorous performance of individual Negro soldiers, ultimately won formal status for Negro troops.

The general's Colonial-style home was completed in 1774. In 1919 a society was formed to restore it as a historic shrine. State birthday exercises and Constitution Day are observed here annually.

NEWPORT

*The Newport Jazz Festival* is held annually at Festival Field, during the weekend closest to the Fourth of July. During its fourteen-year history, the festival has featured most of the great names in jazz music, including many Negro artists.

During the festival the musicians perform, improvise, record, and even compose, as they did in 1960 when it was thought that the festival would be canceled because of rowdyism in the area.

That year the festival had scheduled a program by Negro poet Langston Hughes titled *The Blues.* When it was finally announced that the program was canceled, Hughes gave pianist Otis Spann a telegraph blank on which he had written some lyrics. Spann struck a chord and began singing "What a gloomy day at Newport." The song was recorded and released as "Goodbye Newport Blues."

Fortunately, the difficulties were only temporary, and the festival is still going strong. So many outstanding Negro performers have appeared here that a complete listing is out of the question, but the music lover can whet his appetite on these:

Louis Armstrong, Duke Ellington, William "Count" Basie, Nat "King" Cole, Billie Eckstine, Cootie Williams, Roy Eldridge, Dizzy Gillespie, John Lewis, Milt Jackson, Lester Young, Billie Holiday, Erroll Garner, Joe Turner, Art Farmer, Miles Davis, Max Roach, Mahalia Jackson, Ella Fitzgerald, Ray Charles, and Wes Montgomery.

*Old Colony House,* 155 North Main Street, was built in 1739 and served as the meeting place for the Rhode Island General Assembly until 1900. It has been designated a National Historic Site.

It was here that the first law prohibiting the importation of slaves was passed, on June 13, 1774. More than a century earlier, on May 18, 1650, Rhode Island became the first of the American colonies to pass a law regulating slavery. The action was taken by the General Court of Election at Warwick, but that body did not have a fixed meeting place and the site of this action is unknown.

PORTSMOUTH

*Battle of Rhode Island Monument* near West Main Road and the Portsmouth Expressway honors Rhode Island Negroes who played a historic role in this Revolutionary battle with the British on August 29, 1778.

In February 1778, the Rhode Island General Assembly voted to grant freedom to slaves who enlisted for service in the Continental Army. More than two hundred Negroes joined General Greene's 1st Regiment. They were among a four-thousand-man Colonial army which was organized to attack an equally strong British force at Newport.

The plan provided that the Colonials would receive support from a French force, but the French ships were scattered by a hurricane. Meanwhile, a British fleet was sailing to Newport in hopes of trapping the American army on Aquidneck Island.

The Americans withdrew during the night, and the next day established a defensive line across the island on high ground at Portsmouth. The pursuing British made three charges against the section of the line held by the 1st Regiment, probably expecting that the Negroes, with only three months' training, would yield. After some four hours of bitter fighting the Negroes still held, and the Colonial forces finally effected an orderly withdrawal across the Sakonnet River, only a day in advance of the arrival of the British fleet.

This was the only Revolutionary battle fought in Rhode Island, and one of only two in which Negroes participated as a unit. In other battles they were integrated into units with white troops.

*Overing House,* on Route 114 near the Middletown-Portsmouth town line, was the headquarters of British General Richard Prescott in July 1777 when he was captured by a small band of Colonial volunteers. Much remodeled, it is now a private home.

Among nearly forty Americans who slipped into the headquarters under cover of darkness was a Negro, Jack Sisson. The Americans disarmed the sentinel, located Prescott's bedroom, and captured him after Sisson broke down the door. They then spirited General Prescott away without firing a shot.

The daring capture of a high-ranking officer was a great boost for American morale. Sisson later became one of about two hundred Negroes to serve with the Rhode Island 1st Regiment in the Revolutionary War.

*Brick School House,* built in 1769, was originally used as a school and for town meetings. It was the temporary home of Brown University in 1770, then became a free public school. Prior to the Civil War it was used as a school for Negroes.

Many Rhode Island Negroes fought in the Civil War. The 14th Heavy Artillery Regiment began enlisting men in August 1863, and the first company was mustered in at Dexter Training Ground in Providence on August 28 of that year.

This regiment, which was all-Negro except for its officers, trained at Camp Bailey on Dutch Island in Narragansett Bay. Its eighteen hundred men left in the fall of 1863 from Providence for service at Plaquemine, Louisiana, where they participated in many skirmishes and guerrilla attacks.

# SOUTH CAROLINA

## BEAUFORT

*Smith House*, Bay Street, served as headquarters for General Isaac I. Stevens after his Union forces occupied Beaufort on December 11, 1861. They found the town virtually deserted, and most of the local structures were taken over for various uses as the town became the leave center for the men of the Federal Department of the South.

One of the great moments in American Negro history occurred here on January 19, 1863, when Colonel Thomas Wentworth Higginson brought his 1st South Carolina Volunteers to town for their first public parade. The use of the Negro unit was the first official experiment with the use of Negro troops that was to endure. A previous attempt by David Hunter had ended in failure through no fault of the Negroes involved.

Many of Higginson's men had been with Hunter, and they were determined that the new unit would succeed. They marched proudly in Beaufort, to the music of the 8th Maine Regiment's band. Higginson, aware that the performance of his men would be inspected with a critical eye by Negroes and whites from both North and South, had drilled his men with care, and they fulfilled his expectations. One of the men was later quoted by Higginson as saying, after the march, that every step "was worth a half a dollar."

The men of Higginson's regiment marched in many other places before the war ended. They also died in many of them, covering themselves with glory and providing an example that encouraged the widespread use of Negro troops during the remainder of the Civil War.

*Columbia Museum of Art.* Prominently displayed here is a bronze statue, by C. I. Weston, of the Reverend Charles Jaggers, who was perhaps the most respected Negro in the city's history.

What the minister lacked in education he made up in an over-whelming desire to help people less fortunate than himself. He founded Jaggers' Old Folks' Home, and raised money for its support. Almost invariably he preached from the text: "Let the same mind be in you that was also in Jesus Christ our Lord."

The respect he enjoyed in Columbia was demonstrated on the day of his funeral, when most of the business places closed their doors at noon in his honor. A modern housing development in Columbia was named Jaggers' Terrace in his memory.

## CHARLESTON

*Confederate Museum,* Market and Meeting Streets, has many articles related to the city's role in the Civil War. The city was a secession leader; the first shot of the war was fired at Fort Sumter.

Charleston was under siege for years, and finally fell in February 1865. Leading the Union troops into the city were the men of the 21st U. S. Colored Regiment, with the fabled 54th Massachusetts Regiment hard on their heels. The 54th deserved the honor, for they had their first taste of the siege of Charleston as early as July 1863. James C. Hewett, an Ohio Negro of Company K, described one encounter in a letter to his hometown editor:

"Wednesday morning we were ordered to go out on picket. The rebels kept up a constant hollering all day at us; the boys would occasionally retaliate. They [rebs] kept up a little firing all night, but not very steady.

"About daylight they attacked our whole picket line simultaneously. The 10th Connecticut, being a small regiment, and somewhat detached from the rest of the line, gave way almost immediately, firing but a few shots. Not so with the 54th Massachusetts; they stood their ground, and blazed away until almost surrounded.

"Company K was completely cut off from the rest, and surrounded by rebel regiments formed in a square.

"Finding ourselves in this dangerous condition, we only escaped by desperate fighting, with the loss of five killed, and six or eight wounded. Among the killed was Charlie Holloway, a student of the Wilberforce College. He was shot through the heart."

*County Courthouse,* Broad and Meeting Streets, has a marker noting that it was built on the site of the old State House built in 1752 and destroyed by fire in 1788.

It may have been here that the South Carolina legislature, in

March 1783, cited Antigua, a slave, for "procuring information of the enemy's movements and designs." Antigua had gone within the British lines, often at the risk of his life, and "always executed the commissions with which he was entrusted with diligence and fidelity." As a reward the legislature freed him, his wife Hagar, and their child.

During the Revolutionary War, many Negroes served as spies in support of the American cause.

*Fort Sumter National Monument,* on Sullivan's Island, was the site of the target of the first shot fired in the Civil War. It came from nearby Fort Johnson. Confederate batteries began a bombardment at 4:30 A.M., April 12, 1861, and after thirty-four hours the Sumter garrison surrendered.

A visit here offers the visitor an opportunity to fully appreciate a daring adventure by a Negro pilot, Robert Smalls, on May 13, 1862. Smalls was on board the Confederate steamboat *Planter,* the special dispatch boat of the Confederate port commander at Charleston. The boat was moored in the harbor, and its white officers were all ashore, although the boat was loaded with a cargo of guns and ammunition intended for Fort Ripley.

Smalls seized the opportunity; he and his men gathered their wives and children. At 3:15 A.M. they steamed out of the harbor under the guns of Forts Sumter and Johnson, deceiving the lookouts by imitating the captain, who was normally in command. Once out of the harbor they surrendered the boat to the Union fleet.

Smalls later was elected to Congress, and was much admired by his constituents. Legend has it that two of them got in an argument, with one maintaining that Smalls was a political genius. The second man responded that he didn't think Smalls was quite that good. "He isn't God," the man said. "Yes, that's true," replied Smalls' advocate, "but give him time. He's a young man yet."

*Old Slave Market,* 6 Chalmers Street, is at the site of a warehouse where slave auctions were held.

COLUMBIA

*Guignard House,* 1527 Senate Street. Few of the antebellum homes of Columbia survived the destruction wrought when Sherman's army took the city. If the legends are accurate, many of those that did were saved by Negro slaves. This one is said to be standing because the slave cook, Dilcie, supplied the best food in

Columbia to the Union officers who were quartered here. In gratitude, they did not burn it before departing. Another home said to
have been saved by its slaves was *Pinarea*, located on Lightwood
Creek, below the Falls.

*Old Slave Market*, State and Assembly Streets, is a
small brick building with high, barred windows where slaves were
auctioned by Samuel Mercer Logan. It stands at the rear of the
residence in which the slave merchant lived.

## SILVER BLUFF

*Silver Bluff Baptist Church*, sixteen miles south of
Augusta, Georgia, on the South Carolina side of the Savannah
River, was the first Negro Baptist church in the United States. The
church was organized in 1750 by a white congregation which admitted slaves as members. In 1783 the white members withdrew
and left the church to the Negro members, who outnumbered
them.

When the original site of the church was sold, the Negroes worshiped in goat houses and bush arbors for fifty years until they
were given the land on which the present church stands, in 1866.
The building was erected in that year. The church is now known
locally as the Dead River Baptist Church.

# SOUTH DAKOTA

## CHARLES MIX COUNTY

*Fort Randall*, on U. S. 18. During the Civil War this
was a major post for the troops of the Northwest Military Department. Later, from 1880–82, the 25th Infantry Regiment used the
fort as a base.

The 25th was one of two Negro infantry units that helped maintain law and order to permit settlement of the states west of the Mississippi.

## DEADWOOD

*Adams Memorial Museum.* Deadwood does its best to help tourists relive the days of the early West, although it isn't often, today, that anyone dies with his boots on. This museum has many relics, however, from the days when men did. It also has the original marker from the grave of the first woman, other than the Indians, to enter the Black Hills. She was a Negro. (See Galena.)

Mount Moriah Cemetery, Deadwood's "boot hill," has the graves of such legendary figures as "Wild Bill" Hickock and Calamity Jane.

Deadwood recalls three cowboys who claimed the title, "Deadwood Dick." Forgotten today is a fourth claimant, Nat Love, a Negro who wrote his autobiography at the turn of the century, describing his life in the pioneer West. He said he won the title with an exhibition of riding and marksmanship at the Deadwood Fourth of July celebration in 1876.

Negro soldiers from Fort Meade often visited here in the late 1870s, and at least one gambling house and dance hall was run by a Negro.

There were a number of Negroes in the area during the Gold Rush days. Some of them, like the group that mined at Tinton, found a lot of gold. Several topographical landmarks in the area are named for Negro miners who worked claims here. The Negroes left when the excitement died out, along with most of the other miners. By 1905 the census showed that only 166 Negroes were left in the entire state.

## FORT PIERRE

*Site of Fort Pierre Marker,* on State 514, north of U. S. 14, is all that remains at the site of this old fort, once an American Fur Company post, which was abandoned in 1857. The Negro, York, is mentioned in Lewis and Clark's account of their visit here.

## GALENA

*Aunt Sally Campbell's Grave.* More than fifteen hundred people lived in this mining camp soon after early prospectors found gold, silver, and lead in the surrounding hills. Today only six families remain in a town that once bustled with activity—often violent —and supported two churches and thirteen saloons.

One of the first to come was a Negro, Sarah Campbell, better known as "Aunt Sally" to her many friends. She visited the Black Hills with General Custer's expedition in 1874, as cook for one of the officers in the 7th Cavalry Division. Thus she earned the distinction of being the first woman, other than the Indians, to enter the Black Hills.

It is presumed that she returned to Fort Lincoln with Custer's men, who left her there when they went off to meet their destiny in the Battle of Little Big Horn. At some point Aunt Sally returned to the hills and settled in Galena, where she died in 1888.

Along with others in the Custer expedition, Aunt Sally staked out a gold mining claim in Custer County, but it was never worked. Members of the expedition recalled her as a highly respected woman whose frying pan was often invoked as a weapon when she was displeased with the behavior of one of Custer's troops.

Aunt Sally's grave is well marked in a neglected cemetery at Galena, which is so nearly inaccessible that it is best reached in a four-wheel-drive Jeep. Most of the graves are neglected, including that of a miner who was buried at a forty-five-degree angle so he could continue to look out over his beloved hills. One overturned tombstone bears the ironic epitaph, "Gone but not forgotten."

Aunt Sally's grave is the exception to this scene of general neglect. The old marker, now in the Deadwood museum, was replaced a few years ago by Seth Galvin, whom she cared for when he was a child. Fred Borsch, one of the few remaining lifelong residents of Galena, helped him put it up. Fred still looks in on Aunt Sally now and then.

## MARSHALL COUNTY

*Fort Sisseton,* in Fort Sisseton State Park on State 10, was originally known as Fort Wadsworth. It was renamed in 1876 for a local Indian tribe. The fort served as headquarters for the 25th Colored Infantry Regiment from 1885 to 1888.

## PINE RIDGE

*Holy Rosary Mission,* five miles from town on White Clay Creek, was the site of an engagement in which Corporal William O. Wilson of the 9th Cavalry became the last Negro to win the Congressional Medal of Honor during the Indian campaigns.

The Battle near the mission occurred on December 30, 1890, shortly after the tragic and probably needless slaughter in the Battle of Wounded Knee, in which Sioux Chief Big Foot lost his life. On that morning the troops stationed at Pine Ridge saw smoke rising from the mission, and eight companies of the 7th Cavalry rode out to investigate.

When they arrived at the mission they found one building in flames, and pursued the Indians, who withdrew as they approached. Soon the white troopers found themselves pinned down in a narrow valley, with Sioux warriors pouring bullets on them from the surrounding bluffs.

Back at Pine Ridge were four companies of the 9th Cavalry, who had arrived only two hours before, after marching one hundred miles in a single day. Alerted by the sounds of gunfire, the Negro cavalrymen dragged themselves back into their saddles. They arrived at the battle scene, appraised the situation, and divided their force to charge the Indians on either side of the valley. The Indians fled before their determined attack, and the embattled men of the 7th Cavalry were saved from probable disaster.

This was the last major action for the 9th Cavalry during the Indian wars. Before the end of January more than four thousand Indians had surrendered to the troops at Pine Ridge. On January 21, 1891, General Nelson A. Miles, commander of the Division of the Missouri, reviewed his troops at Pine Ridge. He gave the Negro "Buffalo Soldiers" a special salute as they passed by.

There are several historical markers at Pine Ridge and the mission.

WAKPALA

*Site of Aricara Village*, seven miles east. When Lewis and Clark visited here they found three villages of Aricara living in "a collection of conical lodges made of willow wattles covered with straw and five or six inches of mud, some of them fifty feet in diameter." Indians from all of the villages came to visit the expedition's camp.

The Aricara had seen white men before, for white traders had lived among them, but their curiosity was aroused by the presence of a black man, York. Clark recorded that York, apparently a born entertainer, "did not lose the opportunity of [exhibiting] his powers Strength &c. &c."

York told the Indians that he was actually a wild animal that

TENNESSEE || 187

Clark had captured and tamed. A powerful man, the Negro provided a few demonstrations of his strength, causing Clark to comment that he had "carried on the joke and made himself more turribul than we wished him to doe."

# TENNESSEE

### BRENTWOOD

*Hood's Retreat Marker* in a roadside park near Brentwood is the first of several on U. S. 31 marking Confederate General Hood's retreat to the south after his decisive defeat at Nashville. Among the Federal forces engaged in the pursuit and in numerous actions along the route were the 12th, 13th, and 14th Colored Infantry Regiments.

### CAMDEN

*Gunboats and Cavalry Marker* on U. S. 70 notes the destruction by Forrest's cavalry of the Federal base at Johnsonville Landing, 8½ miles east, on November 4, 1864. Dyer's *Compendium of the War of the Rebellion* describes the same action on the same date, involving the Federal 12th Colored Infantry Regiment, as the "repulse of Hood's attack on Johnsonville."

### CARTER COUNTY

*O'Brien Furnace*, on U. S. 19, east of Valley Forge. The contemporary image of the Negro slave is one of a household servant or a field hand picking cotton. Actually, Negroes worked at occupations of all sorts, many of them highly skilled. On the Doe River here are the ruins of an iron furnace built in 1820, which produced pig and bar iron, using slave labor to man the operation.

*Fort Donelson National Military Park*, U. S. 79, State 49. This Confederate fort was built with slave labor between May 1861 and January 1862, and was captured by Federal forces a month later in General Grant's first major victory of the Civil War. The battleground here is well marked, and many of the earthworks built by Negro labor for the Confederate defenders are still visible.

Negroes did not participate in this action as soldiers, although many were engaged in other capacities. Later in the war, Negro units were stationed here. Negro troops were also recruited here, bringing a complaint in December 1863 from a group of leading Kentuckians that they were losing too much slave property to Federal recruiting officers.

The national cemetery contains the graves of several Negro soldiers, known and unknown, who were brought here after their death at other locations in the area.

GREENEVILLE

*Andrew Johnson National Historic Site* preserves the home of the man who succeeded President Lincoln after his assassination. Like the first Negroes at Jamestown, Johnson was indentured to a tailor at the age of ten. He later entered politics and supported the interests of small farmers and working people against those of the wealthy slaveowners.

As a congressman Johnson avoided discussion of the slavery issue, but he opposed secession at the outset of the Civil War and was later appointed by Lincoln as military governor of Tennessee. As President, he antagonized members of Congress with his conduct of the Reconstruction, and an effort was made to impeach him. It failed by one vote to reach the two-thirds majority required.

Johnson was probably the most controversial of American Presidents. In retrospect, it appears that he made most of his enemies by carrying out the lenient Reconstruction practices already planned by Lincoln before his death, and by failing to establish a vigorous program for rehabilitation of the freed Negroes during the Reconstruction period.

HENNING

*Fort Pillow Marker*, on U. S. 51. Fort Pillow was captured by Federal forces in 1862 and retaken by the Confederates under General Nathan B. Forrest on April 12, 1864. The defending Federal force in the second engagement included 262 Negro and 295 white soldiers. Of these, 231 were killed and 100 seriously wounded.

The opposing commands disagreed on the reasons for the enormous casualties on the Union side. Southerners claimed that the defenders had simply refused to surrender to Forrest's superior force. The Federal Committee on the Conduct of the War reported that Forrest's men massacred wounded and captive Negro prisoners after the fort had been surrendered.

The site, which was eighteen miles west of here, has since surrendered again—to the Mississippi River—but the event lives on as the Fort Pillow Massacre.

## JACKSON

*Home of Casey Jones*, 211 West Chester Street. This is the house where John Luther Jones was living at the time of his death at the throttle of his engine, "Old 382," at Vaughan, Mississippi, April 30, 1900. His name was immortalized in a folk song, which almost everyone knows:

"All the switchmen knew by the engine's moans,
That the man at the throttle was Casey Jones."

What almost no one knows is that the song was written in the Illinois Central roundhouse here by a Negro engine wiper, Wallace Saunders.

There is also a Casey Jones marker at the gate of Calvary Cemetery, where the railroad hero is buried.

## MEMPHIS

*Fort Pickering Marker* on Crump Boulevard west of Pennsylvania Avenue. This is the site of one of many fortifications in the Federal defenses of the city during the Civil War. This one was manned by the 3rd Regiment of Colored Heavy Artillery, but many other Negro units were engaged here and elsewhere in the city. Confederate General Nathan B. Forrest, who led many actions against Negro units during the war, was born and is buried here, and both sites are marked.

*W. C. Handy Park*. A park and a heroic bronze statue overlooking the Beale Street he immortalized are Memphis' tribute to William Christopher Handy, "Father of the Blues." The statue was dedicated in 1960, climaxing a memorial campaign that started shortly after the Negro composer's death in 1958. The drive raised $52,000, most of it through public contribution.

Born in Florence, Alabama, Handy settled in Memphis and called it home throughout his life.

The statue, which shows Handy standing with horn poised, as if ready to play, was executed by Leone Tomassi of Florence, Italy.

*Tom Lee Memorial,* foot of Beale Street on the river-bank. This thirty-foot-high granite replica of the Washington Monument was erected in 1954 in memory of Tom Lee, a Negro who on May 8, 1925 saved thirty-two lives in an excursion boat disaster. The *M. E. Norman* capsized twenty miles below Memphis near Cow Island, dumping its passengers into the water. Lee had just passed the boat in a skiff. He turned back, and pulled thirty-two people out of the water, making four trips to shore.

Another thirty-three were lost, but it is likely that without Lee the loss would have been much higher.

In appreciation for his effort, a fund was raised to purchase a home for Lee, and the Memphis Engineers Club provided money for him as long as he lived. When he died in 1952, a memorial committee raised money to erect this monument.

*LeMoyne College.* Negro education in Memphis had a tragic early history. During the Civil War the American Missionary Association, in cooperation with the Freedman's Bureau, began an educational program for sixteen thousand Negro refugees who had come into the city. By 1866 there were nearly two thousand pupils enrolled in what was the beginning of a fairly good school system. Then a minor incident led to a riot during which four Negro churches and twelve Negro schools were burned. Not a school or church remained for use by Negroes.

The American Missionary Association began again, erecting a six-classroom building which opened in January 1867, for use as both school and church. Within two years, 2000 students were enrolled in a school that was designed to accommodate 150. The school had severe financial problems, and in 1871, through a gift from Dr. Francis J. LeMoyne of Washington, Pennsylvania, it was remodeled and reopened as LeMoyne Normal and Commercial School. The educational offerings have since been broadened to create a liberal arts college.

*Lorraine Hotel.* A plaque here marks the spot where Dr. Martin Luther King, emerging from room 306 on the second-floor balcony, was felled by an assassin's bullet. Dr. King, who was in Memphis to lead a protest in behalf of striking sanitation workers, was still alive when taken to St. Joseph's hospital. He died there, in the emergency room, at 7 P.M. on April 4, 1968.

Less than three months before, Dr. King talked about death to his congregation at the Ebenezer Baptist Church in Atlanta. He said he didn't want a long funeral, or a flowery eulogy, or a recitation of all of his honors and awards. Instead, he said:

"I'd like somebody to mention that day that Martin Luther King, Jr., tried to give his life serving others.

"I'd like somebody to say that day that Martin Luther King, Jr., tried to love somebody.

"I want you to say that day that I tried to be right and to walk with them. I want you to be able to say that day that I did try to feed the hungry. I want you to be able to say that day that I did try in my life to clothe the naked. I want you to say on that day that I did try in my life to visit those who were in prison. And I want you to say that I tried to love and serve humanity.

"Yes, if you want to, say that I was a drum major. Say that I was a drum major for justice. Say that I was a drum major for peace. I was a drum major for righteousness.

"And all of the other shallow things will not matter.

"I won't have any money to leave behind. I won't have the fine and luxurious things of life to leave behind. But I just want to leave a committee life behind.

"And that is all I want to say. If I can help somebody as I pass along, if I can cheer somebody with a well song. If I can show somebody he's traveling wrong, then my living will not be in vain.

"If I can do my duty as a Christian ought. If I can bring salvation to a world once wrought.

"If I can spread the message as the Master taught.

"Then my living will not be in vain."

MURFREESBORO

*Stones River National Cemetery* contains the graves of 182 Negro Union troops from the Civil War years, 101 of them unknown. The Battle of Stones River was fought too early in the war to have engaged any organized Negro units. Most of those buried here are from a later period, when the 111th Colored Infantry Regiment was stationed at Murfreesboro to guard the Nashville and Northwestern Railroad.

NASHVILLE

*Battle of Nashville.* Numerous markers throughout the city note events in this two-day battle between Hood's Confederate army and General George H. Thomas's Federal forces in December 1864.

In the attack on the Confederate positions on Overton Hill, a Negro brigade was supposed to divert Confederate attention from the main attack by white troops on their right. The assault by the white troops was repulsed, but the eager Negro recruits turned their feint into an assault that led to the capture of the hill.

In reporting the casualties, General Steedman observed that the severe loss of 468 men in the Negro regiments "was in their brilliant charge on the enemy's works on Overton Hill . . . I was unable to discover that color made any difference in the fighting of my troops. All, white and black, nobly did their duty as soldiers, and evinced cheerfulness and resolution such as I have never seen excelled in any campaign of the war in which I have borne a part."

*Fisk University.* Founded after the Civil War with aid from the Freedmen's Bureau, Fisk is an outstanding center of liberal arts education and a brilliant example of ingenious self-help. Jubilee Hall, on the campus, was built with part of the funds raised by the school's Jubilee Singers on tours throughout the United States and in Europe, where they charmed several royal audiences with their Negro spirituals and work songs. The group raised $150,000 in seven years to help support the institution.

In the library here are murals painted in 1929 by the outstanding Negro artist, Aaron Douglas. It was also here that James Weldon Johnson, author of such works as *God's Trombones*, became the first Negro poet to teach creative writing at a Negro university.

*Meharry Medical School.* As a young man, Samuel Meharry was befriended and given a night's lodging by a Negro slave in central Illinois. He resolved that when his fortunes permitted, he would do what he could to assist the Negro race. His opportunity came in 1866 when a Union Army corpsman, Dr. George W. Hubbard, with the aid of a Confederate Army surgeon, Dr. W. J. Snead, established medical classes at Central Tennessee College.

The Department of Medicine was formed with an initial gift of five hundred dollars from Sam Meharry. Later he persuaded his four brothers to join him in giving half of their combined assets to the school, and to continue supporting its development.

Throughout a century this medical college—built because of the kindness of one Negro slave—has graduated half of the Negro physicians and dentists in the United States.

# TEXAS

## AUSTIN

*Huston-Tillotson College.* Although it is a small school, this institution has educated many distinguished Negroes. It was formed in 1952 through a merger of Tillotson College, founded in 1877, and Samuel Huston College, founded in 1900. It is operated jointly by the Board of Education of the Methodist Church and the American Missionary Association of the United Church of Christ.

Its graduates include Bishop Price A. Taylor, a former president of the Council of Bishops of the Methodist Church; Dr. James P. Brawley, an outstanding Methodist layman who served as dean and as president of Clark College, Atlanta, Georgia; Dr. Herman A. Barnett, the first Negro to receive a degree from the University of Texas Medical Branch; Dr. Ernest T. Dixon, president of Philander Smith College; Dr. Ray F. Wilson, professor of chemistry at Texas Southern University, who was the first Negro to receive a Ph.D. at the University of Texas; and Dr. Spencer C. Dickerson, Chicago physician who served as a brigadier general in the Illinois National Guard.

*State Capitol.* Sam Houston tried to block secession efforts at a convention held here January 28, 1861. He failed, and was removed from the post of governor. The position of Texas as a slave-holding state probably was instrumental in the decision. During the previous year the assessed value of slave property in the state was sixty-four million dollars.

On June 19, 1865, Major General Gordon Granger declared that all the slaves in the state were free. So much resistance developed that martial law was maintained until 1869. Granger's Emancipation Act unwittingly created an annual holiday for Texas Negroes. They call it "Juneteenth," and still celebrate it as their own Independence Day.

BAY CITY

*"Shanghai" Pierce Grave,* in Hawley's Cemetery, off State 35, five miles southwest of Bay City. Buried here is Abel (Shanghai) Pierce, one of the great early Texas cattle kings who is credited with planning the introduction of Indian Brahma cattle into Texas, to develop a hardier breed.

Pierce started in the cattle business in 1853 as a bronc buster for another cattleman, Bradford Grimes. Grimes owned a number of Negroes who worked as cowboys on his ranch, but he also employed white hands like Pierce at a salary of fifteen dollars a month.

The story is told that shortly after Pierce was hired, he and Grimes were at the corral watching one of the Negro cowhands who was breaking an exceptionally vicious mount. Mrs. Grimes observed the process from the ranchhouse and finally shouted instructions to her husband to "have Pierce ride the bad horses." The Negro cowboys, she reminded him, were worth a thousand dollars apiece.

Negro cowboys, some slave and some free, rode for the men who operated all of the big Texas ranches. Often they were the most valued riders, and the most trusted, yet they rarely were promoted to foremen's jobs. Some of the Negro cowboys, of course, were less competent than others. It was the failure of one of these to brand the calves of his employer, Samuel A. Maverick, on a ranch near here, that led to the use of the term "maverick" to describe unbranded cattle.

BELTON

*Site of Fort Griffin,* five miles southeast on FM 436. Only the outlines of crumbling ruins and a handful of villagers remain at the site of this frontier fort that once bustled with activity.

Located on one of the main cattle trails, the fort was the headquarters for Negro cattlemen and Negro cowboys. The plains surrounding it were once the home of huge herds of buffalo, and some fifteen hundred buffalo hunters once centered here. It is said that the hides of the beasts they slaughtered, and almost made extinct, were once stacked over acres of ground.

The buffalo were huge, stupid, unpredictable, and often ferocious. The town once marveled at a fearless Negro cowboy named Emanuel Jones, who rode into a herd of buffalo and roped two of them.

## BROWNSVILLE

*Fort Brown,* southeast end of Elizabeth Street, is now occupied by Texas Southmost College and a community center. It was once a base for many Negro units who were ordered to Civil War duty in Texas in 1864 and 1865. Later, during the Indian wars, it was frequently an operating headquarters for Negro soldiers of the 24th Infantry Regiment.

*Palmito Hill Marker,* fourteen miles east on State 4. The last engagement of the Civil War was fought here on May 13, 1865, more than a month after Lee's surrender at Appomattox. Lieutenant Colonel David Branson led two white Federal infantry regiments and the 62nd U. S. Colored Troops against a Confederate force under Colonel John Ford.

The two commanders had different versions of the battle. Ford maintained that when the Federals tried to ambush him, he attacked and they broke ranks and fled. "Some of them Yankees could outrun our horses," he said. Branson argued that the attack was under way when he got word of Lee's surrender, and that he retreated while trying to inform Ford that the war was over.

If Ford's account is correct, it is probably the only case in history when an army lost a war and then won a battle. Apparently the dispute wasn't very bitter, because a few days later Branson and Ford had their pictures taken together in Brownsville.

## EL PASO

*Fort Bliss,* northeastern end of Pershing Drive. The 10th Cavalry Regiment was stationed here during part of the Indian wars.

One member of the 10th, Private Fitz Lee, was hospitalized here after the Spanish-American War, and received the Medal of Honor for heroism in Cuba. Curiously, the Negro horseman won the medal by rowing a boat.

Lee was aboard the *Florida* when, after three previous attempts had failed, he and three other Negroes rowed ashore in the dark to attempt the rescue of a landing party. Under constant fire, they reached the shore, located the survivors of the party, and returned them safely to the ship.

The Fort Bliss Replica Museum, in South Fort Bliss at Sheridan and Pleasanton Roads, has numerous exhibits related to the U. S. Cavalry, including the evolution of weapons between 1848 and 1948.

FANNIN

*Fannin Battlefield State Park* contains the site at which Colonel James W. Fannin and his band of Texans and volunteers were overtaken during their retreat from the La Bahia Presidio at Goliad.

Fannin had been ordered by General Sam Houston to abandon Goliad, but failed to do so until Mexican forces under General José Urrea were approaching to attack. Fannin's outnumbered army was overtaken in the open. They hastily erected a defense of wagons and equipment, but soon were compelled to surrender on what they thought were honorable terms. The survivors, including Colonel Fannin, who was wounded, were taken back to Goliad and imprisoned.

Many of the men were newly arrived volunteers from other states, and some were Negro. Texas Supreme Court records reveal that at least one Negro fought with Fannin. He was Peter Allen, who emigrated from Pennsylvania to Alabama in 1835 and there enlisted in a volunteer company that went to Texas. His heirs subsequently obtained the bounty and headright to which he was entitled for his military service.

The Fannin Battlefield Museum has relics recovered from the battleground.

FORT DAVIS

*Fort Davis National Historic Site*, one mile northeast on State 17, was another headquarters for Negro cavalrymen during the Indian wars. Some of the old buildings, built of stone and adobe, still stand in a curve of red rock cliffs.

The endurance of the Indian fighters was remarkable. Lieutenant Henry O. Flipper, the first Negro graduate of West Point, was ordered here in 1880, to campaign against Chief Victorio and the Mescalero Apache. He and his 10th Cavalry unit came from Fort Sill, Oklahoma. What contemporary soldier would feel much like fighting Indians after riding twelve hundred miles on the back of a horse?

A historical museum on the grounds, housed in the reconstructed 1854 barracks, contains artifacts, photographs, and military records of the period between 1854–91 when Negro "Buffalo Soldiers" and other U.S. troops served here.

## FORT MCKAVETT

*Fort McKavett.* Sergeant Emanuel Stance, the first Negro Indian fighter to win the Medal of Honor, was a member of the 9th Cavalry here. On May 20, 1870, on a routine patrol, Stance was the hero of an action in which his unit routed a band of Indians who were stealing government horses. The townspeople are now housed in the old fort buildings.

## GOLIAD

*Goliad State Park,* one mile south on U. S. 183, contains the Presidio Nuestra Senora de Loreto de La Bahia. Fannin's men left this fort in a futile effort to relieve the defenders of the Alamo, returned to it, and then retreated only to be overtaken and killed or captured by Urrea's Mexican army. Urrea brought the prisoners back to Goliad.

On March 27, 1836, those prisoners who could walk were marched from the Presidio in three columns, and about a mile away were shot down by their guards. Fannin, too badly wounded to walk, was taken into the courtyard and shot through the back of the head. More than 330 men were killed, stripped, heaped together, and their bodies partly burned. Two months later they were buried in a single grave, over which the Goliad Memorial shaft now stands.

How many of the men were Negroes is not known, but official records reveal that a Negro volunteer from Alabama, Peter Allen, fought here.

Goliad State Museum here is devoted to the Texas Revolutionary War.

## HOUSTON

*NASA Manned Space Flight Center* is the headquarters for the nation's astronauts, and the command center which will control Americans' first trip to the moon.

The first Negro astronaut was Air Force Major Robert H. Lawrence, of Chicago. An honor student at Englewood High School, Lawrence graduated from Bradley University and received a doctor's degree in physical chemistry at Ohio State University. His announced ambition, in his high school yearbook in 1952, was "to be useful to mankind," but his career was ended in the crash of a fighter aircraft in December 1967.

*Texas Southern University* is one of the newer Negro colleges. Funds for the first building were raised in a door-to-door and school-to-school campaign in the Houston Negro community in 1947. The college has grown rapidly in the past ten years, adding new dormitories, science, library, gymnasium and field house, business school and humanities buildings.

On display here are murals by John Biggers, whose paintings specialized in "social realism," and some surrealism as well. Other Biggers murals are in the Eliza Johnson Home for Aged Negroes in Houston.

## JACKSBORO

*Old Fort Richardson*, one mile south, off U. S. 281, was one of the more elaborate of the frontier posts at which the Negro "Buffalo Soldiers" served. There were about forty limestone buildings at the fort, which was abandoned by the government in 1878. Some have been repaired and are in use. A museum is housed in the old hospital quarters, built in 1867.

## LAREDO

*Site of Fort McIntosh,* west end of Victoria Street. Union soldiers abandoned this fort in 1861, attempted to retake it in 1863, and finally reoccupied it after the Civil War, on October 23, 1865.

Many of the units that reoccupied the fort were Negro. While they operated from here, fighting minor engagements, they found time to plan their future and that of their race. Sitting around a campfire, members of the 62nd Colored Infantry Regiment, originally the 1st Missouri, conceived the idea of a college for Negroes.

When the Negro soldiers returned to Missouri after the war, their dream became a reality: Lincoln University was established with funds that they had saved from their meager military pay.

## PRAIRIE VIEW

*Prairie View A & M College* was established with a legislative appropriation of twenty thousand dollars, and began operations in an old plantation house on March 11, 1878. It had a president, one professor, eight students, a handyman, and a cook.

In 1879 the program was reoriented toward teacher training and, after a number of stormy years, the school began to grow. Today the enrollment exceeds four thousand students.

## SAN ANGELO

*Fort Concho Museum*, 716 Burges Street, is at a fort once garrisoned by the 10th Cavalry Regiment, but closed in 1889. Unlike many of the other old frontier forts, this one is largely in good condition. The museum, which exhibits pioneer relics, is in the old officers' quarters. The fort is a National Historic Site.

San Angelo grew up around the Army post, and was a wild town in the pioneer days. It was on the California Trail and also on the Goodnight-Loving Cattle Trail. This trail, which led to New Mexico and later to Colorado and Wyoming, was opened in 1866 by Charles Goodnight and Oliver Loving. Many Negro cowboys drove longhorn cattle over this trail. The best of them was a Mississippi exslave named Bose Ikard.

Goodnight and Ikard became almost inseparable companions. The cattleman once said of the Negro cowboy, "I have trusted him farther than any living man. He was my detective, banker, and everything else in Colorado, New Mexico, and the other wild country I was in."

Ikard died shortly before Goodnight's own death in 1929. His former boss erected a marker on his grave with this inscription:

BOSE IKARD

Served with me four years on the Goodnight-Loving Trail, never shirked a duty or disobeyed an order, rode with me in many stampedes, participated in three engagements with Comanches, splendid behavior.

C. Goodnight.

## SAN ANTONIO

*The Alamo*, Alamo Plaza. More legend than fact survives about the events leading to the fall of the Alamo before the brutal assault of Mexican General Santa Anna's superior forces.

There were few American survivors of the bloody encounter, and historians are still trying to unravel the events.

It appears that there were at least three Negroes present when the Alamo fell. One was Colonel W. B. Travis' manservant, identified both as Joe and as Jethro. Another was an aide to Colonel Jim Bowie, named Ham. Also present, according to some sources, was a Negro child who, along with the widow of Lieutenant Dickerson, and her daughter, was spared by Santa Anna after the fight. At least one Negro is supposed to have been with the Mexicans—Colonel Almonte's orderly, Ben.

One of the best accounts of the last hours of the heroic defenders of the Alamo came from Joe, who was interviewed by General Sam Houston shortly after the battle. He recalled that the Mexicans "poured over the walls like sheep." Joe emptied his pistol and then turned to see what had happened to his master. Travis had been shot through the head, but he had drawn his sword. As the first Mexican officer came over the wall and charged toward him, Travis ran him through with the sword and then fell dead.

The young Negro, Ham, reportedly was with Bowie, who was lying ill with fever when the Mexicans stormed into his quarters. Bowie killed two before bayonets ripped into his body. Mrs. Dickerson later reported that Bowie's lifeless form was tossed on the bayonets of several soldiers before it finally fell to the floor.

Joe was released by Santa Anna and carried the news of the battle to the Texas forces, which is probably what Santa Anna wanted him to do. There is some evidence that he was re-enslaved soon after. A year later, a newspaper ad offered a reward for a runaway slave named Joe, who had survived the Alamo. He was also accused of stealing a horse on which to make his escape. There is no record to indicate that either Joe, or the horse, was ever found.

# UTAH

DUCHESNE

*Fort Duchesne.* A monument here recalls the men of the 9th Cavalry Regiment who built this fort in 1886 and used it for the protection of settlers throughout the Indian wars. The marker reads:

August 20, 1886, two companies of colored infantry commanded by Major F. W. Benteen and four companies of infantry under Captain Duncan arrived at this site to control the activities of Indians. There were three bands of Utes—Uncompahgres, White-rivers and Uintahs. The troops hauled logs from nearby canyons, built living quarters, commissary, storehouses and hospital, thereby establishing Fort Duchesne. Abandoned in 1912, now headquarters for the Uintah Reservation.

## FORT DOUGLAS

*Old Fort Douglas* was the home of the 24th Infantry Regiment. The survivors of this Negro unit returned to it after serving with distinction in Cuba during the Spanish-American War.

These were the men who swept up San Juan Hill past the faltering 71st New York Regiment, and, along with the Negro cavalry, helped save the day for Teddy Roosevelt.

One of their officers later wrote: "They went out just like it was target practice. They never knew before what it was to be fired at, but they went along, not looking to the right or left as their comrades fell dead at their feet."

When San Juan Hill was taken it was the men of the 24th who first occupied the trenches. Subsequently, they were sent to serve as nurses in the yellow fever hospital at Siboney, where they saw more men die—including their own—than in battle. When they returned to the United States, they could scarcely walk.

Despite their weakness, they participated in a huge welcome in New York. Said one of the 24th's noncommissioned officers of the event: "The men were scarcely able to stand but the band managed to play, though it sounded rather feeble, and we marched somehow. The cheer that went up along the streets made us feel like new men and we shouldered our guns and marched along and felt better than we had in weeks, and I tell you I was sorry for the poor fellow who missed that day. It was worth all the suffering."

## PAROWAN

*Pioneer Rock Church* was built by the pioneer Mormon party that came here in 1851. Most of the Mormon families freed or sold their slaves before coming west, but frequently the slaves were also Mormons and chose to make the trip with them. One pioneer Negro here was John, who came with the Robinson family and played a large role in building this church.

### SALT LAKE CITY

*Brigham Young Monument,* Main and South Temple Streets. The names of the original party of Mormon pioneers who arrived in the Valley of the Great Salt Lake in 1847 are inscribed on this monument. Among them were three Negroes who went on ahead of the families by whom they were employed to establish a place for them.

One of the Negroes, Oscar Crosby, was a servant in the home of William Crosby before the party left for the West. On his arrival in the valley he selected a piece of land and had the first crops growing when the family arrived during the following year.

At least two Negroes died on the rigorous winter trip west. One, Henry, was the servant of John Brown, and the other, his name unknown, was employed by John Bankhead. Both died of "winter fever."

*Mount Olivet Cemetery,* 1342 East Fifth Street. Buried here are several Negro veterans of the Civil, Indian, and Spanish-American Wars.

One of them, Sergeant Thornton Jackson, served in both the 10th Cavalry and the 24th Infantry Regiments. He served from 1880 to 1906, fighting in the Indian wars, Cuba, and the Philippines.

Second Lieutenant Calvin B. Potter, one of the few Negroes commissioned in the Civil War, was with the 45th Colored Infantry Regiment, which battled Robert E. Lee until his surrender at Appomattox.

*Salt Lake City Cemetery* contains the grave of Elijah Abel, the only Negro known to have been ordained in the priesthood of the Church of Jesus Christ of Latter-Day Saints. Abel was an undertaker in Nauvoo, Illinois, before his conversion to Mormonism. He came to Salt Lake City with the pioneers and operated the Farnham Hotel here. He was active in the church, and died in 1884 of an illness arising from exposure during a missionary trip to Canada and Ohio.

Also buried here are Jane Manning James and her brother, Isaac Lewis Manning, two Negroes who were employed by Prophet Joseph Smith in Nauvoo, and later came to the Salt Lake Valley.

When Smith and his brother Hyrum were martyred in the Carthage, Illinois jail, Manning dug the graves in which they were buried at Nauvoo. Fearing that the bodies might be molested, he dug two graves on the riverbank, in which empty coffins were placed. The burial was actually made in two other graves which he dug in the cellar of Joseph Smith's home.

*"This is the Place" Monument*, at mouth of Emigration Canyon. This monument was erected in Utah's Centennial year in honor of the first party of Mormon pioneers. Here, also, are inscribed the names of three Negroes, Green Flake, Hark Lay, and Oscar Crosby. Hark Lay was born a slave, came to Utah in advance of the William Lay family, and eventually went on to California. He had an excellent voice, and was a favorite of Brigham Young's children.

Ultimately, many Negroes accompanied the Mormon parties on their westward journeys. For example, the Mississippi company in 1848 included fifty-seven white members and thirty-four Negroes.

Some of the Negroes were slaves; others were free. In the case of the former, the Negroes were often the most valuable property a family had. Mormon pioneer John Brown, for example, listed in his autobiography an inventory of a gift made to the church. It included real estate valued at $775, a long list of livestock, farm equipment, tools, and household articles, and one "African Servant Girl" valued at one thousand dollars. The value of the slave constituted one-third of the value of the gift.

## UNION

*Union Cemetery* contains the grave of Green Flake, a member of the first company of pioneers, who arrived in 1847.

Green Flake was born on the North Carolina plantation of John Flake, and accompanied the family to the Mormon winter quarters at Nauvoo, Illinois. He was one of a party of men who went on ahead of the main party, and when the Flake family arrived in Utah in October 1848, Green Flake had a log cabin built and waiting for them.

# VERMONT

**BENNINGTON**

*First Congregational Church.* The Reverend Lemuel Haynes, the first Negro minister in Vermont and one of the first in the nation, once preached here to a white congregation.

Haynes was among those who answered Paul Revere's call at Lexington and Concord. He also marched with Ethan Allen's Green Mountain Boys to Ticonderoga during the Revolutionary War. Between 1787 and 1833 he preached and held permanent pastorates in many Vermont towns, including Clarendon, Dorset, Manchester, Pawlet, Rutland, Tinmouth, and Bennington. He was born in West Hartford, Connecticut and died in Granville, New York.

American churches have long been sending white missionaries to black Africa, but in this case the concern of pious people in Connecticut and Massachusetts led to the sending of a black missionary to white Vermont. Haynes was readily accepted in Vermont, and his great eloquence as a pulpit orator was much appreciated. A prominent New York clergyman who once met him commented that "His very colour . . . associated as it was . . . with his high qualifications to entertain and instruct, became the means of increasing his celebrity and enlarging the sphere of his influence."

It is said that when Haynes preached in Torrington to a predominantly white congregation one parishioner was so unhappy about the appointment of a Negro that he wore his hat during Haynes' first sermon. "He had not preached far," said the man later, "when I thought I saw the whitest man I ever knew in the pulpit, and I tossed my hat under the pew."

Services are still held in the old church every Sunday at eleven o'clock.

*Bennington Battle Monument,* on the Old Bennington Village Green, honors those who died in the Revolutionary battle fought here on August 16, 1777. Negro soldiers participated on both sides, each hoping their services would lead to freedom. A mural by Leroy Williams, in the Bennington Museum, shows a Negro among the British prisoners captured in the American victory here.

*Bennington Museum,* in Old Bennington on West Main Street, has many items related to Vermont history. Among them are copies of William Lloyd Garrison's newspapers, *The Liberator* and *The Journal of the Times.* The library also owns a mural of Lemuel Haynes preaching in the pulpit of Old First Church. It is a striking scene, painted by the late William Tefft Schwartz of Arlington, Vermont.

*Dinah Mattis Emancipation.* In September 1777, when the British retreated from Ticonderoga, a force under Major Ebenezer Allen captured about forty of their rear guard. Among the prisoners taken were a Negro slave, Dinah Mattis, and her child.

Ebenezer Allen, one of Ethan Allen's Green Mountain Boys, was a determined foe of slavery, perhaps because he had fought alongside a number of Negroes. He took time out from fighting the British to draw up a written certificate of emancipation for the young woman, and had it recorded in the Bennington town clerk's office. Allen's document, which declared that "it is not conscientious in the sight of God to keep slaves," may still be seen there.

*Garrison Marker,* on Old Bennington Common, is located fifty feet west of the spot where the famous abolitionist editor, William Lloyd Garrison, founded his first newspaper, *The Journal of the Times.* Garrison was later persuaded by Benjamin Lundy, an itinerant anti-slavery editor, to go to Boston. There he founded *The Liberator,* an abolitionist newspaper.

EAST HUBBARDTOWN

*The Hubbardtown Battlefield and Museum.* In July 1877 Burgoyne's Army of British and Hessians pursued the main American army on its flight from Ticonderoga.

The Green Mountain Boys, along with Colonial troops from Massachusetts and New Hampshire, were detached here to hold back the pursuers. They fought the only major battle on Vermont soil during the American Revolution. It was also one of the most successful rear-guard actions in American military history. Burgoyne's forces, having had enough of the rugged Negro and white Colonial soldiers, finally abandoned their pursuit and limped back to Ticonderoga.

The State Board of Historic Sites operates a museum here which includes an animated relief map that reconstructs in miniature the important movements in the battle.

FERRISBURG

"*Rokeby*," the home of Rowland E. Robinson, blind writer of Vermont folklore, was an underground railroad station prior to the Civil War.

WINDSOR

*Site of Constitution House*, on U. S. 5. It was here that Vermont was named and her constitution adopted. It was, in 1777, the first such document to abolish slavery and adopt universal male suffrage without regard to property. The precedent was followed in varying degrees by other New England states which also became strongholds of abolitionist sentiment. The building has been restored by the state as a historic site.

# VIRGINIA

ALEXANDRIA

*Mount Vernon*, south on U. S. 1. George Washington's plantation has been restored and is maintained as a historic site. Thousands of visitors of all races and nationalities visit it each year, and observe firsthand a classic example of the slave-based economy of the Colonial South. The Georgian Colonial mansion is flanked by outbuildings that quartered slaves, and provided services that made the plantation virtually self-sufficient. The buildings include a kitchen, smokehouse, dairy, greenhouse, spinning house, coach house, barn, and stables. The mansion stands on a hill overlooking the Potomac. The first President and Martha, his wife, are buried in an ivy-covered mausoleum on its slope.

Although Washington held slaves throughout his life, and enjoyed the comfort and affluence that their labors provided, his reservations about the practice were revealed in 1799, the year of his death, in these words: ". . . it is my will and my desire that all the slaves I hold in my own right, shall receive their freedom." More than half a century passed before the conscience of the nation he helped establish ended slavery for all Negro Americans.

## APPOMATTOX

*Appomattox Courthouse National Historical Park.* Here, his troops weary, hungry, and pressed by vastly superior Union forces, General Robert E. Lee surrendered to General Grant on April 9, 1865. Among Lee's pursuers was the all-Negro XXV Corps under General Godfrey Weitzel. Weitzel had opposed the arming of Negroes in 1862, but in 1865 commanded a crack Negro unit that had long before proved itself in battle.

## ARLINGTON

*Arlington National Cemetery.* Here lie the honored dead, white and black, of all the nation's wars. The hourly changing of the guard at the Tomb of the Unknowns is one of the most solemnly impressive military ceremonies. The tomb contains remains representative of the unknown dead from World Wars I and II and the Korean conflict.

After it was approved by Congress on Memorial Day in 1921, four unknowns were taken from the four American cemeteries in France. In a ceremony at Chalons-sur-Marne, halfway between Chateau Thierry and St. Mihiel, one was selected and brought to the United States on the cruiser *Olympia*. His name is not known, nor is his color, but he, and the World War II and Korean conflict unknowns placed beside him, are symbolic of the heroes of all races who have served and died in all of the nation's wars and are "known but to God."

## CHARLOTTESVILLE

*Monticello,* the home of President Thomas Jefferson, was designed by him and contains countless examples of his innovative architectural ingenuity. The red brick house with snow-white trim has a fine Roman Doric portico, and is a superb example of Classical Revival design. Many of Jefferson's inventions are housed in the mansion.

Like most ante-bellum mansions of the South, Monticello was largely the product of slave artisans. Life within the mansions was also strongly influenced by the presence of talented slaves. Plantation owners vied with each other in elaborately outfitting their household servants and training them to serve with grace and dignity. Negroes were often encouraged to develop their musical gifts, and many did. When Lafayette visited Monticello in 1825 he was entertained by Robert Scott, a free Negro of Charlottesville, his wife and three sons, all of whom were accomplished musicians.

Although a slave-holder himself, Jefferson was opposed to slavery. His solution was similar to that later considered by Lincoln, that slavery should be ended and colonies established elsewhere for the freed slaves. As architect of the Declaration of Independence, Jefferson had included a clause which indicted the King of England for his role in the promotion of slavery, but it was removed in deference to other signers from slave-holding states who were less troubled by conscience over the slavery question.

Jefferson himself was still troubled over the problem when he died on July 4, 1826. He was carried to his grave here on the plantation by a group of weeping slaves.

*Nat Turner Insurrection.* This town was called Jerusalem in August 1831, when Nat Turner and a band of armed slaves marched on it in a bloody and desperate bid for freedom. Before they were subdued by hundreds of armed troops, Turner and his followers killed every white person in their path, except those who owned no slaves.

Although the rebellion was short-lived, at least fifty-seven white persons died, and countless Negroes were killed in retaliation. Nineteen Negroes were hanged. Turner eluded capture for two months, but finally was captured, taken to Jerusalem in chains, tried, and hanged.

The Turner rebellion was only one of at least 250 similar revolts that have been cataloged by historians—dispelling the myth of the slave as a smiling, contented, and obsequious "Mammy" or "Uncle Tom."

#### FORTRESS MONROE

*Fort Monroe,* on Route 143 near U. S. 60 and Interstate 64 at Old Point Comfort, was one of the few southern military installations not seized by the Confederacy at the outset of the Civil

War. It became a haven for runaway slaves, called "contraband," who sought freedom among the Union troops.

Initially, because of Union policy against use of Negro troops, many of the able-bodied Negroes were impressed for use as laborers in the Quartermaster Corps, mostly to build roads and fortifications, often under fire. However, after initial experiments at arming Negro units demonstrated their valor, the North began actively recruiting Negro soldiers.

McClellan and Grant both headquartered here. Lincoln came in May 1862 to help plan operations against Norfolk and those that resulted in the destruction of the ironclad, *Merrimack*, by her own crew. The Army of the James, in which many Negro units fought in the campaigns leading to the fall of Richmond and other cities, was organized here.

The room where Confederate President Jefferson Davis was imprisoned from 1865 to 1867 is now a picture gallery depicting events in his life. The fort was built in 1819 and named for President James Monroe.

## FREDERICKSBURG

*Fredericksburg and Spotsylvania National Military Park.* Here, General Ulysses S. Grant, as Commander of all Federal forces, engaged Robert E. Lee's Army of Northern Virginia. In the engagements in the Wilderness and around Spotsylvania Courthouse the Union forces, including the Negro infantry brigades of General Ferrero's Division of the Federal IX Corps, won the victories that began the final drive toward Union victory in the Civil War.

*The John Paul Jones House.* This house was owned by the Revolutionary naval hero's brother, William Paul, but it was the only home John Paul Jones ever knew. He first came here from his native Scotland at the age of twelve, when he was apprenticed to a shipmaster. Subsequently he became a ship's officer on slavers and finally master of his own ship. When he killed the ringleader in a mutiny he fled to his brother's home rather than face trial in England, and added the Jones to his real name of John Paul to conceal his identity.

Jones was a brilliant seaman, and is regarded as the father of the American Navy. Crew lists reveal that many Negroes served under him, and on the vessels of his fleet. Cato Carlile and Scipio Africanus enlisted in his service in 1777, and the ship's log of the *Ranger* reveals that Cesar Hodgsdon, a Negro, died on board on February

25, 1780. During both the Revolutionary and Civil Wars many Negroes served as pilots on the East Coast.

*The Slave Block,* Charles and William Streets, is a raised, circular, sandstone platform from which slaves were auctioned before the Civil War. The magnitude of the slave trade was substantial. In 1790 there were less than seven hundred thousand slaves; in 1830 there were more than two million, and the census taken immediately before the Civil War recorded nearly four million of them.

GREAT BRIDGE

*Battle of Great Bridge.* On December 9, 1775, about seven hundred Colonial regulars defeated a force of British regulars, Loyalists, and Negroes under the governor, Lord Dunsmore. Dunsmore lured many Negro slaves to the British ranks with promises of freedom in exchange for loyalty to the British cause. Most Negroes preferred to fight for freedom on the American side, although their services were reluctantly used, and victory did not give most Negroes the freedom they had fought to win.

The hero of the engagement was a free Negro who fought on the Colonial side, William Flora. As the British advanced on the bridge across the Elizabeth River, about twelve miles south of Norfolk, he was the last sentinel to leave his post. An account of the battle says that Flora finally moved back "amidst a shower of musket balls," meanwhile returning the fire eight times. A Negro slave, who slipped into the British lines and persuaded the British that the bridge was lightly manned, is given partial credit for the American victory.

Dunsmore's defeat on this occasion caused him to vacate Norfolk and retreat with his men to British vessels in the harbor.

HAMPTON

*Emancipation Oak Marker,* on U. S. 60 near the entrance to Hampton Institute, points out that "to the west, on the grounds of Hampton Institute, is the tree under which Mrs. Mary Peake, a freedwoman, taught children of former slaves in 1861. Nearby stood the Butler School, a free school established in 1863 for colored children."

Mrs. Peake's pioneering work was under the auspices of the Reverend L. C. Lockwood of the American Missionary Association, who had the full cooperation of General Benjamin Butler, then in command at Fortress Monroe.

*Hampton Institute* was founded in 1868 by General Samuel Chapman Armstrong, in the wartime hospital barracks. Armstrong had commanded two regiments of Union Negro troops during the Civil War and wanted to train young men and women "who should go out and teach and lead their people."

During the first three years the students lived in tents. The first classroom building was built in 1871 with help from the Freedmen's Bureau and northern philanthropists. Booker T. Washington was educated here. Presidents Taft and Garfield served on the board of trustees.

The college museum has an extensive African collection, and the memorial library contains a special collection of books and pamphlets dealing with the Negro and slavery.

## JAMESTOWN

*Jamestown Historical Park.* The seeds of slavery in America were sown in August 1619 when a Dutch frigate entered the harbor here and put ashore a cargo of twenty Africans who were exchanged for supplies—probably with the Colonial government.

The first Negroes in the colonies did not actually become slaves. Instead, like many white immigrants of the time, they were parceled out to Jamestown families as indentured servants, to work until they had earned their freedom.

Their fate is clouded in history, but presumably two of them, Antony and Isabella, were married and gave birth in 1624 to the first Negro child in North America. They named him William Tucker, after a local planter.

An exhibit at the park relates the story of the first Negroes.

## LIBERTY

*Maiden Spring.* Nearby is a marker at the site of the Maiden Spring Fort, built about 1772 by Reese Bowen. In 1776, when the area was being terrorized by Ohio Valley Indians, the men from the neighborhood went in search of them, leaving their families behind.

When Mrs. Bowen found moccasin tracks near the cabin, she urged the other women to put on male attire and take turns walking sentry duty in the hope that the Indians would believe the fort was amply garrisoned. She found only one woman, a Negro slave, who dared join her. With one of them carrying a musket and the other a stick shaped like one, the women guarded the fort all night, and the attack never came.

## MANASSAS

*Manassas National Battlefield Park.* Long before Lincoln and his military leaders decided to accept Negroes for service in the Union Army, Negroes were demonstrating their eagerness to serve in rather spectacular ways.

During the first Battle of Bull Run, William H. Tiflin, a Negro, accompanied Captain Graves of the 1st Regiment, Michigan Volunteers. When the regiment's color sergeant was killed Tiflin dashed forward, picked up the fallen colors, and carried them with pride and courage until he was finally wounded in the action.

## MIDWAY

*Walnut Grove,* one mile off U. S. 11 on County 606, is the restored McCormick family homestead where Cyrus Hall McCormick perfected the mechanical grain reaper in 1831. One of the original binders is in the workshop. Jo Anderson, a Negro, assisted McCormick in developing the device which so revolutionized grain production that McCormick moved west to be closer to the market.

## PETERSBURG

*Petersburg National Battlefield* saw some of the bitterest action of the Civil War. Here the Negro units were tested, won acceptance for their courage, and led the Federal forces to victory. They also died by the hundreds in unflinching charges against heavily fortified Confederate lines.

The year-long siege of Petersburg was the prelude to the fall of Richmond. It involved thirty-two Negro infantry regiments and two Negro cavalry units. Thirteen Negroes won the Medal of Honor during the siege.

The major battles fought here have been marked. One was the famous Battle of the Crater, a costly Union defeat on the road to victory. The Union troops dug a tunnel and planted a huge charge of explosives under the Confederate lines, intending to breach them with the explosion.

In the confused encounter, with men on both sides dazed by the explosion, the Negro units were sent in after the white regiments had been repulsed. They sustained 1234 casualties in a futile effort to save the day. Sergeant Decatur Dorsey of Maryland's 39th Colored Troops won the Medal of Honor in the action.

One of the monuments in the park is the Massachusetts Monument, honoring men from that state who died in the war, many of them Negroes. The monument was erected after negotiations between a Massachusetts commission, headed by Colonel James Anderson, and a Petersburg organization of Confederate veterans.

In the course of the negotiations a delegation of Confederate veterans visited Massachusetts; this prompted a northern lady to criticize Colonel Anderson for allowing a "vile band of rebels" to parade on northern streets. The former Union officer replied: "There will be Confederates in Heaven. If you don't want to associate with Confederates, go to Hell."

*Virginia State College for Negroes*, established in 1882, was established largely through the efforts of public-spirited Negroes. Originally known as the Virginia Normal and Collegiate Institute, its first president was John Mercer Langston, who also served as minister to Haiti. Langston was elected to Congress in 1888.

Another resident of Petersburg who distinguished himself in public affairs was Joseph Jenkins Roberts, the first Negro governor of Liberia. He migrated to Liberia in 1829, and when the country became a republic, he was elected as its first President.

## PORT ROYAL

*Garrett House Marker* on U. S. 17. After President Lincoln's assassination, U.S. troops pursued John Wilkes Booth through Virginia. Among them were men of the 1st Colored Infantry Regiment who had been with Lincoln when he visited Richmond after it was captured with their help.

Booth was finally overtaken here. He took refuge in a barn and refused to surrender. The soldiers sent several shots into the barn and set fire to it. Booth was fatally wounded before he was removed from the barn, and died on the porch of the residence, which has long been in ruins.

## RICHMOND

*City Point National Cemetery* is one of six national cemeteries in and around Richmond that contain the fallen heroes gathered from the numerous battlefields of the year-long siege that led to the fall of Richmond in April 1865. Negro troops were with General Ulysses S. Grant when he crossed the Rapidan River with the Army of the Potomac. They were with Major General Benjamin F. Butler and his Army of the James, and were the first Union soldiers to take the James River points of Fort Powhatan, Wilson's Wharf Landing, and City Point.

Negro cavalrymen of the 5th Massachusetts Regiment were at the head of the Union troops that poured into Richmond after it fell, and members of the all-Negro XXV Army Corps were close behind.

City Point National Cemetery contains a white marble monument erected in 1865 by order of General Butler in memory of the dead of the Army of the James.

*Maggie L. Walker High School* is named in honor of a community leader who also was the first Negro woman bank president. Mrs. Walker organized the St. Luke Penny Savings Bank in 1902. It is now the Consolidated Bank and Trust Company. She died in 1934.

*Monumental Church,* E. Broad Street, stands on the site of the old Richmond Theater, where Governor George William Smith and many other leading citizens died in a fire on December 26, 1811. Gilbert Hunt, a husky slave, saved the lives of about twenty women and children by catching them as they leaped from the upper windows.

*Richmond National Battlefield Park* includes the fortifications that constituted the outer defenses of Richmond during the Civil War. The area around Richmond includes many historic sites of Civil War engagements in which Union Negro forces were deeply engaged. Fort Harrison is now a park headquarters and museum, and Fort Harrison National Cemetery, nearby, is the burial place of the Union troops who died when the fort was taken.

Among the sites marked are those of the bitter battles at Chaffin's Farm and New Market Heights.

General Benjamin Butler was so pleased with the gallantry of Negro troops in these actions that he had two hundred medals made by Tiffany's, and presented them to the outstanding Negro soldiers. He commented that as he "rode among the victorious, jubilant colored troops at New Market Heights, I felt in my inmost heart that the capacity of the Negro race for soldiers had then and there been fully settled forever."

Secretary of War Stanton said of the final assault: "The hardest fighting was done by the black troops. The parts they stormed were the worst of all."

Also in this park is the site of the battle fought at Deep Bottom in July 1864. Four Negro regiments heroically withstood an enemy assault, and Sergeant Major Thomas Hawkins won the Medal of Honor for rescuing the regimental flag. Of the action, in which about three hundred Negroes died, Major General D. B. McBirney, the X Corps commander, said: "It was one of the most stirring and gallant affairs I have ever known."

*Sixth Mount Zion Baptist Church*, Duval and St. John's Streets, once enjoyed the sermons of the famous Negro preacher, John Jasper. Jasper taught himself to read with the aid of a spelling book when he was in his late twenties. He began preaching while still a slave, usually at funerals, and his owner charged a dollar for each workday he missed.

During the Civil War, Jasper preached in Confederate hospitals. When the war ended he had his freedom and seventy-three cents. He founded Mount Zion in a shanty, and it soon grew into a strong and popular church.

His most famous sermon was delivered for the first time in 1879 and was titled, "The Sun Do Move and the Earth Am Square." It captured attention in America and abroad with the theological argument, based on Joshua's saving of the Gibbonites, that Joshua could hardly have made the sun stand still if it wasn't moving in the first place. The church displays a bust of Pastor Jasper, executed by Edward V. Valentine. A memorial to him stands in Woodland Cemetery.

## ROCKY MOUNT

*Booker T. Washington National Monument.* The park grounds contain a replica of the slave cabin in which Washington was born, in April 1856, to Jane Ferguson, a slave and cook on the James Burroughs plantation. After emancipation, his family moved to Malden, West Virginia. He adopted the name Washington, when he entered school, and added the middle initial when he learned that his mother had named him Taliaferro. The two-hundred-acre monument includes the Burroughs plantation.

*Franklin County Courthouse.* Among the historical records kept here is the inventory made in November 1861 of the estate of planter James Burroughs. It included "one Negro boy, 'Booker.' value $400," in a lengthy listing of farm implements and household goods.

Booker may have been worth only four hundred dollars to his owner, but he was far more valuable than that to his country and his race. After emancipation, he and his mother left the Burroughs plantation, near Hale's Ford, and went to Malden, West Virginia. Booker, who had acquired his name because of his love of books, worked in the salt mines by day and studied at night.

Eventually Washington walked to Hampton Institute, graduated, returned to Malden as a teacher in a Negro school, and then went back to Hampton as a faculty member. Tuskegee Institute, which he developed, stands today as a monument to Booker T. Washington, once carried on a planter's books as a four-hundred-dollar slave.

SALTVILLE

*Confederate Salt Works* are recalled on a marker on U. S. 11, four miles west of Chilhowie. During the Civil War they were the principal source of supply for the entire Confederacy and were heavily guarded. The 5th Colored Cavalry Regiment and other Negro and white troops under General George Stoneman finally destroyed them in December 1864.

WILLIAMSBURG

*Colonial Williamsburg.* This magnificent restoration of the Royal Colony of Virginia has been so deeply involved with the great men and events of our nation's history that an effort to list the points of interest would be fruitless. It is a place every American should visit, for it conveys a sense of history that can be found nowhere else.

One role of the Negro in Colonial, slave-holding America can be seen in the fine craftsmanship of the buildings. The Colonial way of life is re-enacted every day of the week. Contemporary Negroes perform roles once held by slaves, but unlike their forebears, they choose to play them and can stop when they want to.

One of the attractions in Williamsburg is the Colonial Capitol, where the House of Burgesses met during the Colonial period. As each white-wigged member entered, the Negro custodian, Bob Cooley, would dust off his seat in a manner that was described as being as solemn "as that of the dignitary that sat in it."

One of the local landmarks is Raleigh's Tavern, once a favorite place for slave auctions. It was also the center of Williamsburg social life.

## WINCHESTER

*First Presbyterian Church,* 304 E. Piccadilly Street, has had a checkered history. Built in 1790, the barnlike fieldstone building was the first Presbyterian church in Winchester, became a Baptist church for white people in 1834, later housed a Negro Baptist congregation, was taken over as a stable by Union troops during the Civil War, was converted into a Negro school in 1925, and later became an armory.

## WOODBRIDGE

*Gunston Hall,* Route 242, 3.2 miles east of U. S. 1. This unpretentious but striking Georgian Colonial home was built in 1755 by George Mason. He was the author of the Virginia Bill of Rights, which served as the model for the first ten amendments to the United States Constitution. When Mason went to Philadelphia in 1787 as a delegate to the Constitutional Convention, he refused to sign the document because it failed to abolish slavery and provided no Bill of Rights.

## YORKTOWN

*Yorktown National Historical Park,* site of the Revolutionary Battle of Yorktown, is another site rich in history. Here, on October 19, 1781, Cornwallis surrendered to Washington and Lafayette. The Colonial Army took eight thousand British prisoners after a ten-day siege, and the Revolutionary War, for all practical purposes, was over.

Yorktown can be visited conveniently on a trip that also encompasses Jamestown and Colonial Williamsburg. One of the tales about Yorktown involves a man named James, a Negro slave of William Armistad, who joined Lafayette as a spy when the French general came to Williamsburg in March 1781. Lafayette used him to gather information about Benedict Arnold's Portsmouth base.

When Lord Cornwallis visited Lafayette at Yorktown after the British defeat, he was surprised to discover James, whom *he* had been paying to spy on Lafayette. The praise of Lafayette won freedom for James by Act of the Virginia Assembly in 1786. The ex-slave idolized the Frenchman, and was reunited with him briefly when Lafayette visited Richmond on his return to the United States in October 1824. Long before, when he was freed, the ex-slave had taken the name of James Lafayette.

The number of Negroes involved in the actual siege of Yorktown is not known, but an occasional official record reveals their presence. Thus, nearly two centuries later, we know that Bristol Rhodes, a Negro soldier from Rhode Island, lost a leg and an arm in the fight. Today, visitors can walk over the peaceful battlefield where this patriotic Negro made his contribution to the cause of liberty.

# WASHINGTON

## CENTRALIA

*George Washington Park* honors a revered Virginian, but not the one who cut down the cherry tree. This one was the son of a Negro slave who grew up to found this city and became one of its most respected citizens.

As a child, George Washington escaped a life of slavery when he was adopted by a white couple and taken to Missouri. His color denied him a formal education, but he was tutored by his foster mother and eventually operated a sawmill at St. Joseph, Missouri. At thirty-three he joined a wagon train for a perilous 117-day trip to the Pacific Northwest. There he established a homestead, on the Chehalis River, which ultimately lay in the path of the Northern Pacific Railroad.

George did not neglect this good fortune. He laid out a town, first called Centerville, and began selling lots. He set aside park land, two acres for a cemetery, and dedicated generous streets and alleys. Lots were also donated for the establishment of churches. Within fifteen years, two thousand lots had been sold and Centralia became a thriving city.

Then came the Panic of 1893; the mills shut down, and to save his town George Washington became a one-man relief agency. He took wagons to Portland and bought rice, flour, and sugar by the ton. A packing plant sold him huge quantities of meat and lard. George loaned money to many with no interest or terms for repayment. But mostly, he managed to give people work. He saved the town.

In 1905, at eighty-eight, George Washington was a wealthy—and, more important—respected businessman. Then, unexpectedly, he was thrown from a buggy and died.

The mayor of Centralia proclaimed a day of mourning. The funeral was the biggest in the city's history. It was held in a church that Washington built on ground that he donated, and he was buried in the cemetery that he had given to the city. More than sixty years after his death, he is still honored in this park—also his gift—which bears his name.

## OLYMPIA

*Simmons Party Memorial,* in Tumwater Falls Park, is a monument to a rare instance in which the racial prejudice of a few resulted in benefit for many.

The Simmons party joined the great migration on the Oregon Trail in the spring of 1844. Among the group seeking new opportunities in Oregon was the family of George Washington Bush a free Negro born in Pennsylvania. Bush had settled in Missouri after serving under Jackson in the Battle of New Orleans and venturing in 1814 into the wilderness as a fur trader with the French trader, Robideau.

He had more reason than most to go west. Although he had become fairly prosperous as a cattle trader in Missouri, the state had recently passed a law excluding free Negroes from the state. Bush helped guide the party to Oregon, only to discover on arriving that free Negroes had recently been forbidden to settle in Oregon, as well.

The Simmons-Bush party decided to cross the Columbia River and go on north into what was then regarded as British territory. The others had developed such respect and affection for George Bush during their perilous journey that they did not want to stay where he was not wanted. After spending the winter at The Dalles, the whole wagon train pushed on north in 1845, arriving eventually at this point on Puget Sound. They were the first American settlers in the area.

When the western boundary between the United States and Canada was finally determined, the presence of George Bush and his fellow pioneers was an important factor in the decision of the British to yield the territory north of the Columbia River, to the Forty-ninth Parallel. Thus the prejudice that forced George Bush to leave the settled part of Oregon Territory may well have made Washington part of the United States.

Simmons persuaded the Oregon provincial government to permit Bush to remain in the Territory, north of the Columbia. In the years that followed, Bush, and later his son, became leading citizens of the area. George Bush staked out a homestead and soon had a prosperous farm which he almost lost because of his color. It took an act of the first Washington territorial legislature in 1854 to persuade Congress to grant Bush the claim on which he had settled in 1845.

Bush and his family were skillful and intelligent farmers. Crops raised by his son, William Owen Bush, won prizes at expositions throughout the country. They brought attention—and settlers—to the new territory. George Bush brought the first reaper and binder to the area, and established a reputation as a provident and generous man. Dozens of migrants who arrived, destitute, on Bush Prairie were indebted to George Bush for counsel and supplies.

In the near-famine during the winter of 1852, Bush proved to be the only man on Puget Sound with a surplus of wheat. Seattle speculators offered him a fortune for it, but he stubbornly refused to profit from the misfortune of others, having already had too much experience with others who were eager to profit from his. He kept his wheat, and apportioned it to the hungry on the basis of need.

George Washington Bush remains one of the most respected of the early Washington pioneers. He has often been suggested as a candidate as Washington's representative in the National Capitol's Statuary Hall.

# WEST VIRGINIA

## CHARLES TOWN

*Jefferson County Courthouse*, George and Washington Streets, contains the room in which John Brown was tried and sentenced to hang.

*Site of John Brown Gallows*, South Samuel Street near McCurdy Street. The noted abolitionist became a martyr here, in the presence of Lincoln's assassin, John Wilkes Booth, who was a member of the militia. Also present was Major Thomas J. Jackson, guarding Brown with a troop of twenty-one Virginia Military Institute cadets. As General "Stonewall" Jackson, he later returned to Harpers Ferry, the scene of Brown's defeat, at the head of victorious Confederate troops who captured the city for the Confederacy. On that occasion, instead of guarding one prisoner, he captured eleven thousand.

## HARPERS FERRY

*Harpers Ferry National Historical Park.* Its location at the junction of the Potomac and Shenandoah Rivers inevitably made Harpers Ferry an important strategic prize in the Civil War. The town changed hands nine times and never fully recovered from the destruction wrought by both northern and southern forces.

The most significant role of Harpers Ferry in the Civil War actually was achieved before the war began. It was here that John Brown made his famous raid (immortalized in the song "John Brown's Body"), which crystallized the division of North and South over the slavery issue.

Brown, an ubiquitous abolitionist whose activities are marked by monuments and onetime residences in half the states of the Union, chose Harpers Ferry as the site for his final, most ambitious, and probably least sensible plan. He came here on October 15, 1859, to set up a fortress and refuge for fugitive slaves, in which they could defend themselves against attack, and from which they could escape into Pennsylvania.

After recruiting and training his private army at several other locations, Brown hired a farm near Harpers Ferry in June 1859 and settled there with twenty-two men, including two of his sons. On Sunday evening, October 16, Brown and a force of thirteen white men and five Negroes seized the armory of the U.S. arsenal and took possession of the village.

Brown apparently thought that others would rally to his cause. Instead, the local citizens turned on him and fired at his men. Ironically, the first man killed by Brown's raiders was a free Negro, Heyward Shepherd, who was baggagemaster at the train depot.

At dusk on October 17, Brown and his surviving men were besieged in the armory enginehouse. All but five of his raiders were dead or wounded, including his two sons, one of whom died during the night, and the other later. During the night Colonel Robert E. Lee and Lieutenant J. E. B. Stuart, both of whom became Civil War generals, arrived from Washington with ninety U.S. marines. On the morning of the eighteenth they stormed Brown's "fort" and ended the insurrection.

Ten of Brown's party were killed, seven captured, and five escaped. Brown was hanged at Charles Town on December 2.

Harpers Ferry today looks much as it did then, with many old buildings still standing, and a breathtaking view of the valley from Jefferson Rock.

INSTITUTE

*West Virginia State College.* Founded in 1891 under the second Morrill Act, this school began as the West Virginia Colored Institute, a grammar school, high school, normal, and vocational school. In 1915, the name was changed to West Virginia Collegiate Institute, and college programs were begun. After accreditation in 1927, the name was again changed, to West Virginia State College. The institution was desegregated in 1954 and, in the words of its president, "today is an outstanding example of what a former Negro institution may become when it enters the mainstream of American life."

MALDEN

*Booker T. Washington Monument.* This monument was erected in 1963 to mark the site where Washington lived for many years. The noted educator worked here in the salt works and also in the home of General Lewis Ruffner.

During Washington's years in Malden it was the scene of several racial conflicts inspired by the Ku Klux Klan. In one of them, General Ruffner defended several Negroes from attack and received injuries from which he never fully recovered.

Washington credited Mrs. Viola Ruffner with inspiring him to seek an education at Hampton Institute. He taught in Malden briefly before returning to Hampton and going on to found the Tuskegee Institute that brought him fame.

TALCOTT

*Big Bend Railroad Tunnels.* The first of the tunnels, driven in the 1870s, produced a bit of folk music that has remained popular for nearly a century. It was inspired by John Henry, a giant Negro who allegedly drove steel faster than a newfangled drill.

> "The men that made that steel drill
> Thought it was mighty fine;
> John Henry drove his fourteen feet
> While the steam drill only made nine, Lawd, Lawd,
> While the steam drill only made nine.
> John Henry was a steel-drivin' man . . ."

UNION

*Bishop Mathew Clair Marker,* on U. S. 219, honors a Negro Methodist bishop who was born here October 21, 1865. He was a member of the local Methodist Church before he entered the ministry.

Mathew Clair, Sr. experienced many difficult years before he achieved stature in the ministry. He worked at a succession of unskilled jobs, including one as a dishwasher at the Hale House in Charleston, West Virginia. But Clair persevered, and by 1889 had become a minister in the Methodist Conference of Washington, D.C.

During his career Bishop Clair served in Liberia as well as in the United States, and was consecrated a bishop in 1920. One of his achievements while in Washington was the rebuilding of the Asbury Methodist Church, at a cost of eighty thousand dollars. He died in Covington, Kentucky, in 1943, and was buried in Washington.

# WISCONSIN

### CHILTON

*Calumet County Courthouse* stands as a sort of local monument to a pioneer couple whose determination led to the selection of Chilton as the county seat.

Chilton was founded by a Negro, Moses Stanton, and his Indian wife. She was a descendant of Massasoit, the Indian benefactor of the Pilgrims at Plymouth. Her husband was known as Elder Stanton, and served as both preacher and physician for the area. During the election campaign to determine the county seat they divided the county between them and secured a vote in favor of Chilton.

Mrs. Stanton was also involved in raising the funds for the building of Chilton's first church, now called the Trinity Presbyterian. A few years later the men of the town offered to veneer it with brick if the women would agree not to hold temperance meetings in it. As might have been expected, the women raised the money and did it themselves.

### JANESVILLE

*Tallman Homestead*, 440 North Jackson Street, was built from 1855–57 by William M. Tallman. It had served as an underground railroad station for many years before Abraham Lincoln slept here in October 1859, when he visited Janesville to give a political address. The home has been restored.

MADISON

   *Executive Residence,* 101 Cambridge Road, is the lake-
shore home of Wisconsin's governors. The residence was restored
and refurnished during 1966 and 1967 under the direction of Mrs.
Dorothy Knowles, the wife of the incumbent governor. A professional interior decorator, she enlisted the aid of Links, Inc., a Milwaukee women's service club, to obtain a painting by an outstanding
Negro artist for permanent display.

   The group selected the painting "Songs of the Towers," by Negro
artist Aaron Douglas. It is a representation from one of his four
murals in the Countee Cullen Library in New York, and depicts
Songs of Deliverance, Songs of Joy and the Dance, and Songs of
Depression or the Blues.

   Douglas says he selected the theme because "the song is the most
powerful and pervasive creative expression of American Negro life
. . . a natural instrument for representing all of the other arts as
well as a perfect vehicle for conveying all of our various moods and
conditions of life."

   The artist, who recently retired as head of the Art department
at Fisk University, Nashville, Tennessee, is now a professor emer-
itus. He was on hand when the presentation ceremony was held in
the residence in 1967. His work will be viewed by thousands of
people every year, for the residence is open to visitors at specified
times.

   *Vilas Park,* one of the nation's finest small city zoological
parks, stands on a site donated to the city by William F. Vilas, a
United States senator from Wisconsin who made a fortune in the
timber industry.

   Thousands of children enjoy the park each year, and some grow
up to benefit from another of his gifts. When Vilas died in 1908, his
will provided that upon the death of his daughter his estate should
be held in trust for the University of Wisconsin. A portion of the
estate was to be used to establish fellowships and scholarships for
"worthy and qualified" Negroes.

   What prompted the interest of Senator Vilas in advanced education for Negroes is not clear, but the bequest was unusual because
there were few Negroes in Wisconsin in his day. One family legend
holds that the bequest stemmed from his exposure to escaping slaves
during a period when his parental home was an underground railroad station. Another possibility sometimes offered is that he was

influenced by his association with Negro soldiers during his service in the Civil War.

At any rate, many Negroes have advanced their education at the University of Wisconsin because of his farsighted bequest.

*State Historical Society of Wisconsin,* State and Langdon Streets, has begun the collection of documents and materials related to the efforts of contemporary Negroes in the struggle for equal rights. The collection, part of a larger unit on contemporary social movements, covers activities since 1960, and already includes the papers of more than three hundred Negro civil rights workers and organizations. The society hopes to build a resource that will aid future historians in gaining perspective on the current civil rights movement.

The society also maintains extensive general historical collections, specializing in papers related to Wisconsin history. It maintains a museum featuring Wisconsin historical events. Included are broadsides relating to the Negro in the Civil War, and items concerning the period of Negro slavery.

### MILTON

*Milton House Museum,* the oldest cement building in the United States, has a tunnel which was used to hide fugitive slaves escaping on the underground railroad.

In 1964 Milton College awarded a Doctor of Humanities degree to Edward Kennedy "Duke" Ellington, one of the greatest and most durable of Negro musicians.

### MILWAUKEE

*Kosciuszko Park* was named in honor of the great Polish patriot, Thaddeus Kosciuszko, who fought with the Continental Army during the American Revolution.

Many Negro soldiers fought in the war with Kosciuszko; in fact, when he led the last skirmish of the war at Port Johnston, South Carolina, a Negro soldier in his command was among those killed.

The Polish hero believed in liberty and opportunity for his own people and all others. It was probably his wartime exposure to the inequities suffered by Negro Americans that prompted the disposition of his American estate. He left a handwritten will with his friend, Thomas Jefferson, whom he also named as executor. In it he directed that his American funds be used to buy freedom for Negro slaves, and provide for their education.

*Milwaukee Art Center,* 750 N. Lincoln Memorial Drive, has two oil paintings by Henry Ossawa Tanner. The Negro artist's works are titled "Sunlight Tangiers" and "Moonlight Hebrun."

PORTAGE

*Silver Lake Cemetery.* Flags flew at half mast and the whole town turned out in April 1967, on the thirty-fifth anniversary of the death of Ansel Clark. By proclamation of Governor Warren P. Knowles, it was "Ansel Clark Day" throughout Wisconsin. Clark was unknown outside Wisconsin, but the inscription on his tombstone summarizes how people felt about him here. It says, simply:

ANSEL CLARK
Born a slave, about 1840
Died April 18, 1932
"A Respected Citizen"

Clark got his last name from Cletcher Clark, who bought him in a Memphis slave market when he was very young. He served on both sides in the Civil War, first as an impressed laborer for the Confederates, and later for the Union Army after it captured him. During the siege of Vicksburg, Clark served as a nurse in a Union hospital, and one of his grateful patients, a Wisconsin officer, brought him back to Wisconsin after the war.

Eventually "Anse" settled in Portage, where he became town constable, deputy sheriff of Columbia County, and the county's first humane officer, a post he held for thirty years. One local resident, recalling "Anse" on the day of the 1967 celebration, said of him:

> Where Anse's marker reads 'respected citizen,' it means just that—and that in every respect. Anse had quick hands and a hard fist and was not afraid to use them when the occasion warranted. Portage was a river town with its share of rough characters. It was part of Anse's job as a law-enforcement officer to keep them in line, a task he performed with firmness and dignity.

Another resident recalled another side of the Negro's character:

> Clark was a gentle man, as well as a gentleman, and the suffering of any animal at human hands caused him extreme anguish. Usually calm and agreeable, he could be goaded into a cold and relentless

fury over the neglect or abuse of animals. I think he linked animals and children together, for he had an abiding and indiscriminate love for both.

They tell the story here that at Anse Clark's funeral the undertaker expressed gratitude that he was not driving a horse-drawn hearse.

"If I cracked the whip just once, Old Anse'd be out of that box and on my neck," he said.

# WYOMING

**BUFFALO**

*Site of Fort McKinney,* Highway 16, 2½ miles north. This old fort was once the headquarters for units of the 9th Cavalry Regiment, and the territory surrounding it is famed as the site of the Johnson County War.

In the late nineteenth century a conflict developed between the large ranchers and the settlers, who claimed that they were persecuted by the cattlemen. The ranchers allegedly cut the settlers' fences, and the settlers, in turn, were accused of rustling the ranchers' cattle.

Finally, in 1892, a small army was recruited by a group of wealthy cattlemen, with the avowed purpose of stamping out cattle rustling. They moved secretly into Johnson County and killed two homesteaders at the KC Ranch. When news of the episode reached the sheriff at Buffalo he set out after the cattlemen and their party, which included several professional gunmen. They were surrounded at the TA Ranch, near here.

A siege ensued, with the sheriff's posse determined to take the vigilante party, dead or alive. When news of the event reached Cheyenne the governor ordered out the cavalry. A company of Negro troopers arrived in time to rescue the cattlemen and return them to Fort McKinney under arrest.

The episode persuaded most of the large ranchers that the days of the open range were over and that they would have to accept settlement of the West.

## CHEYENNE

*First Public School Site Plaque* at Nineteenth Street and Carey Avenue. The town turned out here on January 5, 1868, for the dedication of Cheyenne's first public school, their enthusiasm chilled only slightly by the temperature, which was twenty-three degrees below zero. They were warmed by the speakers, who spoke with pride of the fact that the town's first public school would be open to all, "rich or poor, black or white."

Cheyenne was remarkably free of prejudice in its pioneer days. Barney Ford, the Negro who built and operated the Inter-Ocean Hotel, ran a social gathering place that was considered one of the finest hotels in the West.

W. J. Hardin, a popular Negro barber, was elected to the territorial legislature in 1879. The Cheyenne *Daily Leader*, on December 16, 1879, credited the Negro legislator with making "the most forcible speech delivered in the House during the session . . .

"He has . . . sustained the *Leader's* promise, made before election day, that he would prove to be one of the best members of the legislature," the paper commented. At that time there was only one other Negro legislator in the North.

## FORT LARAMIE

*Fort Laramie National Historical Site* is one of the best-preserved and most completely restored of the old pioneer forts. For forty-one years it served as headquarters for white and Negro soldiers who watched over the safety of the wagon trains traveling west.

The Indian wars were about over when the fort was abandoned in 1890. Today, many of the twenty-one historic structures have been restored and are open to the public.

## FORT WASHAKIE

*Fort Washakie Blockhouse* served as headquarters for units of both the 9th and 10th Cavalry Regiments during the Indian wars.

The 9th Cavalry left here on one occasion to rescue a party of infantry from Fort Steele which was ambushed and besieged by a Ute Indian war party on the Uintah River in Utah. The infantrymen had dug in and had been in their trenches for three weeks. They were running out of food and ammunition when the 9th arrived with plenty of both, plus two light revolving field cannons. The Indians were quickly driven off, but the 9th remained at the site to build what became Fort Duchesne.

The grave of Sacajawea, the Indian woman who, with the Negro, York, helped guide the Lewis and Clark expedition, is marked in the nearby Wind River Cemetery. Whether this is her actual burial place is a matter of dispute among historians.

### JACKSON HOLE

*Jackson Hole Wildlife Park.* This area, and the adjacent Grand Teton Mountains, offer some of the most picturesque scenery in America. Perhaps this is why, a century and a half ago, it was visited and revisited by trappers and guides whose names have become legends of the West.

The hole was named for David E. Jackson, an associate of fur trader William H. Ashley, who came here in the 1820s with such rugged mountain men as Jim Bridger, Kit Carson, and Jim Beckwourth. Beckwourth, a Negro, trapped and explored in this area in the early part of the nineteenth century, and subsequently served as a guide for fur traders, trappers, and wagon trains. He was with Ashley when he established a Rocky Mountain Fur Company trading post on the Yellowstone River in 1822.

Another Negro of the same era was Edward Rose, a sullen but expert guide whose personality was the antithesis of the garrulous Beckwourth's. Rose lived among the Crow Indians for a time, and later guided the fur-trading expeditions of Thomas Fitzpatrick and William Sublette.

Rose was the first settler in the Big Horn Basin, where he came to trap in 1807.

### LARAMIE COUNTY

*Texas Trail Marker*, Highway 30, west side of Pine Bluffs. Many of the trail herds coming north from Texas paused at Cheyenne to give the cowboys a break from the monotonous ordeal in the saddle. Many of the cowboys were Negroes who apparently differed little from the white riders in their tastes, desires, and behavior.

It was while refreshing himself in Cheyenne that a Negro cowboy called "Bronco Sam," renowned as a broncbuster, accepted a challenge to ride the biggest Texas longhorn in the herd down the town's main street. The ride went well until the steer saw its reflection in the plate glass window of the clothing store—the only such window in town. The animal charged through it, with Sam still aboard, made a circuit of the store, and then came back out through the empty window frame.

The Negro cowboy's employer, Bill Walker, recalled years later that when the steer emerged, "Sam was still in the saddle, the steer's horns decorated with pants, coats, underwear, and other odds and ends . . ." Sam returned to Cheyenne the next morning and peeled off three hundred and fifty greenbacks to pay for the damage he had done.

## SHERIDAN

*Fort MacKenzie Historic Site* is another of the pioneer forts from which the 10th cavalrymen protected settlers, cattle drives, and wagon trains during the Indian wars. Later they were used primarily to enforce law and order in the territory.

## SINCLAIR

*Remains of Old Fort Steele,* U. S. 30, nine miles east. In September 1879, Major T. T. Thornburgh left here with a party of about 450 soldiers, in pursuit of renegade Ute Indians. He found too many of them near the Milk River in Colorado. Thornburgh was killed, and his men were about to be annihilated when the Negro 9th Cavalry Regiment came to their rescue. (See New Mexico.)

# ACKNOWLEDGMENTS

THIS GUIDE WAS INSPIRED BY A BOOKLET describing some sixty monuments to Negro achievements in the United States, which was published by the American Oil Company in 1963. Although it was limited in scope and content, that pioneering effort was enthusiastically received, and widely adopted in public and private schools to supplement American History and Social Science textbooks.

Many teachers noted that the association of historical figures and events with existing monuments, structures, and marked sites gave physical reality to the historic role of Negroes in American history. It was this discovery of the value of relating events of the past to the physical present that prompted the three years of research and writing involved in this far more comprehensive guide.

Included in this volume is much of the American Oil Company material, for which the author is indebted to many persons at American Oil who have been associated with the project over the years, and particularly to James M. Patterson, Director of Public Relations, and Dolphin Thompson, a consultant of the firm, who were largely responsible for the birth of the idea.

The hundreds of additional listings are the result of the patient and determined research of my wife, Jayne, and the generous cooperation of hundreds of private citizens, librarians, and staff members of state and local historical societies and other organizations. Their assistance often exceeded what could reasonably be expected of them.

The author's debt to these helpful strangers cannot be repaid. How do you thank someone like Mrs. Agnes V. Calkins, of Bella Vista, California, who devoted weeks to the search for Alvin Aaron Coffey's grave? How do you acknowledge the generosity of Mrs. Kate B. Carter, President of the Daughters of Utah Pioneers, who generously made available the fruits of her own extensive research and writing about the Negroes who migrated westward with the Mormon pioneers? How do you adequately recognize the contributions of busy professional historians, such as Edwin C. Bearss, of the National Park Service, who shared his intimate knowledge of Negro participation in the Civil War?

You cannot thank them adequately, of course. But for the vast majority of these people, who expended extraordinary effort because of their deep convictions regarding the need for a book of this kind, the publication of the book will probably be thanks enough. Nevertheless, the interest and help of the following cannot go unmentioned:

Milo B. Howard, Jr., Department of State Archives and History, Montgomery, Alabama; Mrs. Ruth Warren, Mobile Public Library, Mobile, Alabama; Joseph W. Hurt, State Highway Department, Montgomery, Alabama; Richard DeRoux, Alaska Department of Education, Juneau, Alaska; Paul McCarthy, University of Alaska, College, Alaska; Bert R. Coleman, State Development Board, Phoenix, Arizona; Marguerite B. Cooley, Department of Library and Archives, Phoenix, Arizona; Bert M. Fireman, Arizona Historical Foundation, Tempe, Arizona;

Lou Oberste, Arkansas Publicity and Parks Commission, Little Rock, Arkansas; Mrs. Margaret E. Lambert, Downieville, California; Mrs. Carma R. Leigh, California State Library, Sacramento, California; Miss Ruth I. Mahood, Los Angeles County Museum of Natural History, Los Angeles, California; Allen W. Welts, State Park Historian, Sacramento, California; Dr. James Abajian, California Historical Society, San Francisco, California; Delores W. Bryant, Society of California Pioneers, San Francisco California; Mrs. Laura Allyn Ekstrom, State Historical Society, Denver, Colorado;

Miss Jane R. Hayward, Village Library, Farmington, Connecticut; William D. Farnham, Yale University Library, New Haven, Connecticut; Lieutenant Michael D. Jacobs, Coast Guard Academy, New London, Connecticut; Leon de Valinger, State Archivist, Dover, Delaware; Richard S. Maxwell, National Archives and Records Service, Washington, D.C.; Stanfield S. McClure, National Society, Daughters of the American Revolution, Washington, D.C.; Hal V. Kelly, Georgetown University, Washington, D.C.; Richard H. Howland, Gordon D. Gibson, Elizabeth Phillips, Smithsonian Institution, Washington, D.C.; Mrs. Virginia Newman, Florida Board of Parks and Historic Sites, Tallahassee, Florida; Miss Dena Snodgrass, Florida State Chamber of Commerce, Jacksonville, Florida; James H. Sayes, Florida Development Commission, Tallahassee, Florida; Mrs. N. Penney Denning, Florida State Museum, Gainesville,

Florida; Miss Margaret L. Chapman, Florida Historical Society, Tampa, Florida;

Mrs. Ann R. Harrison, Georgia Historical Commission, Atlanta, Georgia; William H. Vickery, Department of the Army, Honolulu, Hawaii; Merle W. Wells, Idaho Historical Society, Boise, Idaho; Brocket R. Bates, Illinois Information Service, Springfield, Illinois; Helen R. Guilbert, Chicago Historical Society, Chicago, Illinois; the Reverend Landry Genosky, Quincy College, Quincy, Illinois; Wayne D. Herrick, Farmer City, Illinois; Clyde C. Walton, State Historian, Springfield, Illinois; Hubert H. Hawkins, Indiana Historical Bureau, Indianapolis, Indiana;

William J. Petersen, State Historical Society of Iowa, Iowa City, Iowa; Elizabeth Sloan, Lida Lisle Green, State Department of History, Des Moines, Iowa; Jack Siefkas, Simpson College, Indianola, Iowa; Superintendent Elbert W. Smith, Fort Larned National Historic Site, Larned, Kansas; Mark C. Endsley, Fort Riley, Kansas; Francis M. Brooke, Fort Leavenworth National Cemetery, Fort Leavenworth, Kansas; Robert W. Richmond, State Archivist, Topeka, Kansas; P. O. Crawford, Fort Scott, Kansas; Francis L. Wilson, Ellsworth County Historical Society, Ellsworth, Kansas;

G. Glenn Clift, W. A. Wentworth, Kentucky Historical Society, Frankfort, Kentucky; Forrest J. Wilson, Department of Parks, Frankfort, Kentucky; Robert F. Wachs, Lexington National Cemetery, Lexington, Kentucky; Miss Joyce N. YelDell, Louisiana Tourist Development Commission, Baton Rouge, Louisiana; Mrs. Susan B. Judice, Louisiana Landmarks Society, New Orleans, Louisiana; Mrs. Peggy Richards, Louisiana State Museum, New Orleans, Louisiana; Arthur Hehr, Chalmette National Historical Park, Arabi, Louisiana; A. Otis Hebert, Jr., State Archives and Records Commission, Baton Rouge, Louisiana;

Kenneth J. Boyer, Robert L. Volz, Bowdoin College, Brunswick, Maine; Richard N. Dyer, Colby College, Waterville, Maine; John Quentin Fuller, Archdiocese of Baltimore, Baltimore, Maryland; George W. Hubley, Jr., William B. Braun, Department of Economic Development, Annapolis, Maryland; John T. Dowd, Annapolis National Cemetery, Annapolis, Maryland; Miss Mary Carter-Roberts, Maryland Hall of Records, Annapolis, Maryland;

Frank Harris, Governor's Office, Boston, Massachusetts; Mrs. Margaret Flint, Lincoln Center, Massachusetts; Mrs. Virginia A. May, Curator, Groton Historical Society, Groton, Massachusetts; Mrs. Ruth Sampson, Arlington Historical Society, Arlington, Massachusetts; Mrs. Mary P. Sherwood, The Thoreau Lyceum, Concord,

Massachusetts; Bartlett Hendricks, the Berkshire Museum, Pittsfield, Massachusetts; Philip F. Purrington, Old Dartmouth Historical Society, New Bedford, Massachusetts; Raymond J. Callahan, Framingham *News*, Framingham, Massachusetts;

Foster L. Fletcher, City Historian, Ypsilanti, Michigan; Kurtz Myers, Detroit Public Library, Detroit, Michigan; Donald Chaput, Michigan Historical Commission, Lansing, Michigan; Jerome Irving Smith, Librarian, Greenfield Village, Dearborn, Michigan; Miss Christine McCarthy, Detroit Historical Commission, Detroit, Michigan; Professor Earl Spangler, Macalester College, St. Paul, Minnesota; Beverly J. Bergman, Governor's Human Rights Commission, St. Paul, Minnesota; Russell W. Fridley, Minnesota Historical Society, St. Paul, Minnesota; Theartrice Williams, Phillis Wheatley Community Center, Minneapolis, Minnesota;

David C. Corson, Natchez National Cemetery, Natchez, Mississippi; Ernest L. Fusse, Corinth National Cemetery, Corinth, Mississippi; Charlotte Capers, Mississippi Department of Archives and History, Jackson, Mississippi; A. P. Marshall, Lincoln University, Jefferson City, Missouri; Philip C. Brooks, Truman Library, Independence, Missouri; Patsy D. Santagato, Jefferson Barracks National Cemetery, St. Louis, Missouri;

Mayor Cecil R. Kirk, Cascade, Montana; J. H. Vanderbeck, Virginia City, Montana; Orvin B. Fjare, State Highway Commission, Helena, Montana; John R. Hallowell, Governor's Office, Helena, Montana; Paul D. Riley, Nebraska State Historical Society, Lincoln, Nebraska; James D. Sims, Fort McPherson National Cemetery, Maxwell, Nebraska; Samuel J. Cornelius, Nebraska Technical Assistance Agency, Lincoln, Nebraska;

Miss Stella J. Scheckter, New Hampshire State Library, Concord, New Hampshire; Mrs. Nancy T. Stevens, Philbrick-James Library, Deerfield, New Hampshire; Mrs. Isabel C. Brooks, New Jersey Department of Conservation and Economic Development, Trenton, New Jersey; Frances R. Goodman, Camden, New Jersey; William W. Barnes, Eric B. Chandler, State Division of Civil Rights, Trenton, New Jersey; Mrs. Rebecca B. Muehleck, Free Public Library, Trenton, New Jersey; Miss Ann H. Benson, New Jersey Historical Society, Newark, New Jersey; Bernard Bush, New Jersey State Library, Trenton, New Jersey;

Dr. Myra Ellen Jenkins, Dorotha M. Bradley, State Records Center and Archives, Santa Fe, New Mexico; Bruce T. Ellis, Museum of New Mexico, Santa Fe, New Mexico; Paul D. Guraedy, Historian, El Morro National Monument, Ramah, New Mexico; James J. Heslin, New York Historical Society, New York City; Edward J. Gaumond, U. S. Mission to the United Nations, New York City; Ken Smith, National Baseball Hall of Fame, Cooperstown, New York; Lieutenant Colonel Robert E. Kern, United States Military Academy, West Point, New York; Harry S. Douglas, County Historian, Arcade, New York; Rear Admiral Gordon McLintock, United States Merchant Marine Academy, Kings Point, New York; John F. Von Daacke, University of the State of New York, Albany, New York; Grove McClellan, Old Fort Niagara, Lewiston, New York; Kelso Sturgeon, Ted Worner and Associates, New York City; Catherine W. Taggert, Curator, Remington Art Memorial, Ogdensburg, New York; Agnes M. Gahagan, Curator, Hall of Fame of the Trotter, Goshen, New York;

Dr. Richard Bardolph, University of North Carolina, Greensboro, North Carolina; Miss Elizabeth W. Wilborn, Department of Archives and History, Raleigh, North Carolina; Craig A. Gannon, State Historical Society, Bismarck, North Dakota; Myrl G. Brooks, Theodore Roosevelt National Memorial Park, Medora, North Dakota; Daniel R. Porter, Ohio Historical Society, Columbus, Ohio; John R. Earnst, Robert J. Dodge, Perry's Victory National Monument, Put-in-Bay, Ohio; Walter E. Reeves, Oberlin College, Oberlin, Ohio; Elizabeth Lupton, Historical Society, Mount Pleasant, Ohio; Mrs. Ruth W. Helmuth, Western Reserve University, Cleveland, Ohio;

Elmer L. Fraker, Oklahoma Historical Society, Oklahoma City, Oklahoma; Mrs. Jean Brownell, Oregon Historical Society, Portland, Oregon; Irene Payne, State Highway Department, Portland, Oregon; Robert W. Smith, Lafayette College, Easton, Pennsylvania; Joseph R. Fugett, George Washington Carver Library, Valley Forge, Pennsylvania; Maxwell Whiteman, Elkins Park, Pennsylvania;

George T. Wein, Newport Jazz Festival, Newport, Rhode Island; Leonard J. Panaggio, Rhode Island Development Council, Providence, Rhode Island; Michael S. Van Leesten, Rhode Island Commission Against Discrimination, Providence, Rhode Island; Clarkson A. Collins, 3rd, Rhode Island Historical Society, Providence, Rhode Island; Mrs. Grace M. Haire, Newport, Rhode Island; Charles E. Lee, South Carolina Archives Department, Columbia, South Carolina; Will G. Robinson, South Dakota Historical Society, Pierre, South Dakota; Fred G. Borsch, Galena, South Dakota; Mary E. Harlan, Deadwood, South Dakota;

R. G. Hopper, Carlon Sills, Fort Donelson National Military Park, Dover, Tennessee; Sherman W. Perry, Stones River National Battlefield, Murfreesboro, Tennessee; Robert H. White, State Historian, Nashville, Tennessee; James M. Day, University of Texas, El Paso, Texas; Karen Hackelman, Utah State Historical Society, Salt Lake City, Utah;

Hugh D. Gurney, Saint Gaudens National Historic Site, Windsor, Vermont; T. D. Seymour Bassett, Curator, Wilbur Collection, University of Vermont, Burlington, Vermont; Charles T. Morrissey, Director, David D. Warden, Vermont Historical Society, Montpelier, Vermont; Frank A. Nuzzolo, Fair Haven, Vermont; Allen D. Hill, The Bennington Museum, Bennington, Vermont; John T. Willett, Martin R. Conway, Petersburg National Battlefield, Petersburg, Virginia; William R. Holloman, Fredericksburg and Spotsylvania National Military Park, Fredericksburg, Virginia; Ervin N. Thompson, Historian, National Park Service, Arlington, Virginia; Mrs. Mildred L. Harris, Department of Highways, Richmond, Virginia;

Mrs. Hazel E. Mills, Washington State Library, Olympia, Washington; B. N. Stratford, Seattle Historical Society, Seattle, Washington; Frank L. Green, Washington State Historical Society, Tacoma, Washington; James M. Hupp, State Historian and Archivist, Charleston, West Virginia; Leslie L. Fishel, Jr., Director, Miss Margaret Gleason, State Historical Society of Wisconsin, Madison, Wisconsin; Miss Lenore B. Lee, Milwaukee Art Center, Milwaukee, Wisconsin; William F. Steuber, State Highway Commission, Madison, Wisconsin; Mrs. Katherine Halvorson, Viola McNealy, Wyoming State Archives, Cheyenne, Wyoming.

# INDEX

Homestead National Monument, 119
Honey Springs, Battle of, 162
Hood, General John B., 192; Retreat Marker, 187
Hooker, George, 163
Houston, Sam, 193, 196, 200
Houston-Tillotson College, 193
Howard, O. O., 86, 145
Howard University, 37, 86; Founders Library, 37; Moorland Collection, 37
Huachuca, Fort, 10–11
Hubbardtown Battlefield and Museum, 205
Hughes, Langston, 103, 177
Hunt, Gilbert, 214
Hunt, Richard, 57
Hunter, David, 180

Idaho, 54–57; Historical Society, 54
Ikard, Bose, 199
Independent Kansas Colored Battery, 72
Indian Wars, xi, xii, 115–16, 128–29, 130–31, 229–30; Arizona, 6–12; Colorado, 26–29; Kansas, 71–74; New Jersey, 126; Vermont, 204–6; Virginia, 217
Iowa, 65–68; State University, 65

Jack, John, 96
Jackson, Andrew, xi, 21, 80–81
Jackson, C. T., 26
Jackson, David E., 230
Jackson, Saunders, 18–19
Jackson, Thomas J. ("Stonewall"), 221
Jackson, Thornton, 202
Jackson, Waller, 18
Jackson Hole Wildlife Park, 230
Jackson, Miss., State College, 107
Jacksonville, Ore., Museum, 166
Jaggers, Charles, 180–81
James, Isaac L., 202
James, Jane Manning, 202
Jamestown, Va., Historical Park, 211
Jasper, John, 215
Jayne, William, 151
Jefferson, Thomas, 134, 226–27; Monticello, 207–8
Jefferson Barracks National Cemetery, 112
Jeffries, Jim, 121
Jenkins Ferry State Park, 15
Jocelyn, Simeon S., 31
Johnson, Andrew, 144, 172; National Historic Site, 188
Johnson, Henry (Indian Wars), 26
Johnson, Henry (World War I), 139
Johnson, J. Rosamund, 97
Johnson, Jack, 121
Johnson, James Weldon, 31, 42, 97, 192
Johnson, John, 157
Johnson, Jubilee, 120
Johnson, Lyndon B., 59, 103
Johnson, Sargent, 21
Johnson, T. W., 61
Johnston, Joseph E., 144, 148–49
Johnston, Joshua, 38
Jones, Absalom, 173, 174
Jones, Caesar, 92

Jones, Emanuel, 195
Jones, John, 24, 57, 135
Jones, John L. (Casey Jones), 189
Jones, John Paul, 88; House, 209
Jones, Laurence C., 101
Jones, Mary Richardson, 57
Jordan, George, 130–31
Jordan, Noble, 80, 81
Jubilee Singers, Fisk University, 192
Julian, Percy L., 64

*Kearsage*, U.S.S., 124
Kennedy, John F., Memorial Library, 95
Kennedy, Nancy, 75
Kennedy, Thomas, 74–75
Kentucky Derby, 76–77
King, Dr. Martin Luther, 37, 46–47, 191
King, Mrs. Martin Luther, 38
Kings Mountain National Military Park, 146
Kings Point, N.Y., Merchant Marine Academy, 135
Kitty's Cottage, Oxford, Ga., 51
Korean War, xii, 8, 53
Kosciuszko, Thaddeus, 226

Lafayette, James, 218
Lafayette, Marquis, 93, 126, 169, 208, 217
Lafayette College, 170
Lambuth, Walter R., 47
Lancaster, Ky., 74; Kennedy House, 74–75
Lane, James, 71
Langston, John M., 162, 213
Langston, Okla., All-Negro Town, 162
Laramie, Fort, 229
Larned, Fort, 71
Last Chance Gulch, 116, 117
Latham, Lambert, 30
Latimer, Lewis H., 82
Lawrence, Jacob, 38, 39, 101, 102, 133, 137
Lawrence, Robert H., 197–98
Lawrence, Kans., 71; Oak Hill Cemetery, 71
Lawson, John, 2, 107–8
Lawson, Marjorie M., 140
Lay, Hark, 203
Leavenworth, Fort, 71
Ledyard, William, 30–31
Lee, Fitz, 195
Lee, Jerry, 28
Lee, John Wesley, 64
Lee, Robert E., 3, 58, 171, 207, 209, 222
Lee, Tom, Memorial, 190
Lee-Smith, Hughie, 102
Leidesdorff, William A., 23
LeMoyne College, 190
L'Enfant, Pierre, 38, 88
Leslie, Frank, 12
Leutze, Emanuel, 126, 172
Lew, Barzillai, 59, 93
Lewger, John, 91
Lewis, Meriwether, 55, 116. See also Lewis and Clark expedition
Lewis and Clark expedition, 55, 56, 116, 117, 152–53, 164, 166, 186; Markers, 116; State Park, 167
Lexington, Battle of, 92, 97

Tallent, Annie, xv
Tallman, William M., Homestead, 224
Tanner, Henry O., 4, 57, 127, 175, 227
Taylor, murder of, 70
Taylor, Richard, 78, 79
Temple, Lewis, 99
*Tennessee* (ship), 2, 4
Texas Southern University, 198
Thackeray, William M., 47–48
3rd Colored Cavalry Regiment, 108
3rd Louisiana Native Guards, 84
3rd Wisconsin Cavalry Regiment, 68–69
10th U. S. Cavalry, 6–11, 29, 44, 73–74, 129, 164, 196
369th Regiment Armory, N.Y.C., 139
Thomas, Fort, 9
Thomas, George H., 48, 192
Thompson, James, 105
Thompson, William, 8, 53
Thompson's Museum, 118
Thoreau, Henry David, 96, 97, 98
Thornburgh, T. T., 26, 231
Thornburgh Battlefield, 26–27
Ticonderoga, Fort, 142
Tifftin, William H., 212
Tolton, Augustus, 62
Tougaloo College, 109
Towson, Fort, 162
Trail, William, 63
Trenton, N.J., Battle Monument, 128
Truman, Harry S., Library, 111
Truth, Sojourner, 101–2; grave of, 101
Tubman, Harriet, 89–90, 101; home of, 132–33
Tucker, William, 211
Tupelo National Battlefield, 109
Tupper, H. M., 149
Turner, James M., 111
Turner, Nat, insurrection, 208
Tuskegee Institute, Ala., 4–5
21st U. S. Colored Regiment, 181
24th Colored Infantry Regiment, 6–8, 44, 128–29, 162, 164, 195, 201
25th Infantry Regiment, 6, 44, 106, 115, 117, 183–84, 185
Tyler, John, 152

Ullman, General, 84
Uncles, Charles Randolph, 88, 89
*Uncle Tom's Cabin*, 64, 75, 90–91, 154, 158
Underground Railroad: Colorado, 24–25; Connecticut, 30, 31; Delaware, 32, 33; Illinois, 59; Indiana, 63; Iowa, 65–66, 67; Massachusetts, 96, 97; Michigan, 102, 104; Nebraska, 120; New Jersey, 127; New York, 132–33; North Carolina, 146; Ohio, 153, 155, 156; Rhode Island, 178
United Nations, 140
Urrea, José, 196, 197
Ursuline Convent, New Orleans, 83
Ute Indians, 7, 26, 27, 119, 230, 231

Valley Forge, Pa., 175–76; State Park, 175–76
Vicksburg National Military Park, 109–19

Victorio (Apache Chief), 11, 130
Vietnam, xii, 58
Vilas, William F., Park, 225–26
Villa, Pancho, 9, 129
Virginia State College for Negroes, 213

Walden State Reservation, 97
Walker, Jonathan, grave of, 103
Walker, Maggie L., High School, 214
Walker, Moses "Fleet," 156–57
Walker, "Silver," 56–57
Wallace, Fort, 73–74
War of 1812, xi, 80–81, 87, 134, 157, 170
Warsaw, N.Y., Presbyterian Church, 142
Washakie, Fort, 229–30
Washington, Booker T., 110, 215–16, 223; monuments to, 215, 223; statues of, 46; at Tuskegee, 4; *Up from Slavery*, 26
Washington, George, 38–39, 126, 141, 142, 169, 172, 177; Mount Vernon, 206–7; Valley Forge Headquarters, 176; White Plains Headquarters, 143
Washington, George (Negro captor of Billy the Kid), 131
Washington, George (Negro founder of Centralia, Wash.), 218–19
Washington Crossing State Park, 172
Watie, Stand, 161, 162
Wayne, Anthony, 126, 141, 142
Weaver, Robert C., 40, 95
Wells, Ida B., 60
Wesley, Charles H., xiv, 34, 159
West, John, 54
West Point Military Academy, 7, 143
West Virginia, 221–24; State College, 222
Whaling (whalers), 31, 99
Wham, J. W., 7
Wheatley, Phillis, 38–39, 95; Community Center, 104–5
Whipple, Prince, xi, 172
White, Andrew, 36
White, Eartha M., 42
White, George H., 37
White, Walter, 37
White Plains, Battle of, 143
Whittemore, Cuff, 92
Wiggins, Thomas ("Blind Tom" Bethune), 48–49
Wilberforce University, 159
Wiley, Fletcher H., 25
William Penn, Camp, 171
Williams, Daniel H., 39, 59–60
Williams, Franklin H., 140
Williams, Mr. and Mrs. G. Mennen, 102
Williams, James M., 13, 69
Williams, Paul R., 17
Williams, Tom, 61
Williamsburg, Va., 216
Willis, Ed, 76
Willis, Minerva and Wallace, 163–64
Wills House, Gettysburg, Pa., 171
Wilson, William O., 185
Wimberly, Dred, 150
Wood, Cato, 92
Wooden, "Aunty," 67